Nostradamus
The
Next 50 Years

Other books by Peter Lemesurier

Nostradamus

The
Next 50 Years

COVERING *the*

FORTHCOMING

INVASION

of EUROPE

PETER LEMESURIER

PIATKUS

*Neither the author nor the publishers are
responsible for the expressed views or
predictions of Nostradamus, nor do they
necessarily subscribe to them. Reader's reactions
to the prophecies are entirely their own
responsibility. While all interpretations are
offered in good faith, no guarantee is implied or
should be inferred regarding their predictive
validity.*

© 1993 Peter Lemesurier

First published in 1993 by
Judy Piatkus (Publishers) Ltd of
5 Windmill Street, London W1P 1HF

Reprinted 1996
This edition 1997
Reprinted 1998

The moral right of the author has been asserted
under the Copyright, Designs and Patents Act 1988

A catalogue record for this book is available
from the British Library

ISBN 0-7499-1744-X pb

Set in 11/13 Sabon by
Phoenix Photosetting, Chatham, Kent
Printed & bound in Great Britain by
Mackays of Chatham PLC,
Chatham, Kent

CONTENTS

A Word of Thanks

Grateful thanks to Susan Mears for proposing this book, to Elen Sandhu and Hywel Edwards for reading it, to Max and Jean-Charles de Fontbrune for showing me the way to go, and to Erika Cheetham for drawing my attention, in her *Final Prophecies of Nostradamus*, to the 1568 edition of Nostradamus's original French text in the Taylorian Library, Oxford.

INTRODUCTION:
A NEW
TRANSLATION

WHEN IT WAS FIRST SUGGESTED that I write a book on Nostradamus, I was extremely dubious. I had become familiar with existing commentaries on the celebrated French seer during the course of my earlier studies of prophecy and its workings, and had been left with the impression of a dark and possibly confused mind whose claimed accuracy I doubted, and whose motives I frankly distrusted. Who was this sombre entity who was prepared to shed gloom over the world with such apparent abandon? Did he not realise what damage he could possibly cause, what fears he could engender, what dangerous ideas he could stir up?

The most widely-accepted recent translations insisted, after all, that what Nostradamus foresaw for our next decade or so was a time of sheer horror for the world at large. There were to be Antichrists and Armageddons, nuclear war between the Western powers and the Warsaw Pact, world-wide famines, pestilences and the whole terrifying, apocalyptic, Pandora's box of the Bible's Revelation of St John – and all this by around the end of the twentieth century. Indeed, it was in 1999 (according to most existing versions of the seer's prophecies) that a great 'King of Terror' would finally come from heaven to wreak destruction on a doomed world, even if humanity was apparently destined to stagger on amid mounting terrors for a little while longer.

1

Whether there was anything in all this I, of course, did not know. But I did wonder whether the prophecies of Nostradamus could themselves help to bring it all about. Might not the efforts of latter-day interpreters to spread his message anew serve to rekindle such expectations in our minds and actually precipitate the events predicted? Might not the whole scenario, in short, become a self-fulfilling prophecy, with any additional interpretative efforts on my own part merely helping to oil the wheels?

I need not have worried. By this time, after all, it was the autumn of 1992. The Cold War had recently come to an end. There was not even a Soviet Union or Warsaw Pact to fulfil the gloomy predictions any more. While there were still plenty of nuclear weapons about, none of the major world powers had any further reason to use them on each other, or seemed even remotely likely to do so. Nuclear Armageddon, consequently, seemed highly improbable. Apart from the comparatively impotent Saddam Hussein, there was no sign of any world leader who could come anywhere near to playing the role of universal Antichrist. Suddenly the end of the world had retreated into the far distance, transmuted itself into a large question mark. If there was to be any Last Judgement at all, it seemed likely to be on the translators and interpreters — unless, of course, it was Nostradamus who was wrong.

A new approach

In consequence, it made sense to examine the seer's writings again — and this time from a totally new perspective. For, as I started to look again at the familiar French verses in my role as a professional translator, it quickly became obvious that many of them were not, after all, saying what earlier commentators had long assumed. The dreaded 'King of Terror', in particular, was nothing of the kind. Instead, I discovered that he was no more than a major leader with money to spend (see page 74). Indeed, though translations of the prophecies had been appearing for centuries, all too often, it now emerged, they had contained a surprising number of linguistic errors.

. But why should all this be? Possibly because, although Nostradamus's prophecies clearly belong together, they do not follow any kind of logical sequence (see page 11, 'Disguising the prophecies'). Most commentators, as a result, have attempted to interpret each stanza more or less in isolation, when in fact one can no more do this with Nostradamus's scrambled verses then one can interpret the individual pieces of a jigsaw puzzle of which one has lost the picture on the box. True, some interpreters did endeavour to fit them together into some kind of logical sequence – but then they insisted on using their own dubious preconceptions as a kind of template for the process, thus invalidating the whole exercise.

Clearly both approaches were unsatisfactory. For this book I therefore had to start all over again virtually from scratch. I went back to the original sixteenth century French texts. I had to lay aside all my own preconceptions and instead base any presumed sequence purely on which verses appeared to go together with which on the basis of common themes, phrases, place names and time references, together with Nostradamus's letters and his occasional helpful summary verses. And, indeed, pairings did soon lead to groups, and groups to larger clumps, until in the end an overall sequence emerged that had little to do with what previous commentators had suggested.

The forthcoming invasion

Its message for our own immediate future was – and is – astonishing. According to Nostradamus, we have (it seems) to expect a massive invasion of Mediterranean Europe by hordes from the East who will be Asiatic, Muslim *and red* (whatever Nostradamus means by the term).

Reaching Italy by the year 2000, the insurgents will also spread along the North African coast and, via Spain, into southern France. The Pope will be forced to flee to the Rhône valley, where he will be pursued, captured and eventually killed: *moreover, he will apparently be the present Pope* (this detail alone cannot help but emphasise the imminence of the events described). The Vati-

3

can will subsequently be destroyed. From southern France the invaders – looting and raping, as well as persecuting the Catholic Church in particular – will advance steadily northwards in their millions. With the aid of some kind of aerial fire-weapon they will overrun major defence-lines on the Rivers Garonne and Loire, until they eventually reach the English Channel coast. Only at the last moment will an invasion of England be averted, and then more as a result of dissension in the Asiatic ranks than of any efforts on the part of the defenders.

Then Second World War history will repeat itself (Nostradamus clearly believed implicitly in the idea), as a massive, allied counter-invasion is launched. In this case, though, it will set out both from Britain and from Germany. Thanks partly to brilliant invasion tactics, the invaders will be chased out of a now desolate and largely depopulated France, then out of Italy and finally out of Spain. Later they will be pursued to the Middle East by a charismatic new Western leader who will go on to crown himself king of most of Europe after the manner of the former Emperor Charlemagne. An era of unprecedented peace and prosperity will then ensue that will last for over half a century.

Yet even this will not be the end of things. For the eventual inception of earth's long-awaited Millennium – the gospels' Kingdom of Heaven on earth – will not be due (according to Nostradamus) for another seven hundred years at least, following a whole new range of heavy trials and tribulations for humanity at large . . .

This, then, is what I found Nostradamus to be saying – and he says it repeatedly, vividly and in immense detail. The picture is dramatic, even horrific at times, yet it is by no means all gloom. Moreover, it has next to nothing to do with the picture that emerges from most of the existing accounts. So far as I am aware, it has never been revealed before. Only with the *ending* of the much-vaunted Cold War and the associated nuclear threat, in fact, has it at last been possible to bring the picture clearly to light in the first place. Only the enforced death of the old interpretations has made it possible for the new to come to birth.

Could it come true?

Fact or fiction, then? Is such a scenario even remotely possible? Even as I write, it is easy to assume that it is not. And yet, extraordinary things are starting to happen. In Central Asia, the newly-independent Muslim republics of the former Soviet Union are slowly finding their feet, aided by Turkey and other Muslim countries. Their combined potential oil wealth is already considerable, their store of armaments (left over from the former Cold War) immense. Islam is recovering its former power by leaps and bounds. There is a longing for a new, charismatic leader who will set everything to rights. And already there is talk of founding a new United States of Central Asia. Meanwhile, in the Middle East, the conditions are becoming ever more ripe for some kind of ultimate confrontation between militant Islam and the West, while in the former Yugoslavia the temptation is growing for the Arab world to intervene in the very heart of Europe itself . . .

I cannot, of course, say with any degree of certainty that any of these developments is necessarily relevant to Nostradamus's prophecies. Nor is it for me to comment at this point on the Jewish/Christian Nostradamus's characteristically hostile attitude to Islam, other than to say that I do not share it. Yet I cannot help feeling that there may be some kind of link here, just waiting to be established. And, if so, then the rationale for Nostradamus's efforts will start to become increasingly obvious. For he makes it repeatedly clear in his verses that the future lies very largely in our own hands. It is for us, in other words, to take warning from his prophecies, to make due preparations for what is likely to happen and to take what counter-measures we can while there is still time.

Of course, it is always possible that he is wrong. But if he is, then he has to be wrong in a big, big way – utterly, hopelessly and comprehensively wrong, indeed – which would hardly square with the fact that he is generally credited (as we shall see) with a remarkable number of past successes.

It seems to me to be of the utmost importance, then, to

establish just what it is that Nostradamus predicted for the coming years. I have therefore rendered his verses in the clearest and most appropriate way I can – namely in rhymed verses of the same type that Nostradamus himself used. So far as I know, this is the first time that this has been done, at least in recent years. I have also endeavoured to keep my own comments simple and to the point, relegating the more academic material to the back of the book. Indeed, I have not reproduced the original French verses at all, since these are quite easy to find in other editions and are in any case far too obtuse to be of any help to the majority of readers.

The result is, I believe, the first accessible English translation of Nostradamus of recent years. But then, if he is right in predicting the events he does, it may well need to be.

About this book

To start with, then, I propose to look briefly at Nostradamus the man and to tell the story of his life. Following this, I shall examine his prophetic and writing career and some of his working methods. In Chapter 2, I shall go on to look at how interpreters and commentators have struggled to make some sort of sense of the baffling riddles left by the prophet of Provence. I shall also examine the laws of prophecy and outline my proposed principles for interpretation and explain briefly how I arrived at the sequence suggested. Chapter 3 will take a look at a selection of the most successful of the seer's predictions and, finally, in Chapters 4, 5 and 6, I shall for the first time set out in verse his astonishing prophecies for the coming years.

> Up! Flee away o'er field and fen!
> And let this dark, mysterious tome
> From Nostradamus' very pen
> Suffice to guide you as you roam.
>
> Goethe, *Faust* (I, 1)

1

THE SEER

Seated at night, the studious eremite
On brazen tripod stares with steady sight.
What flickers forth out of the lonely night
Bids fair to bring what none should doubt to light.

Centuries: I.1

UNEASE, FEAR, FATALISTIC DREAD — these are among the most usual reactions of people today when the name of Nostradamus is mentioned. The mysterious medieval doctor and seer has acquired something of the aura of a magician, a dark and threatening master of the occult, a delver into unspeakable realms of astrology and witchcraft. Many have come to class him with Mephistopheles himself.

Not because he was necessarily anything of the kind, but because that is how his crabbed and curious verses have come to be seen — especially by those who have never read them.

It is almost as though this eminent, sixteenth-century physician and occultist — the contemporary of his British near-equivalent, Queen Elizabeth I's celebrated court astrologer Dr John Dee — were, through his verses, not only predicting the

7

future, but actually controlling it from his grave, dead though he has been now these four hundred years and more.

Certainly, the former leaders of Nazi Germany seem to have believed as much. Either that, or they were determined cynically to exploit popular superstition to that effect. Not only Dr Goebbels's ministry of propaganda, but also Himmler's SS delved into the prophecies in a big way. Their aim seems to have been first to descry the future destiny of the world in general and of the Third Reich in particular, and then to convince that world of their conclusions. The British and Americans, no less cynically, retaliated in kind. So, much more genuinely, did one of the greatest of French Nostradamus scholars, Dr Max de Fontbrune. His book on the prophecies of Nostradamus, published in 1938, admittedly foretold the German invasion of France, but it also predicted the subsequent victories of the Allies in North Africa, their invasion of Italy, the disgrace of Marshal Pétain, the triumphant return of General de Gaulle to France, and the defeat and partition of Germany. Not surprisingly, the occupying German forces banned the book almost as soon as they arrived in France in 1940. De Fontbrune himself was persecuted by the Gestapo. It was as though they believed that attacking the prophetic conclusions – blaming, as it were, the messenger for the message – would somehow alter the world, too. And, strangely enough there is actually more than a grain of truth in the idea. Prophecies do seem to have a role in conditioning events.

But if so, then it is literally vital that we should not draw the *wrong* conclusions. If we somehow manage to convince ourselves – as many have – that what Nostradamus foretold for the few remaining years of the present century was an era of nuclear war, widespread genocide and general hell on earth, then just possibly that is precisely what we shall inherit. Equally possibly, if we discover that his original, semi-trancelike oracle foretold nothing of the kind – whatever the more conscious Nostradamus himself may have thought about it afterwards – then that realisation, too, may have its tangible, practical consequences.

Hence, of course, the urgent need for a new and more coolheaded investigatory book such as this.

Student and doctor

Michel de Nostredame (the name seems simply to derive from the day of his grandfather's conversion) came of humble Jewish–French stock. Born in St Rémy-de-Provence on 14 December 1503 (Julian), he was brought up in the Roman Catholic faith, to which the family had recently converted from their ancestral Jewish religion out of understandable concern for their own survival amid an age of growing religious bigotry.

The eldest of seven or eight sons, he was educated by his mother's grandfather, a doctor and herbalist, who also taught him Greek, Latin, Hebrew, mathematics and astronomy, which at the time was still inseparable from astrology. An early convert to the Copernican theory that the earth went around the sun and not vice versa, the young Nostradamus went on to study at Avignon and Montpellier Universities, at the latter of which he took up medicine as his main subject. Before doing so, however, he spent nine years as a wandering physician. The plague was rife at the time, and Nostradamus soon gained considerable renown for his unorthodox methods of treating it. He insisted on good hygiene, used primitive antiseptics, seems to have had more than a passing suspicion as to just how the disease was transmitted and was reluctant to bleed his patients as tradition demanded. More than that, he was actually prepared to attend them. Not for him the accepted notion that the disease was some kind of well-deserved Divine curse, and that those suffering from it should be avoided, as we still say, 'like the plague' – the equivalent, perhaps, of the almost fatalistic attitude towards the Aids epidemic that is so often adopted by today's Christian fundamentalists.

All of this was, of course, anathema to the reigning medical establishment. Indeed, such ideas were regarded at the time as being of the devil. It was something of a miracle, then, that the young man was allowed to go up to Montpellier in 1529 to take his doctorate. Nevertheless, he successfully completed his studies there. Then he took to the road once more.

By 1534 he was living in the house of the well-known philosopher Jules César Scaliger at Agen, where he prospered, married and produced two children. His good fortune was to be short-lived, however, for soon the plague put in its appearance in the town – and both wife and family promptly died from it. This personal disaster not only nearly destroyed Nostradamus himself; news of it all but destroyed his practice too. What price, after all, the doctor who himself survived, but could not even save his own nearest and dearest?

Further calamities followed. He quarrelled with his host, was persecuted by his late wife's family and, to crown it all, started to be hounded by the Inquisition for heresy. Nostradamus's reaction was predictable. He took to the road again. During the next six years he wandered all over France and possibly Italy, everywhere gathering material from local apothecaries for a proposed medical book. Most of his life at this time, however, is a complete blank to us, and so almost inevitably raçonteurs and romancers have been drawn to fill the vacuum with fanciful tales of startling personal predictions and pieces of almost magical precognition.

By 1544 the wanderer had returned – this time to Marseille, where that winter's unusually severe floods, flushing out the rodents from their nests, brought renewed plague in their wake, and consequently more work for Nostradamus too. By 1546, it was the stricken town of Aix-en-Provence that was appealing to him for help. As ever, Nostradamus willingly responded, insisting particularly on fresh air and clean water for his patients. Working almost entirely alone, he became the acknowledged hero of the hour.

Prophet and writer

His second marriage followed, this time to a rich widow by the name of Anne Ponsarde Gemelle (their house in Salon, which still stands to this day, has been renovated in his honour). But now he largely abandoned medicine in favour of writing. Long aware that he was one of a line of natural clairvoyants – though always careful (for obvious reasons) to describe his skill as a gift from God and to link it with the Bible's prophecy that 'your old men shall dream dreams and your young men see visions' – he had already been producing an annual *Almanac* ever since 1550. Now, having converted the top floor of the house into a study, he committed himself to a much more all-embracing work: a vast collection of general prophecies called *Centuries*. It was designed to consist of ten books of one hundred four-line verses each – a thousand quatrains in all – predicting in some detail all the major events leading from Nostradamus's own time to the end of the present age and the inception of the Millennium.

His exact working methods are fairly obscure, though they are sketched vaguely in the very first two quatrains (the first of which is reproduced in translation at the head of this chapter). Most of his insights he seems to have gained by 'scrying' – in his case, contemplating the images that appeared in a water-filled vessel mounted on a brass tripod, either before or after using a wand to sprinkle his feet and the hem of his garment with some of the contents of the vessel. He also appears to have induced within himself semi-magical trances in the course of which he heard mysterious voices. For months on end he seems to have spent much of each night doing all this, since it was the best time to obtain the total silence and solitude he needed. Next, he used a variety of techniques – ancient books and astrological calculations among them – in an effort to obtain greater precision regarding the resulting insights, no doubt particularly in respect of their siting and timing. And finally he deliberately imposed on the resulting visions the discipline of working them into rhymed quatrains of a type that would not only render them memorable and difficult to tamper with, but also lend them a fine, incantatory air such as was formerly associated with the ancient Sibylline oracle.

Disguising the prophecies

Intuitive insights being intuitive insights, of course, Nostradamus's visions came in no particular order. Clairvoyant images rarely do, any more than do those of nightly dreams. The later tradition that he deliberately scrambled them, consequently, seems to have little basis in fact. With the ever-watchful Inquisition in mind, though, and with the risk that he might be accused of witchcraft if the predictions subsequently proved too obviously accurate, he not only burnt his written sources, but also took good care that his own predictions would not be too clear or specific – 'written in terms that are cloudy rather than plainly prophetic', as he himself was later to put it. We shall see in the next chapter just how he achieved this and how in consequence we might hope to decode them.

However valid the original insights might be, there were a whole host of dangers inherent in the subsequent 'tidying-up' exercise. As we shall also see in our next chapter, one particular risk was the contamination of the original vision with established religious expectations and eschatological beliefs. Indeed, the more Nostradamus's conscious mind became involved in the exercise, the more was this potentially the case. Certainly, when he eventually concluded his *magnum opus* by writing a preface in the form of a straight, prose letter to his new son César (presumably named after his former host at Agen), the preconceptions took over almost completely. There were to be untold catastrophes, plagues, famines, revolutions, floods and holocausts 'more terrible than there have ever been'. As had already happened with the plague itself only some two hundred years before, humanity's numbers would be so reduced that there would be scarcely anybody left to work the fields. Only then, after all this period of doom and gloom, would the final, golden age or Millennium arise.

This was all very well, but it had all been either said or done before. The Bible's Revelation of St John was full of it. History, equally, was full of it. Moreover, it was a fair bet that the future would be full of it, too – possibly on a repeated basis. Indeed, much of it has already come true once again in our own century. Whether the letter's gruesome end-time scenario has anything to do with what Nostradamus's original nightly visions actually revealed, consequently, is something that we shall need to establish on our own account by looking carefully at what the quatrains themselves say, while making due and cautious allowance for the seer's subsequent exercise in 'tidying up'.

And we shall not need to take too seriously his claim in the same letter that the prophecies were intended to cover the period up to the year 3797. In terms of his own abstruse calculations involving biblical chronology and the alleged date of the creation of the world he may well have been right, of course. But the verse-prophecies themselves mention no such date. What they do seem to be particularly concerned with is the years up to and including 1999 (a date that they refer to specifically).

On various occasions Nostradamus was also to suggest that he saw them as stretching as far as what he called the 'seventh millennium' – which, on the basis of his own version of biblical chronology, could indicate any date between 1827/8 and 2827/8 (he also made it clear, incidentally, that he expected time itself to go on for a good deal longer than that). Nevertheless, that a good many of the as-yet unfulfilled prophecies refer to our own time and the early years of the twenty-first century can – as we shall see in Chapter 4 – hardly be in doubt.

Fame and fortune

The great project, however, was never to be fully completed. When first published in 1555, it consisted of only the first three *Centuries*, plus part of the fourth (the old French word *'centurie'* here designates a group of one hundred verses, and has nothing to do with hundreds of years). Even the 1568 edition lacked over fifty of the seventh *Century's* intended quatrains – though it did contain the prefatory letter to Nostradamus's young son César and an odd, imprecatory quatrain in Latin doggerel at the end of *Century* VI. Also included was a bafflingly symbolic prose synopsis of his predictions in the form of a rambling screed entitled *Letter to Henri King of France the Second*. In addition, 141 *Présages* (Portents) and 58 *Sixains* (six-line verses) were incorporated into various subsequent editions, as well as eight additional quatrains for *Century* VIII and thirteen new ones apparently intended for two extra *Centuries* that were never completed.

Completed or not, however, the effect of the whole compilation was both immediate and electric. At once Nostradamus was summoned to the royal court, where he was fêted and consulted by every man and his dog, and not least by Queen Catherine de Médicis herself. He was required to draw up horoscopes for all the royal children – a difficult and delicate task in view of the ill-fortune that (unbeknown to the Queen) he had already predicted for almost all of them in his *Centuries*, albeit in his customary covert form.

If he had been unsure before of just how personally dangerous for him his chosen task might turn out to be, no such doubts could now remain – especially when news suddenly reached him that the Justices of Paris were starting to make serious enquiries about his alleged magical practices. Nostradamus reacted in his usual way. He simply hit the road. Hurriedly he returned home to Salon, where his newly-acquired fame easily swamped any darker suspicions that might be circulating about him. Indeed, that renown steadily increased as prophecy after prophecy now apparently started to come true – especially in respect of the French royal family.

So impressed was the Queen by now that she even called on the seer at his home in Salon during one of her royal progresses. Word has it that he used the occasion to identify among her retinue the relative nonentity who would become the future King Henri IV.

A few days later Nostradamus was again summoned to attend the Queen and her son, the new King Charles IX, at Arles, where Nostradamus was awarded a grant of 300 gold crowns. His triumph, clearly, was complete. True, he was becoming increasingly ill with gout, arthritis and dropsy, but with the *Centuries* already being reprinted both at home and abroad (indeed, they have never been out of print since), at least he could die rich, famous and content.

And this he duly did, at the age of sixty-two, during the night of

1/2 July 1566, just as he had predicted to his local priest the evening before, and in exactly the manner that he had apparently already described in *Présage* 141:

> *Once back from embassy, once garnered in*
> *The kingly gift, all's done: his spirit sped,*
> *The dearest of his friends, his closest kin*
> *Beside the bed and bench shall find him dead.*

It had been a remarkable, if turbulent life, and one that would reverberate around the world for centuries to come. As he lay dying amid the silence of the night that he so loved, Nostradamus may well have allowed himself a secret smile at the thought that the world had yet to hear the last of him.

2

FISHING IN THE DARK

Think on this, reader, sagely as you may,
But shun my verse, you mob profane and shallow.
Star-gazers, stupid philistines, away!
Let those more reverent my office hallow.

Centuries: VI.100 (the Latin quatrain)

Nostradamus really had no choice in the matter. His message had to be deliberately garbled – or at very least made ambiguous, arcane, obscure. The whole thing must be written (to recall once again his own words) 'in terms that are cloudy rather than plainly prophetic'. With both the law and the Inquisition constantly on his trail for suspected witchcraft and heresy, his very survival – and that of his prophecies themselves – depended on it.

The *Centuries* show the results of this. They are arcane to the point of bafflement. Often they seem to be all but devoid of meaning. Frequently they are difficult to square with normal French syntax – even though Nostradamus is nearly always extremely careful with his grammatical agreements (a good deal more so, it has to be said, than most of his would-be interpreters).

The words themselves are little better. It is not just that they are often archaic, or borrowed from Greek or Latin. It is not even that their spelling (not unusually for the period) is inconsistent and chaotic. Quite often they are wilfully distorted and mangled, whether to fit the demands of Nostradamus's rhymed decasyllabic lines or merely to hoodwink the reader. A favourite trick is to disguise words as their homonyms, rather as in English 'tiers' might be substituted for 'tears', or even 'wear' for 'where'. Thus, *son oeil* ('his eye') is first elided into one and then respelt *seul* ('alone' – I.1); *très* ('very') becomes *trois* ('three' – VIII.77); and *sang humain* ('human blood') takes on a new life as *cent, main* ('a hundred, hand' – II.62).

But that is not the half of it. Names of places are frequently replaced by ancient and unfamiliar equivalents. Names of people are equally frequently disguised under abstruse mythological or biblical pseudonyms – then, for good measure, scrambled into anagrams. Except in a handful of cases, dates are either entirely lacking or (occasionally) encrypted into complicated astrological paradigms. The whole thing is presented in loosely constructed rhyming verse rather than plain prose (and even Nostradamus's *prose* is generally far from plain), with all the strange, elliptical constructions and other unfamiliar turns of phrase which such an approach allows. And the predictions, as we have seen, are not presented in chronological order.

Moreover, to cap it all, Nostradamus (in the scholarly manner of his day) was from the start evidently thinking in Latin rather than French and phrasing his ideas accordingly, rather as though he were Virgil or Ovid.

'They will be neither too obscure nor too clearly revealed', wrote the sage rather optimistically to his son César. César, thanks to his closeness to his father, obviously had the advantage of us. To modern readers, who live at a much greater cultural and temporal remove from Nostradamus, they can seem only *too* obscure. And at this point, of course, it apparently becomes permissible – if not irresistible – for commentators to read almost anything they like into them.

As, indeed, they repeatedly have.

17

Nostradamus seems to have been aware that this would happen. 'Be alive to the fact,' he wrote to his son César, 'that men of letters will make grand and for the most part overblown claims about the way in which I have interpreted things.'

Thus, French commentators tend to site many of the allegedly predicted events confidently in France, American ones equally confidently in America, British ones in some uneasy space between the two. The religiously-minded persist in interpreting the predictions in largely eschatological terms, the scientifically-minded in terms of advanced technology, the ufologically-minded in terms of awesome visitors from outer space. It is all heady, exciting stuff. Can it, though, be squared with what Nostradamus actually says? It is here that the doubts start to creep in.

Why, then, all the self-delusion? Why the desire to read into the prophecies what manifestly is not there? Presumably because, in attempting to make sense of any unknown quantity, we always try to make *our* sense of it. We attempt, in other words, to relate it to what we know. And so, if we are keen observers of the current world scene, we tend to see future events as mere extensions – however improbably – of present ones, forgetting that there may be no discernible links between them at all. In Arthur C. Clarke's words, 'The one fact about the Future of which we can be certain is that it will be utterly fantastic.'[5]

And so, to take one example, the published commentaries on Nostradamus of only a few years back are full of third world wars and nuclear confrontations between the Soviet Union and the Warsaw Pact on the one hand, and West Germany and its allies on the other. Little had the commentators foreseen that none of the countries or organisations just mentioned would still exist to take part in their colourful scenario in the first place.

Again, those who are conventionally religious may be inclined to see the future foretold by Nostradamus exclusively in terms of the biblical apocalypse as described in St John's Book of Revelation – famines, pestilences, Antichrist, Armageddon, Last Judgement and all. That, indeed, was how Nostradamus himself, as a devout Catholic, clearly saw that future when in full waking consciousness. Yet the results of such an approach are likely to turn out to be no more reliable than the Last Times scenarios dreamt up by well-meaning fundamentalist Christians who are convinced that the events predicted by the Bible refer to *present-day* powers and alliances, and interpret them accordingly.[15] Amid the curiously comforting certainties of the former Cold War and the murderous, if reliable, confrontation between Communism and Capitalism, such expectations may have seemed reasonable enough. Now, however, things have changed – and not necessarily for the better. Ever and anon, consequently, such ideas will have to be drastically revised as the map of world politics constantly changes, dissolves and reconstitutes itself into new and totally unexpected configurations.

And always the excuse will be, '*Then* we were wrong. *Now* we are right.'

You can believe that if you like.

The Laws of Prophecy

What, then, is the underlying problem? Evidently it lies in the fact that expectation and prophecy simply do not mix. Clairvoyant insights, such as most of Nostradamus's evidently were, do not come supplied with datelines, thematic links or bibliographical references. They come, if at all, as instant, disconnected snapshots which may or may not contain some clue as to the where and when and how. They may as easily be about the past as about the future. And they are curiously one-dimensional.

It is rather as though a person were to attempt to map the heavens by looking up the chimney.

Nostradamus himself, admittedly, tried to make good the deficiency with the aid of astrological calculations and references to ancient books – not excepting the Bible itself. This may have helped. On the other hand, to the extent that both astrology and ancient books come with their own constellations of expectations, it may just as well have hindered.

Prophecies, in other words, simply cannot be interpreted in terms of past or present expectations. The expectation predicts its own future: the prophecy may well refer to quite another.

But if this is the case, what other bandits might not be lying in wait to waylay the prophetic caravan? Unfortunately, there are all too many of them. In my book *The Armageddon Script: Prophecy in Action* (Element, 1981)[12] I set out the more obvious of them in terms of eight proposed Laws of Prophecy. They run as follows:

1 **The Law of Surprise Fulfilment**
The most likely outcome is the one that nobody has anticipated.

2 **The Law of Thwarted Expectation**
The most obvious interpretation is likely to be the wrong one.

3 **The Law of Prejudicial Interference**
Preconception and prophecy do not mix.

4 **The Law of Self-fulfilment**
Prophecies tend to be self-fulfilling (here I would merely add to my original text the word 'repeatedly').

5 **The Law of Diminishing Accuracy**
A prophecy's accuracy decreases as the square of the time to its fulfilment.

6 **The Law of Divided Functions**
Prophecy and interpretation are incompatible activities.

7 **The Law of Prophetic Foreshortening**
Clairvoyance foreshortens the future.

8 **The Law of Non-existent Impossibility**
If it can happen, it will; if it can't happen, it might.

Readers will not expect me to expatiate on these eight prophetic laws here. Most of them are pretty self-evident and even those that are not will soon become clear, once they are experimentally applied to a few specific examples.

Given, however, that there is some merit in my analysis, it will be seen that most existing would-be interpretations of Nostradamus immediately fall foul of Laws 1, 2, 3 and 6. They also tend to ignore at least the second half of Law 8, which Arthur C. Clarke has likewise proposed in his stimulating book *Profiles of the Future*. Under the title 'Clarke's Law', this runs: 'When a distinguished but elderly scientist states that something is possible, he is almost certainly right. When he states that something is impossible, he is very probably wrong.'[5] For 'scientist', we could, of course, in the present case equally well read 'Nostradamian commentator'.

Not that commentators usually deal specifically in impossibilities. Nevertheless, their very tendency to propose one particular scenario tends by its very nature to preclude all others. And yet, as my earlier quotation from Arthur C. Clarke affirms, the one thing that is certain about the future is that it will be quite different from what we anticipate.

Or at least it might be, were it not for the baleful – yet by now widely recognised – operation of Law 4. For one result of the commentators' efforts is that their interpretations have long since come to take on the aura of prophecies in their own right. People have come to assume that what Nostradamus is supposed to have meant is what he *did* mean. To the extent that Law 4 is valid, therefore, there is a danger that this very assumption will cause people, however unconsciously, to help bring to pass what is assumed.

Putting Nostradamus in context

Any new interpretation of Nostradamus, therefore, has to avoid these obvious pitfalls. Eschewing preconceptions, avoiding all past or present assumptions, it needs to decode his quatrains purely in terms of what is known about Nostradamus himself – his working methods, his arcane literary tendencies, his keenness to condense and veil what he wrote 'somewhat obscurely' in order to protect the prophecies from the ignorant and himself from the hands of the Inquisition.

Above all, it needs to interpret Nostradamus as a man not only of his age, but of his place and creed as well. The seer, after all, was not merely a Renaissance scholar, imbued through and through with classical mythology. He was also something of a medieval mage, a contemporary of both John Dee and Paracelsus. His sixteenth-century mind inevitably contained an extraordinary mixture of the educated, the everyday and the purely fantastic. Medically enlightened as he undoubtedly was, he was every bit as prone as his contemporaries to see the future in exclusively biblical terms – and overwhelmingly dark and threatening ones at that. He lived, after all, amid an age of plagues and pestilences that had decimated Europe's population only a couple of centuries before, and constantly threatened to do so again. As a Jew, he was privy to many of the ancient secrets of Jewish occultism, not least the kabbala. As a Catholic, he was naturally liable to relate his insights regarding the future to Catholic apocalyptic teaching, as well as to the fate of the Church and its leaders. He was also prey to every kind of religious superstition in an age when such superstition was rife – rife enough, in particular, to fire the revolutionary Protestant initiative of Martin Luther. Above all, as a Frenchman, he was prone to relate world events mainly to his own country and those bordering it, while also casting a wary eye on events in and around his ancestral Holy Land.

And so we should positively *expect* him to write in terms of alchemical notions, hermetic symbols, kabbalistic codes, biblical doctrines, mythological entities, plagues, epidemics, famines, floods, conflagrations, Armageddons, Second Comings and Last Judgements. If he did not, it would actually be surprising.

For obvious reasons, too, we should expect him to describe future national leaders as 'kings' or 'princes', to disguise their names even when he anticipates them, to use classical or contemporary – rather than modern – names for countries and cities, and to set his ultimate predictions within the framework of some kind of Last Times scenario. And we should expect him to apply such words as *viendra* (will come) and *terre* (land, world) to France itself, rather than to the world as a whole.

In all these respects, indeed, Nostradamus was *himself* only too prone to the baleful operation of Laws 1, 2, 3 and 6. However accurate his intuitive insights, the conscious man who wrote them down almost inevitably allowed them to be coloured by all of the factors mentioned – to say nothing of his astrological work and other studies. Moreover, by casting his predictions in rhyming verse rather than clear, straight prose – not something of which Nostradamus ever seems to have been particularly guilty at the best of times – he inevitably drew a further veil of obscurity over the insights that he was seeking to convey, even if we leave out of account his further, more deliberate efforts in that direction.

Principles of interpretation

From all of this three major interpretive principles seem to follow.

1 Since all translation relies for its success on an awareness of overall context, it will be no more possible to interpret individual stanzas *in isolation* than it is possible to interpret the individual pieces of a jigsaw puzzle. In the absence of the original 'picture on the box', we have no option but to reconstruct it gradually for ourselves from first principles, piece by apparently meaningless piece. Preconceptions as to what the outcome will be are likely to get in the way. Possibilities can of course be indicated, but only as possibilities among other possibilities, and then only in so far as is warranted by what Nostradamus actually says.

2 It then has to be our major objective to relate each verse, once roughly decoded, to other decoded verses by spotting common themes, phrases, place names and time references, so as to establish roughly what the correct sequence is. In this way it should then become possible gradually to discover what the

true overall context is, too, and thus eventually to put ourselves in a position to interpret Nostradamus *in terms of
himself*.

3 Finally, the usual, literal, word-for-word type of translation
  will actually be counterproductive, since it merely reproduces
  the original surface lexicon without giving any flavour of its
  sense, shape, vigour or flow, still less of the former complex
  semantic associations which have long since become lost to us.
  In short, it is not translation at all, but semi-legalistic nonsense
  − and anybody who had ever attended a court of law will know
  what travesties of justice such insensitivities to linguistic
  nuance can produce.

In view of this, I propose in the following chapters to render
Nostradamus's verses in just the same memorable, rhythmic
form that he himself adopted − rhymed, decasyllabic lines (i.e.
pentameters) of precisely the type that were also being written in
English at the time by the immediate precursors of Shakespeare.
Not that Nostradamus was himself in any sense a Shakespeare.
His verse is generally terse in the extreme, often telegrammatic,
sometimes clichéd, even crude at times. Much of it is so bald and
garbled as to read rather like semi-dyslexic newspaper headlines.
Nevertheless, it follows its own distinct (if Latinate) grammatical
rules, generally scans and virtually always rhymes − and any true
translation will therefore need to do the same.

I do not propose, though, any more than most other commentators, to reprint the original, sixteenth-century text, or even (as
most of them do) an edited version of it. Readers wishing to
compare my translations with the French would probably be best
advised to go directly to the original version, as most recently
republished by Erika Cheetham.[3] (For the 'extra' quatrains and
translations of the two letters, see Roberts:[19] some of the *Présages* and *Sixains* will be found in de Fontbrune.[7]) A set of
academic notes, designed to explain one or two of the more
abstruse and unfamiliar points, will be found at the end of the
main text. More general explanatory comments will be found

appended to each verse. Numbered references are to the bibliography on page 287.

In this way I hope to put readers in the best possible position to assess the various prophecies for themselves, first checking the claimed accuracy of those that are supposed already to have come to pass, and then matching those that are still unfulfilled with actual events as they unfold. But actually *anticipating* those events is something that will depend heavily on just how far it turns out to be possible to reassemble into its original sequence the prophetic jigsaw puzzle that Nostradamus's inner visionary source itself so determinedly disassembled all those years ago.

3

A SHORT COURSE IN PROPHECY

On numerous occasions and over a long period I have predicted well in advance specific events, . . . however unexpected they may have been, which have already come to pass in various parts of the world.

Letter to César Nostradamus

IF THERE IS ONE THING for which Nostradamus is more widely renowned than for the fearsomeness of his predictions concerning our future, it is the uncanny and unerring accuracy of his predictions of events that now belong firmly to our past. If popular mythology is to be believed, almost every event of any note that has happened since his death has been found to have been foretold in his enigmatic verses. That, indeed, has to be his prime qualification for offering himself as a guide to our future.

To take the *Centuries* proper, for example, out of a total of some 940 or so quatrains (the exact number varies with the edition) around 420 have been identified by one commentator or another as having already come to pass — which means, incidentally, that rather more than half of them are still awaiting fulfilment.

However, this figure – and with it the implied success rate – is actually far from being what it seems. For the fact is that, out of the 420 or so proposed 'hits' *only some 50* are interpreted in more or less the same way by most commentators. Of the other 370, different interpreters frequently disagree over which events should be linked with which verses. Any two commentators may well apply a given verse to quite different countries and even centuries. Indeed one of them may well apply verses to the future that the other would confidently apply to the past.

But that is not the last of the surprises. *Of only a dozen or so of the allegedly 'fulfilled' predictions can it be said that all the major commentators agree in their identification.*

This fact is something of a bombshell. It means that Nostradamus's alleged past accuracy has far more to do with popular belief – perhaps even with a popular *need* to believe – than with actual fact. You may insist, of course, that the commentators – or some of them, at any rate – must be wrong. Alternatively you may deduce, possibly with a sigh of relief, that it was Nostradamus himself who was wrong after all.

What the figures really suggest, however, is something much less satisfying to those who like final answers. It is the sobering thought (sobering, that is, for would-be commentators) that the seer's predictions, interpreted in isolation, are in most cases cast in far too vague a form to permit much in the way of positive and final identification even of *past* events – to say nothing of their future equivalents.

Nor would this necessarily have been a bad thing from Nostradamus's point of view. The possibility always deserves to be borne in mind that history is in some degree cyclic, and that the same or similar events do tend to return again and again, much as Nostradamus clearly believed, and as the author of the Book of Ecclesiastes (allegedly King Solomon himself) likewise suggests:

> To *everything its season, and to every activity under heaven its time* ... *Whatever is has already been, and whatever will be has already been, and God recalls each event in its turn.*

. In this chapter, then, I propose to quote a selection of what are generally agreed to be the more strikingly successful of the predictions (Roman numerals will refer to the number of the *Century* or book; Arabic ones to that of the verse quoted). You will note that a common feature of many of these is the mention of specific times and place names – the latter especially being a feature which Nostradamus himself recommended to his son César as a vital key to interpretation. I also include one or two others which commentators have all too easily consigned to a familiar apocalyptic future, but which seem to me already to have been fulfilled in terms at least as clear as those applying to most of the other agreed 'hits'.

On this basis, hopefully, you will gain a much clearer idea in your mind of the kind of predictive features to look for in the as-yet unfulfilled prophecies. You will then stand a better chance of using them, if not actually to anticipate future events, then at least to recognise them when they come.

What follows, in other words, may be regarded as a kind of short course in prophecy – or at least in prophetic decipherment – conducted in terms of practical examples from Nostradamus himself.

I.35   *The younger lion shall surmount the old*
       On martial field in duel man to man.
       Twice challenged, thrice; eyes pierced in cage of gold,
       Death shall come hard as only dying can.

It was with the success of this quatrain that Nostradamus originally made his name as a seer. As soon as it came to the ears of Queen Catherine de Médicis, she immediately sensed that it applied to her husband the King. This was the main reason why Nostradamus was summoned to attend the court within weeks of the publication of his first edition. The King, however, was less impressed, and during the combined marriage celebrations for his daughter and sister in 1559 insisted on tempting fate by taking part in a series of three jousts. His opponent was the captain of his Scottish guard, the Conte de Montgomery. The king, clad in full armour and golden helmet, bore a shield whose device was a lion rampant. Montgomery's shield, too, allegedly bore a lion rampant. The first two encounters were indecisive, but the King demanded a third. During the course of it, Montgomery's lance shattered and splintered, part of it entering the king's throat and the other penetrating his visor, piercing his eye and eventually entering his brain. The King died from his wounds after eleven days of agony, plunging France into half a century of crisis.

III.30   *He who by force of arms in martial fight*
From greater man shall steal away the prize
Shall by six men be piked from bed at night.
Naked, unarmed, how sudden his surprise!

I cannot resist including this quatrain, as it predicts the historical sequel to the first one in unmistakably specific terms (always a vital key where interpretation is concerned).

Montgomery, who had fled to England and converted to Protestantism following his unfortunate killing of the King, eventually returned to France to lead the Huguenots of Normandy in a revolt. Defeated and captured, his life was officially spared. But the Queen had a long memory and a longer arm. In May 1574 six of her men broke into his bedroom at night and dragged him off naked. Eventually he was executed on her orders. Whether or not this was all in conscious response to the prophecy or despite it we shall probably never know.

Sixain 52   *Another blow, great town, half-starved anew,*
The feast of blessed Saint Bartholomew
Shall grave into the bowels of your heart.
At Nîmes, Rochelle, Geneva, Montpellier,
Castres and Lyon, Mars on his Arian way
Shall wager all on noble lady's part.

Allegedly found among Nostradamus's papers on his death in 1566, this prediction was to come horribly true six years later in the form of the now-infamous Saint Bartholomew's Day Massacre. Apparently carried out at the Queen's behest, this was an attempt to massacre all the Protestant leaders in France at one fell swoop. In the course of it some eight thousand died, not only in Paris, but in other towns and cities as well – though not, it seems, in Geneva. Note that it is the specific details of time and place that ultimately validate the prediction. Once again, though, prior knowledge of this prediction by the Queen cannot be ruled out.

III.51   *Paris shall plot grand murder to commit.*
Blois shall contrive to bring the deed to pass.
Orléans would restore its leader's writ.
Angers, Troyes, Langres shall make them pay, alas!

Here again, it is above all the place names that make it possible to identify the prophecy – this time with the celebrated murder of the Duc de Guise on the King's orders in the royal château at Blois on 23 December 1588. (Tourist guides at the castle still lovingly recount the gory details to this day.) This bloody deed was to prove a crucial event in France's sixteenth-century wars of religion. Its immediate effect was to produce general unrest throughout the country, during which the citizens of Orléans replaced their governor with a Guise supporter. Only the predicted reaction of the three towns in the last line is at fault: Nostradamus failed to foresee that Angers and Langres would support the Guise cause, while Troyes would stay neutral. Nostradamus, it seems, was not infallible, any more than anybody else ever is. The point is doubtless worth remembering.

IV.18   *Of those most learn'd of facts celestial*
          Some shall by ill-read princes be impeached,
          Proscribed, then hounded as though criminal
          And put to death where'er they can be reached.

Though lacking much in the way of specific detail either of time or of place, this quatrain accurately foresees the persecution by the reigning establishment of the post-Copernican astronomers for a good while to come – not the least of them Galileo. But then perhaps it was not too difficult for Nostradamus, as a post-Copernican himself, to anticipate this probability.

IX.49   *Brussels and Ghent shall march against Anvers*
          And London's parliament its king shall slay.
          Wine shall be ta'en for wit: confusion there,
          With government in deepest disarray.

This quatrain, it is generally agreed, constitutes a clear prediction of the death of Charles I of England in 1649 – though once again the lack of specific dating means that Charles himself would have had the greatest of difficulty in taking warning from it, even had he been inclined to. Nevertheless, Brussels, Ghent and Anvers (Antwerp) were indeed all in contention between the three great powers of France, Holland and England in 1648/9, so that it could be said that the warning signs were there, however

31

indistinctly. Moreover, a second look reveals that the year of 1649 is possibly foreshadowed after all – in the number of the quatrain!

VIII.76   *More cudgeller than ever English king*
          Base-born, by force the wretch in power shall sit.
          Sans law, sans faith, blood from the land he'll wring.
          His time's so close I sigh to think of it.

Nostradamus's description of a non-Catholic commoner seizing power in England seems to offer a more or less perfect fit with Oliver Cromwell, who was born only thirty-three years after the death of the French seer. It must by now be starting to become apparent, meanwhile, that the latter was particularly sensitive to future acts of *lèse-majesté*, as of antireligion or heresy of any kind.

II.51   *Innocent blood is laid at London's door,*
        Consumed by lightning-bolts in '66,
        And ancient lady, falling to the floor,
        Kills several of that sect of heretics.

Numerous commentators have identified this prediction with the Great Fire of London in 1666. If the 'lightning-bolts' seem slightly off-beam in the light of the established explanation, the 'ancient lady' does seem to link in with the great statue of Our Lady that formerly stood in the porch of the then St Paul's cathedral. During the fire the statue collapsed on a number of people who were seeking refuge there, prior to the destruction of the entire building which to this day is for many people the most memorable feature of the catastrophe.

IV.89 *Thirty from London secretly lay schemes*
By sea to act against their king anointed.
His circle has no taste for death, it seems.
From Friesland a fair-headed king's appointed.

Here it is the place names that give the game away. In 1688 a group of leading noblemen (whether thirty in number or not is not recorded) left England by sea to seek the assistance of the Dutch William of Orange against their King, James II. The latter conceded defeat with remarkable alacrity, first fleeing, then accidentally captured by William's forces and finally gratefully accepting the chance that he was offered to escape again to France. And to crown Nostradamus's evident prediction of England's so-called Glorious Revolution, William had indeed been born, if not in Friesland, at least in the region corresponding to the modern Holland.

. . . And starting in that year there will be greater persecution of the Christian Church than ever took place in Africa, and it will last until the year 1792, which will be thought of as the beginning of a whole new order.

Quite what the beginning of this extract from Nostradamus's *Letter to Henri King of France the Second* refers to is anybody's guess, but his pinpointing of 1792 as the start of a new dispensation seems to be an accurate prediction of the start of the antireligious French revolutionary republic in that year. But then leading astrologers had already been predicting a major social turnabout at this time for around a century before Nostradamus's day. Perhaps it is significant, then, that this prediction comes, not in one of the quatrains, but in Nostradamus's fully conscious prose writings.

IX.20   *Through woods of Reims by night shall make her*
            way
         Herne the white butterfly, by byways sent.
         The elected head, Varennes' black monk in grey
         Sows storm, fire, blood and foul dismemberment.

Of the numerous predictions that seem to apply to the future
French Revolution of 1789 onwards, none is more famous than
this extraordinary bull's-eye. The surprising mention of the insig-
nificant town of Varennes (the one near France's eastern border,
presumably) immediately points to the sole historical event of
major note that ever seems to have happened there – namely the
celebrated night-time arrival of Louis XVI and his queen, Marie
Antoinette, on 20 June 1792, in the course of an attempt to flee
the country that was to prove the final nail in the coffin of the
French monarchy and its credibility. It is this identification in
turn – and this alone – that then makes it possible for us in
retrospect to decode the rest of the quatrain. 'Herne', via the
form 'Ierne', decodes anagrammatically as *Reine* (queen). The
route to Varennes had indeed been largely circuitous ('two parts
devious', as the French puts it), taking the royal couple through
the forest near Reims (suggestively spelt *Reines* in the original).
The King, who (unusually) was an elected one, and a Capet to
boot – the French has 'cap.' which could as easily be short for this
as for the Latin *caput* ('head') – is known to have been wearing
grey, while the Queen (certainly a frivolous butterfly at the best
of times) was, as predicted, clad in white – the same colour that
her hair allegedly also turned following the incident. Despite
determined efforts by some commentators to explain the kingly
'black monk' as an 'impotent aristocrat', though, this expression
seems to be yet another demonstration of Nostradamus's
endearing fallibility. The last line is just as difficult to decode –
though not, in this case, because its meaning is entirely inacces-
sible. It is merely that it is so cryptic – more a list of disconnected
words than a sentence. Consequently a measure of hindsight has

to inform the final line of the translation. Dismemberment (my admittedly free interpretation of the French *tranche*) is certainly what awaited the kingly 'head' and that of his consort: in the form of the guillotine it is also a fair description of what was to befall countless numbers of their subjects, too, during the next few years.

I.60   *Near Italy an emperor is born*
         Who'll cost the Empire dear; and ever since
         Those even who his hand decline to scorn
         Shall say he is more butcher than a prince.

As in the case of the French Revolution, Nostradamus seems to devote an extraordinary number of quatrains to the Corsican-born Napoleon Bonaparte, at least if the commentators are to be believed (Erika Cheetham[3] lists no fewer than fifty-five references to him, plus a further nineteen devoted to the Napoleonic wars). In one of them (VIII.1) the seer apparently even tries to spell out the future emperor's name in the capital letters that he tends to reserve for such exercises in literary clairvoyance: PAU, NAY, LORON – which resolves anagrammatically into 'Napaulon Roy'. Given Nostradamus's main prophetic concerns (king, country, religion), this emphasis on Napoleon – whom he seems to regard as some kind of Antichrist, though he never actually uses the word of him – would not be too surprising. Nevertheless it has to be said that few of the proposed identifications are as detailed or consequently as convincing as they might be. The above verse could be seen as a case in point: it fits, but it could equally well fit any other major leader born in the Mediterranean area. Indeed, under intense pressure to identify quatrains that predict such major events as Trafalgar, Waterloo or the Retreat from Moscow, a good many commentators all too readily resort to highly dubious methods, forcing meanings on to quatrains that patently cannot bear them – mainly by dint of totally ignoring or even blatantly misrepresenting Nostradamus's syntax (he may have been deliberately devious, but he was certainly not illiterate!). This naïve tendency to corral his quatrains around favourite, pre-selected themes – especially present-day ones that for obvious reasons loom much larger in our own consciousness than they are likely to do in that of posterity – is a common tendency against which we shall need to be constantly on our guard when attempting to decipher what appear to be Nostradamus's predictions for our future.

I.25   *For finding what was lost for many an age*
         Shall Pasteur be as demigod acclaimed.
         Then, as the moon ends her great pilgrimage,
         Shall he by currents contrary be shamed.

On the face of it, this piece represents an extraordinary prophetic bull's-eye. According to Erika Cheetham,[3] the moon's last great astrological cycle ran from 1535 to 1889. In the light of VI.100 (quoted at the beginning of Chapter 2), I would not presume to disagree or even to express an opinion on the matter. But true it undoubtedly is that the years 1888–9 marked the establishment by Louis Pasteur of his famour Paris institute, dedicated as it was to his discovery that many diseases were partially caused by micro-organisms. The prediction (if that is indeed what it is) suggests that this was known about in ancient times, too. Modern medicine has since rather gone overboard in this direction, almost as though Pasteur had suggested that infectious diseases were caused by nothing else – when in fact he adduced environmental, emotional and psychological factors as well. As in the case of Nostradamus himself, in other words, the guru was more or less turned into a god and his words were taken by devotees to ridiculous extremes. Not so his immediate contemporaries, however. As always, the reigning establishment opposed his views. Hence, presumably, the last line. But then all this is to assume that Nostradamus was really talking about Pasteur in the first place. My guess is that, had he been asked, he would have taken the view that the word *Pasteur* in fact referred to a future pastor of the church – or even a simple shepherd – who would rediscover some ancient artefact or holy relic (he elsewhere seems to refer to the expected rediscovery of the tomb of St Peter, for example). In this case we should have an interesting example of prophetic intuition – or even plain chance – triumphantly transcending the prophet's own conscious expectations. Even more important, however, we have an example of a quatrain that offers us both a name and a date as a means of identification. For our current purpose, such things are worth a ton of general speculation.

VII.25   *Long-drawn-out war the army's strength so saps,*
To pay the soldiery shall nought remain.
Instead of coins they'll issue parchment-scraps.
French bronze shall face the crescent flag again.

Among the various quatrains that commentators commonly assign to the First World War, this one is little more specific or convincing than most (one or two of the others will in fact be listed as *future* predictions in the next chapter). Nevertheless, it does seem to reflect the enormous drain of the war, both in men and in materials. Indeed, Nostradamus seems to imagine that this is why people are starting to be paid in paper money rather than coinage ('gold', as he puts it) – a detail which certainly does seem to date the prediction to the fairly recent past rather than to the future. If the term 'parchment' (*cuir* in later editions) seems slightly odd, one only has to ask oneself what paper money looks like once it has acquired a goodly layer of grime. Line four also seems accurately to anticipate the use of French cannon in the war against the Turks in the Middle East.

. . . In the month of October a great revolution shall take place, so profound as to convince people that the earth has ceased to move naturally and has descended into everlasting darkness. Following warning signs the previous spring, extraordinary changes shall occur, kingdoms be turned upside down. There shall be great earthquakes, too. And all this shall be accompanied by the creation of a New Babylon, a despicable whore pregnant with the abomination of the first holocaust. This shall last no more than seventy-three years and seven months. At that time, from the stock that has so long been barren, originating in the 50th degree, shall come one who shall restore the entire Christian Church. Then a great peace shall ensue . . . The countries, towns, cities and provinces, having quit their original state in an effort to set themselves free – but having thereby imprisoned themselves all the more firmly – shall experience a secret rage at the loss of their freedom and religion, and shall start to strike from the left to return once again to the right.

This extraordinary piece of prediction from the *Letter to Henri King of France the Second* – which in the interests of readability I have been forced to render fairly freely – immediately begs to be identified with the Russian Bolshevik Revolution of October 1917, which had indeed been preceded by a preliminary rising the previous spring. Seventy-three years and seven months from that date takes us up to the spring of 1991, when the emergence of the new order in the Soviet Union was in full swing, and was about to lead on that summer to the sudden rightward lurch that Nostradamus had predicted over four hundred years before (however he may have understood the idea). Since the 50th degree of latitude passes almost directly through Cracow in Poland, the great restorer of the Christian Church (in the East especially, presumably) is seemingly identified as Pope John Paul

II, who was formerly the city's archbishop – even though in those days religion in the Eastern bloc had, as foreseen, perforce been something of a 'barren plant'. The Great Whore I shall have to leave readers to identify for themselves.

Allowing for the seer's customary exaggeration, however, it has to be said that the accuracy of the whole forecast, especially for a 'clear consciousness' one, is astounding – always assuming that we have identified its correct fulfilment. (The prediction, after all, is immediately surrounded by others that seem to refer to nothing recognisable at all. Indeed, the groups of predictions contained in the letter seem to be both scrambled and inserted back-to-front, almost as though Nostradamus was determined not to reveal his hand too clearly, even in his letter to the King. As he himself writes: 'By this discourse I put everything predicted confusedly as regards its timing . . .')

This problem of identification is always where the danger lies. The actual words of the prediction, after all, say nothing whatever about Russia, still less about Communism. Even with the text in front of them, nobody could have used it to forecast the events in question until at least the year 1917, when they had already started to happen, simply because the identification of any prophecy has to depend on whether details can be found to fit it – but then, actual events are so complex that it is nearly always possible to find details that do, however obscure they may be. The chief merit in the present identification is that the details are not obscure at all, but large and plain for all to see – and consequently it is for similarly large and plain facts that we shall need to look as we attempt to identify Nostradamus's most important predictions for the future. Meanwhile we can at least gain from the current exercise a better idea of the scale on which to interpret Nostradamus's use of such familiar apocalyptic notions as the Great Whore of Babylon, for example – presumably a much less vast and even cosmic concept than religious tradition might have led us to suppose.

IX.16   *From Castile's council Franco shall set out:*
The legate, loth to please, shall split away.
Those of Riviera shall join in the bout
And entry bar to the great gulf that day.

Albeit translated with the benefit of a fair amount of hindsight, this quatrain not only magnificently pinpoints Franco's epic Spanish coup of 1936, but seems to name several specific names – not only Franco himself, but the former dictator, Primo de Rivera, and Castile too, in whose ancient capital of Burgos the original revolutionary *junta* named Franco head of government. The last line seems to refer either to his exile in the Canaries or to his difficulties in getting his forces across the Mediterranean from Morocco at the time of the coup. Either way, however, the prediction is a devastatingly effective one, even in the absence of dates: if enough names are openly named, it seems, a prediction can be a useful pointer to events even in the absence of other information.

X.22   *For lack of will to let divorcing be*
Which aftertimes unworthy should be deemed,
The Islands' king shall be constrained to flee,
Replaced by one who never kingly seemed.

Widely regarded as predicting the abdication of Edward VIII in 1936, this quatrain once again gets it slightly wrong. It was the government and church who objected to the King's marrying the divorced American Mrs Wallis Simpson, not the young monarch himself. The last line well describes his unwilling brother who was to become George VI as a result of the abdication. Here, once again, Nostradamus shows his extreme sensitivity to any threat to what he seems to regard as the 'divine right' of monarchy, even in a foreign country.

III.35   *In occidental Europe's deepest heart*
To poorest folk a little child is born.
Such throngs he shall beguile by speaker's art
As even Eastern kingdoms to suborn.

It seems to be widely agreed that this quatrain predicts the birth
and life of Adolf Hitler. On the other hand it is so general that
almost any great central European orator would fit: he would not
even need to be a dictator. In the event, it is the man's clearly
nefarious nature that tends to clinch the issue. As a guide to the
future, however, the prediction – even as I have fairly freely
translated it with the benefit of hindsight – would have been
valueless, lacking as it does either names, dates or (except in the
vaguest terms) places.

V.26   *By accident of war the Slavic race*
Shall come to be raised up to high degree.
One rustic-born their leader shall replace.
His forces, mountain-raised, shall cross the sea.

With its evident reference to Russia (see, though, the 'Academic
Notes' at the end of the book), this quatrain seems to predict the
rise of Stalin to world power largely as a result of the Second
World War. In this case, though, the last line is somewhat
dubious. Even where Nostradamus does get it right, it seems, we
cannot expect him to be correct in every detail.

X.100   *For all-commanding England there shall be*
More than three hundred years' imperial sway.
Great armies shall go forth by land and sea.
The Portuguese shall sorely rue the day.

Nostradamus's very last quatrain in the original collection of ten *Centuries* is a perfectly clear and unambiguous prediction of the future British Empire. The fact that the Empire finally collapsed around the middle of the twentieth century would suggest that he foresaw it as having its origins around or shortly before the year 1650 – some half a century or more after his own death, say. This ties in well with the founding of England's first successful colonies in North America in the early 1600s. The rather more dubious last line might then refer to colonial rivalry between England and Portugal. For Nostradamus's day, of course, the whole idea was a quite extraordinary one: England was then little more than a medium-sized power on the fringes of Europe. Note, though, that the dating of the prediction can, as usual, only be established *after* the event.

Sixain 54   *Six hundred, fifteen, twenty then again,*
Great Lady dead, a long and deadly rain
Of fire and iron shall hurt those countries sore.
Flanders is of their number, England yet:
Long shall they by their neighbours be beset
Until to them constrained to take the war.

This verse has been identified by some commentators as predicting the Second World War and the so-called Blitz mounted by the German Luftwaffe on Britain in the early stages of it: certainly the details are evocative. In this case the death of the 'Great Lady' would refer to the capitulation of the French Republic in June 1940. Since, however, the Flanders reference would have to be to the earlier German attack on the Low Countries, Nostradamus seems to have his facts in slightly the wrong order. But then we are already becoming used to the seer's fallibility in matters of detail, even in his more successful predictions: timing is not always a strong point where clairvoyance is concerned.

This brings us, though, to the intriguing first line. Evidently this is meant to be some kind of dating, yet clearly the numbers, if our identification is the right one, cannot refer to years. Counting backwards six hundred years or so from the time of the Blitz, after all, would place us well *before* Nostradamus's time. Bearing in mind, though, his statement in the *Letter to Henri King of France the Second* that 'everything has been worked out and calculated right down to the day and hour assigned to it,' we should not ignore the possibility that his text may imply smaller units.

If, in other words, we take the 'six hundred, fifteen' to signify *months*, say, and the remaining 'twenty' (which are presumably meant to refer to a unit of a different order) to *days*, then counting backwards from the beginning of the Blitz on Britain in August 1940 brings us to a much more promising date – namely April of 1889. This – believe it or not – coincides with the birth of Adolf Hitler. Could it be, then, that it was from this ominous date that the seer was actually calculating some of the predictions contained in his Sixains? It may seem unlikely, yet he seems to have used exactly the same system to determine, in Sixains 14, 21, 25 and 53, the dates of the German attack on Poland (said by Pitt Francis[17] actually to have been planned by Hitler on the basis of a contemporary misreading of *Century* III.57), the start of the Second World War, the German occupation of Paris and the death of Hitler respectively.[7] At all events, all of these seem to be recognisable from the text *in retrospect*, and all of the figures quoted in it then lead us back once again from those events to that decidedly inauspicious spring of 1889.

Certainly Nostradamus seems to have taken a great interest in the future German Fuµhrer – not least because (as we shall see later) he seems to have seen him, like Napoleon, as some kind of Antichrist. But then you can believe all this if you like. The verse may well apply to later events entirely. One lesson, though, that we should perhaps glean from this unlikely exercise is that Nostradamus's figures – even when he is generous enough to supply any – are not necessarily pure rigmaroles: they may well have some relationship to fact, even though it may be of an unexpected order.

IV.15   *From thence where famine shall be thought to lie*
Shall come instead recovery long-sought:
Past sea-wolf's covetous and hungry eye
Shall oil and flour from land to land be brought.

This quatrain has for some time now been widely recognised as describing the Atlantic convoys of the Second World War bringing supplies from America to a beleaguered Britain. The 'sea-wolf's eye' (Nostradamus actually writes 'dog' – or rather 'bitch' – rather than 'wolf', but in English 'sea-dog' has quite another connotation) is seen as an inspired prediction of the submarine periscope, and since the Germans themselves were to refer to their U-boat fleet in terms of packs of sea-wolves, the line naturally begs to be so applied too. On the other hand, it is not at all certain from the French that Nostradamus did not foresee the submarines as actually doing the bringing, rather than desperately trying to prevent it. Once again, in other words, he seems to have 'got' the picture as a whole, while failing fully to understand the true relationship of its details to each other. Also worth noting is the extraordinary way in which Nostradamus seems to pick up on widely used expressions and relevant turns of phrase centuries in advance, almost as though by clairaudience, and then to transform them into actual images, We should be wary of this tendency, then, in our future consideration of his unfulfilled quatrains: the seen and the heard (even, quite possibly, the *read*) are quite liable to become confused.

I.29   *When fish aquatic and terrestrial*
Through mighty waves shall land upon the beach
In form horrific, sleek, fantastical,
The seaborne foes the wall shall shortly reach.

It is natural to assume, of course, that of all Second World War images Nostradamus would have picked up on the horrific nuclear destruction of Hiroshima and Nagasaki that effectively ended it. Such events, after all, seem truly apocalyptic in scale. II.6, indeed, is often interpreted in this way (see 'Index of Predictions Quoted'), even though it in fact refers to 'gates' (*portes*) rather than 'ports' (*ports*), and the twin 'scourges' that are described as afflicting the two unnamed cities concerned seem to be specifically designated as *plague and famine* rather than 'fire from heaven'. Nostradamus could quite easily have drawn on the biblical Sodom and Gomorrah episode to invoke celestial fire and brimstone, in other words – yet he chose not to. What he does seem to have picked up on, however, was (not untypically) something much nearer to home – namely the war's numerous amphibious landings, and especially perhaps (Nostradamus being a Frenchman), the massive allied invasion of Normandy in 1944, in part using inflatables. Hence, conceivably, the current quatrain. However, Nostradamus once again seems to have got one of the details back-to-front in describing the liberating invaders as 'foes' when they are supposed to have been friends – which could conceivably suggest that the quatrain really refers to some future occasion when such will indeed be the case (see Chapter 4). The term 'wall' may seem slightly odd, too, until it is realised that the Germans' term for their massive coastal defences around the French coast was precisely that – the 'Atlantic Wall'. Once again, in other words, the seer seems to have 'heard' or 'read' an expression which he has then translated into an actual image.

III.97   *A new law in a new land shall hold sway*
        Over by Syria, Palestine, Judea.
        Dominion Arabic shall melt away
        Ere Phoebus shall complete his long career.

If the last line is a reference, as Erika Cheetham claims,[3] to the twentieth century as the 'century of the sun' (an astrological notion on which I do not propose to comment), then this prediction would appear to be describing the future re-establishment of the state of Israel in 1948. Whether the quatrain envisages an expected collapse of Arab power generally, or merely in Palestine, is not entirely clear. Once again, however, the possibility cannot be excluded that it really applies to much later events, and specifically those described towards the end of Chapter 5 of this book.

II.89   *One day the two great masters yoked shall be,*
Yet greater power on great brows seen to sit.
The New World's stars shall be at apogee:
The bloody one shall take account of it.

Once upon a time this quatrain was confidently applied to Mussolini and Hitler (the 'bloody one'). Nowadays it is more fashionable to apply it to the revolutionary series of summit meetings between Ronald Reagan and Mikhail Gorbachev which started in November 1985, and which certainly led eventually to a major realignment of world power and an enhancement of American influence at the expense of the then Soviet Union and her allies. The prominent red birthmark on Gorbachev's brow then becomes a real gift for the interpreters. Who knows – they may even be right.

I.70   *Rain, hunger, endless warfare Persia knows:*
Faith overdone the monarch shall ensnare.
What starts in France there to its ending goes.
To him it touches, so the Fates declare.

Nowadays this quatrain is widely applied to the Iranian revolution and the overthrow of the former Shah by the forces of Islamic fundamentalism ('faith overdone'). In this case, the moving force did indeed come from France, where the Ayatollah Khomeini, who was the revolution's inspiration and figurehead, was in exile at the time.

VIII.70   *Wicked and vile, a man of ill repute,*
The tyrant of Iraq comes in apace.
With Babylon's Great Whore all plead their suit.
Horrid the land shall be, and black its face.

Until quite recently nobody had managed to decode this prediction satisfactorily. With the recent advent and rapid passing of the so-called Gulf War in Kuwait, however, its fulfilment seems all too obvious. Despite the intervention of undisguised biblical imagery, everything seems well described – even the almost apocalyptic scenes of darkened skies and oil-covered desert which filled the television screens for days on end. As usual, though, there is some ambiguity in the text – this time as to whether the country that the 'tyrant' is entering is Mesopotamia (Iraq) itself or some other country. At the same time Nostradamus seems to have been at pains to disguise the word for 'land' in the last line (see 'Academic Notes'), almost as though he assumed that the latter applied to the 'tyrant', rather than to the land itself – even though the linguistic context itself firmly suggests otherwise. This might suggest in turn that not merely his visions, but even a good deal of the actual *wording* of his predictions, tended to come through to him in trance – and that he consequently preferred to disguise them not by replacing their words, but simply by respelling them. It is almost as if he regarded the words themselves – or at least the sounds of them – as somehow holy or sacred, and not to be changed in any way (compare the attitude suggested by the last line of the quatrain

47

quoted at the beginning of Chapter 2, for example) – a fact which might then help to explain the often apparently 'crude' and 'unedited' quality of the whole Nostradamian opus.

VIII.15   *Great efforts by a northern woman mannish*
Europe shall vex and nearly all Creation.
She'll hound failed leaders till they're fit to vanish,
With life and death facing the Slavic nation.

Most of this stanza seems uncannily, if wryly, predictive of Britain's so-called 'Iron Lady', former prime minister Margaret Thatcher – as popularly perceived, at least – yet only recently has it been possible to decode it satisfactorily. This is partly because, on the basis of the Latin word *dux* ('leader' or 'general') Nostradamus has – not for the last time – characteristically disguised the word *ducs* in line three as *deux*, thus contriving to fool generations of astrologically-minded interpreters into imagining that he is talking about 'two eclipses' instead of 'failed leaders'. (Well might we recall his warning words quoted at the beginning of Chapter 2!) Puzzles of this type nearly always indicate that Nostradamus is writing in code.

VI.74   *Once hounded out, she shall return to power,*
Her foes revealed conspirators to be:
More than before above her age she'll tower,
All too assured 'till death from seventy-three.

Finally, a piece of delicious speculation. Formerly applied (albeit with some difficulty) to Queen Elizabeth I, this quatrain has recently been discovered by the British media, who have promptly assumed that it, too, applies to Margaret Thatcher.

They may or may not be right. Even though this quatrain may currently be in process of fulfilment, in other words, we still cannot be sure about it until the outcome of line four has finally been established. If this is the case the prediction (to say nothing of the proposed identification) will, as so often happens, be unverifiable until *after* the event . . .

Learning the lessons

At this point, then, we come to the end of our brief survey of a few of the more striking of Nostradamus's already fulfilled predictions. To be sure, there are plenty of others, but very few of them match the best of those that I have quoted for clarity or specificity. That these others are adduced at all often owes much more to almost obsessive interpretational bias and distortion than to their genuine predictive quality. Nor is this the only influence that has been at work.

No complete edition including the last three *Centuries*, for example (and none at all of the *Sixains*) was officially published until after the prophet's death – a fact that allowed ample opportunity for other hands to edit Nostradamus's work, or even to insert 'predictions' of their own. Most of the predictions suspected of having suffered this treatment contain factual errors, however – not, on the whole, what one would expect informed hindsight to produce (unless, of course, the perpetrators were clever enough to include deliberate mistakes to give the *impression* of authenticity!). Consequently the possibility of such interference is not now too important to our investigation, especially as the vast bulk of the prophecies have necessarily been immune from it for some centuries now.

Again, just as we have referred to the possibility that Queen Catherine de Médicis may have acted in full knowledge of the predictions, so others may have done so too. The Bourbon kings, Napoleon Bonaparte and the Adolf Hitler of the 1930s (thanks to the intermediary of Frau Goebbels) are all suspected (*cf* Pitt Francis[17]) of having regarded them as a kind of 'omen' and thus of having used them as a guide to their own actions. Deliberate self-fulfilment, in other words, starts to muddy the waters further.

But all this is as nothing compared with the prolonged exercise in misinterpretation that has dogged the predictions ever since they first appeared. Generation after generation of interpreters, endlessly repeating each other's mistakes, have determinedly misread what the verses actually say in their desperate efforts to make them mean what they wanted them to mean. An almost infallible sign of this approach has been the tendency to use the predictions to blow up recent or contemporary events out of all reasonable historical proportion, irrespective of the fact that they in no way gel with what Nostradamus's overriding concerns seem to have been.

That tendency still continues today. To support it, words are ignored, tenses scrambled, whole phrases taken as if they were nothing more than magic rune-spreads and all interpretational level-headedness thrown to the winds.

But to the extent that all this is so, it is all the more incumbent on us not to fall into the same trap ourselves. Giving Nostradamus the benefit of the interpretational doubt (as I have sometimes done above) is one thing: the wholesale distortion of what he clearly says to fit our own preconceptions is quite another. Indeed, as we noted earlier, preconceptions of any kind are a luxury with which we can quite simply not afford to indulge ourselves in the first place. Initially at least, the seer's words have to be taken at face value, *though always in context* – right up to the point where we are faced with some piece of obvious nonsense that leads us to suspect that he has been tampering with his own spelling for reasons of concealment or even plain contrariness. Only at this point are we entitled to review the text, experimentally investigating what other word or expression might reasonably underlie the 'sticky patch' in question. And even then we are in honour bound to admit the fact, exposing for all to see precisely what changes or substitutions we have assumed (see the 'Academic Notes' at the end of the book).

And, meanwhile, we shall need constantly to bear in mind the other lessons that we have learned from the predictions quoted in this chapter. Nostradamus, as we have seen, is not infallible. He frequently fails to recognise how the detailed parts of his picture relate to each other – indeed, he sometimes gets them entirely back-to-front. He sometimes makes generalised predictions that could refer to almost anybody, and that are likely to be fulfilled somewhere in the world at almost any time or place. He is possibly over-sensitive to any threat to the established order, as well as to matters concerning the Christian religion and any betrayal of it. He is sometimes so cryptic that a measure of conjecture needs to be locally applied – always, though, in context, and never as a general principle. He tends to see disasters and catastrophes in terms of biblical eschatology – to which he often assigns a larger-than-life scale that it possibly does not merit. He occasionally names names, though he is also prone to resort to anagrams. Occasionally, too, he specifies exact times, though care needs to be taken in establishing the exact *terminus a quo*, as well as the precise scale involved (years, months, days). He is almost never capable of final interpretation until after the event – or at least until that event is already plainly in the offing. He seems to be clairaudient as well as clairvoyant, frequently picking up topical expressions and turns of phrase that not only are of no interpretational use to us beforehand, but are actually turned into concrete images capable of bamboozling us afterwards – just as they possibly bamboozled Nostradamus, too. And, finally, he is first and foremost a Frenchman, so that events in and around France always tend to loom especially large in his vision.

Armed with this knowledge, then, we can now proceed to examine some of his apparent predictions for our future with a view, not so much to anticipating in any detail the events involved (even though it may be possible to establish a rough sequence, and thus some sort of generalised interpretation), as to recognising them when they come. It may not be an easy exercise. But at least we can take some comfort from the fact that Nostradamus, unlike many of his would-be interpreters, seems always to have remained true to his vision, resolutely refusing to replace or tamper materially with the words that it dictated. It is almost as though he were aware of the immortal words of *The Rubáiyát of Omar Khayyám*, as later rendered by Fitzgerald:

> *The Moving Finger writes; and, having writ*
> *Moves on; nor all thy Piety nor Wit*
> *Shall lure it back to cancel half a Line*
> *Nor all thy Tears wash out a Word of it.*

4

THE COMING YEARS

At that time great ships from Turkey shall make their way to Italy thanks to the help of powers to the north . . . Craft built by the former military shall accompany them through Neptune's waves. In the Adriatic there shall be such great conflict that those who were united shall be torn apart and, to a house, cities shall be destroyed (including the former omnipotent Babylon of Europe) on the 45th, 41st, 42nd and 37th degrees of latitude.* In a sea-battle the sea shall become red . . . And at that time and in those countries the power of hell shall rise in opposition to the Church of Jesus Christ. This shall be the second Antichrist, which shall persecute the church and its rightful Vicar thanks to the power of world leaders who in their ignorance shall be seduced by tongues sharper than any madman's sword . . . Then shall come an unprecedented persecution of the church . . . And that persecution shall last eleven years or a little less . . . Then a united southern leader shall take over who shall persecute the church's clergy even more severely for a further

---

* Presumably Turin, Naples, Rome (the European 'Babylon') and Syracuse in Sicily.

three years ... This leader shall commit unbelievable
crimes against the church ... At the same time there shall
be so great a pestilence that two-thirds of the people shall
be wiped out, such that none shall be able to identify the
owners of homes or fields, and grass shall grow knee-high
in the streets of the cities. The clergy shall be totally
desolate, and military men shall seize all the revenues
from the City of the Sun† and Malta and the offshore
islands of Hyères, and the great chain of the port shall be
broken that takes its name from the sea-bull‡ ...

Extracted from the *Letter to Henri King of France the Second*

QUITE LITERALLY with the wisdom of hindsight, we are now in a position to apply our acquired knowledge of Nostradamus and his working methods to the majority of his predictions that have not yet been fulfilled.

I use the phrase 'not yet' advisedly. It is an old and well-worn formula among those who cannot quite bring themselves to believe that their favourite prophet might just possibly be wrong. Who is to say, after all, that Nostradamus might not prove as wrong as anybody?

Curiously enough, Nostradamus himself seems to have agreed. 'If I should have worked out the timings wrongly, or should fail to satisfy in any way, may it please Your Most Imperial Majesty to pardon me,' he wrote in his *Letter to Henri King of France the Second*, clearly anticipating his own due ration of abject flops. 'I protest before God and His saints,' he went on, 'that it has not been my intention to write anything that is contrary to true Catholic faith, even though I have applied such astronomical calculations as my learning permits.'

---

† Lyon (the Lion – astrological or otherwise – has always been associated with the sun).
‡ Lat, phoca = *seal*; Phocaea = *Marseille*.

The point is well taken, for we have already seen how many of Nostradamus's more apocalyptic prophecies are inevitably vitiated by his own pre-existing religious beliefs and his urgent need to stand by them publicly.

The upshot is clear. We do not have to assume that all five hundred or more of the unfulfilled prophecies refer to the future at all. Many of them may turn out to be no more than the confused ramblings and hallucinations of a half-deluded obsessive. Some may refer to events that were already long in the past even when they were first made. *Others, though, will almost certainly turn out to be just as startlingly accurate in predicting events in our own future.*

How, then, are we to recognise the latter?

For the purposes of the present exercise, a number of basic principles seem to be worth applying throughout.

1 Look for predictions that are in some way unexpected or striking. This at least means that they are unlikely to be of a type that happens somewhere or other in the world at least a hundred times a year.

2 Pinpoint those that refer to particular times or places (whether astrologically or otherwise), or that name names where people are concerned, however symbolically or anagrammatically. Take careful note, too, of those that relate to other quatrains, whether thematically or temporally.

3 Treat with the greatest suspicion (curiously enough) all those that sit too neatly with received biblical expectation, and avoid like the plague any temptation to treat the rest as if they did.

4 Take the whole exercise with more than a pinch of salt: the infallibility of Nostradamus is not an article of faith.

5 Finally, remember constantly that the initial object of the exercise is not to anticipate events at all, but merely to gain some idea of what to look out for and how to recognise it when

it comes. If it then turns out to be possible to establish a rough sequence – and thus some kind of overall context – a measure of interpretation may start to prove possible.

So much for the proposed approach. It is one, clearly, that demands both time and patience. Having produced English versions of all the prophecies concerned, it becomes necessary to group them into subject areas and mini-sequences if the resulting chapter is not to prove disordered and obtuse. These mini-sequences lead quite naturally to larger groupings, those groupings to yet larger groupings, and so on until – *mirabile dictu* – one finds that one has arrived at something that looks suspiciously like Nostradamus's original, overall sequence. Consequently, one suddenly has a general context within which to attempt some kind of interpretation – and one that is based on Nostradamus himself, rather than on imported preconceptions, at that.

The jigsaw pieces having at last been joined up together, the picture on the box at last becomes clear – and so, consequently, does the relationship of each individual piece to it.

Thus it is that I am now able to present the relevant quatrains in what appears to me to be more or less their correct order and (more important) their correct sense. We can, in short, begin our survey of our Nostradamian future more or less at the beginning, starting with its seeds in the earlier part of our own century (for cross-references please refer to the 'Index of Predictions Quoted').

III.44   *When the dumb beast that is domesticate*
After great toils and strides shall find its tongue,
The lightning-rod it shall so harm and hate
That, lifted up, on high it shall be hung.

We join the prophetic sequence at a point where Nostradamus, in apparently science-fiction vein, seems to be predicting the attainment of speech by the animals at some far-distant point in the future. However, like a good many of his apparently futuristic quatrains, this one is not at all what it seems. Its strangeness arises purely because the contents of the vision on which it is based were themselves necessarily strange and puzzling to Nostradamus himself, and he therefore lacked the vocabulary to describe it. In fact, the prediction has been fulfilled long since. The subject is not, after all, the bizarre product of some kind of genetic engineering, nor even (as Dolores Cannon suggests[2]) recent successes in teaching primates to use sign-language, but something with which we are all strangely familiar, as careful study of the details makes quite clear. Perhaps the first remarkable thing to notice is that he 'gets' – and names specifically – the lightning-rod almost two hundred years before it was invented, even though he cannot quite bring himself to believe the words that have 'come to him', and so substitutes for *verge de foudre* ('lightning-rod') the more familiarly religious, if no less strange phrase *vierge de foudre* ('Virgin of lightning'). Apparently he then confuses it (quite understandably) with the radio-aerial, which he therefore sees as posing such danger to the strange 'talking creature' to which it is attached, that 'it' (the aerial, that is) has to be strung up among the chimney-pots, well out of harm's way. In which case the creature itself – the brutish servant of mankind that eventually learns to speak, as Nostradamus describes it – begs to be identified *with the primitive wireless-set.*

I.64   *The sun at night they'll wager to espy*
When pig half-human his expression finds.
Songs, loud alarums, battles in the sky,
And brutish beasts are heard to speak their minds.

Once again we seem to be confronted with a startling picture of the horrific effects of genetic engineering in the far-distant future, with half-human pigs and talking animals. Once again, though, things are likely to be quite other than they seem. Unless it is the purest, futuristic science-fantasy, there has to be a simple explanation for this startling piece of prediction, too. Erika Cheetham suggests that it is a forecast of modern aerial warfare, with oxygen-masked (and thus 'pig-snouted') pilots dodging night-time searchlights while speaking to each other on the radio-telephone. The suggestion is ingenious – perhaps even a little *too* ingenious. (In this case a familiar piece of folk-wisdom might also be said to be predictive: 'Pigs', it goes, 'might fly'.) Nevertheless, she may just be right – though my own feeling is that the prediction better describes people wearing gas-masks on the ground by the light of marker-flares, possibly during the London Blitz of 1940. This might then explain the 'songs', as people in the communal air-raid shelters were much given to hearty community-singing to drown the noise and keep their spirits up.

VIII.77 *The Antichrist is very soon laid low.*
Seven years and twenty shall his battle stand.
Dissenters dead, captives to exile go.
Blood, corpses, reddened water pock the land.

This quatrain is commonly the cause of much apocalyptic dread, not least because of the suggestive word 'Antichrist' in the first line. Surely, it is argued, this prophecy must be either of the end of time, or at least of the dread events predicted by the Bible as taking place during the immediate run-up to it? Fortunately, we can relax. There really is no warrant for jumping to such epic conclusions. For a start, it needs to be remembered that, to Nostradamus, *any* major atheistic or anti-Christian leader would have merited the title of 'Antichrist' – even, perhaps, a leader who was merely violently hostile to the established world order as represented by traditional Christendom. This, together with the fact that the last line is curiously reminiscent of an early twentieth-century European battlefield, gives us the vital clue and leads us to the usual, sobering conclusion: namely that the prediction has in fact already been fulfilled – in this case *twice over*. Joseph Stalin, the renegade former candidate for the priesthood who became notorious as one of the most powerful and repressive atheistic dictators that the world has ever known, was dominant in Soviet politics from 1927 until his death under dubious circumstances in 1953. His struggle (the French word *guerre* means not only 'war', but any kind of quarrel or feud) thus lasted twenty-six years, so apparently fitting the requirements of the original text, which seems to see twenty-seven years as some kind of maximum. Responsible for the successful, if exceptionally brutal, fightback against the invading German armies of the Second World War, he nevertheless exterminated millions of his own compatriots too, while consigning countless others to the vast system of so-called *gulags*, or internal prison camps.

However, in this he was all but outdone by an even earlier candidate, Adolf Hitler, who used the German Nazi party to achieve his nefarious dreams of world power from the time he joined it, in 1919, until his defeat and death in 1945. His fight too, then, lasted some twenty-six years – though in his case he himself described it in terms which bore out Nostradamus's prediction with startling exactness, actually entitling his book and political testament *Mein Kampf* ('My Fight'). Meanwhile Hitler, like Stalin, was responsible for the deaths of millions during the Second World War, in his case taking on very nearly single-handed almost the whole of the rest of the civilised world. At the same time he was sending Jews from all over his ill-gotten domains to the concentration camps of Eastern Europe, where most of them were exterminated in the infamous gas-chambers. Small comfort as it may be to those who actually suffered at his hands, then, Hitler seems on the basis of the details to be marginally the better candidate for identification as the object of this quatrain – which means that, since both outrageous monsters are in any case long dead now, we can all sleep soundly in our beds again, for the moment at least . . .

I.50 *From triad watery he'll take his birth,*
And from that one where Thursday is made feast:
His fame, praise, rule and power shall spread on
earth,
By land and sea storming the farthest East.

Yet again, this quatrain is widely assumed to refer to the future Antichrist, intent on desecrating all the major Western sabbaths (Friday, Saturday, Sunday) in favour of an antireligious one of his own (Thursday). The first line, it is claimed, merely pinpoints his nativity astrologically – a fact which might, I suppose, prove useful to anybody who wanted, rather like Herod, to strangle him at birth: the *aquatique triplicité*, it is alleged, refers to the three water signs of the zodiac. But Nostradamus is rarely as astrological in outlook as many of his commentators would have us believe. The proportion of clearly astrological stanzas starts low and gets less throughout the *Centuries* – amounting to less than one in ten overall.[17] It seems far more likely, then, that the current prophecy simply refers to an alliance of three major naval powers, one of whose national feast-days will fall on a Thursday. This last detail is the real giveaway. It would be difficult for it to pinpoint more clearly the present United States of America, whose national Thanksgiving festival always does precisely that. The picture we are given, then, is of a major American leader who brilliantly wages war in the Far East, both by land and by sea, and who achieves considerable fame and stature there as a result. As such, he has a perfect fit, not in the future but (not for the first time) *in the past*. He is General Douglas MacArthur (1880–1964), former Allied Commander-in-Chief in the Far East who, at the head of a massive amphibious task-force headed by American, British and Australian forces, finally conquered Japan during the Second World War and ruled over it for many years as a particularly resplendent and charismatic dictator. Once again, in other words, a supposedly 'apocalyptic' prediction turns out (whether accidentally or otherwise) to be nothing of the kind –

unless, of course, we are positively determined that history shall repeat itself.

VIII.59 *Twice raised to giddy height, then twice brought*
        low,
    The East shall weaken and the West shall pall.
    After so many battles shall the foe,
    Pursued at sea if need be, slip and fall.

Tempting as it is to see this prediction as a mere description of the two world wars, complete with the defeat of Hitler and the pursuit and sinking of his capital ships, it now begins to look more like a general, long-term forecast for the entire twentieth century. Neither East nor West, it seems, has anything to be cock-a-hoop about, let alone any justification for American presidents to talk about the dawning of a New Era – as, indeed, events are already starting to make clear at the time of writing. Perhaps it is significant that, to British ears, the American pronunciation of the term sounds suspiciously like 'New Error' . . .

II.28 *The last but one the prophet's name to bear*
    Shall take Diana's day to rest in peace.
    He'll roam, frenetic, here, there, everywhere
    And multitudes from tribute shall release.

Yet again a fairly non-committal stanza is widely taken by the commentators to refer to the expected Antichrist, mainly because they read the verse to mean that the figure described is, like the one mentioned above, determined to replace the accepted Sabbaths of the three major Western religions with a secular one of his own – this time Diana's day, or Monday. In fact, nothing so drastic is suggested. He is merely described as taking Mondays off – and personally I have to say that I can see little that is particularly satanic about that. The fact that he travels frenetically all over the world to release a 'great people' from financial bondage does not seem particularly sinful either. To me he seems merely to be a harassed leader, politician and/or financier with decidedly good intentions. It is the first line, though, that is the real puzzle – and is evidently intended to be so. We are given no idea of which prophet is being referred to – it could be one of the Old Testament prophets (of whom the next to last was Zechariah, incidentally), or Jesus' messianic forerunner John the Baptist (either as 'John' or as 'Baptist/Baptiste'), or Muhammad, or even Nostradamus himself – and certainly no explanation is offered of how anybody is expected to identify the *last but one* to take any particular name. Nevertheless it is this very phrase that turns out to be the vital clue. Of those who regularly adopt a special name (or a *surnom*, as the text specifically puts it), among the most prominent are the popes – and Nostradamus, as we shall see, had a special interest in predicting the future of the papacy. If, then, there turns out to be only one more pope who adopts the name of John (most psychic predictions suggest that there will be only one or two more of them in any case), the next-to-last would inevitably be the present incumbent, the intensely nomadic John Paul II, intent on his former efforts to rescue his beloved Poland and the rest of the Eastern bloc from beneath the Soviet Communist heel – in which case the prophecy, like the others already listed, has long since been triumphantly fulfilled. (One would love, in this case, to know more about how he normally organises his week: certainly it would be quite understandable if he put his feet up on a Monday, in common with a good many other clerics who spend Sunday hard at work!) As ever, then, the prediction is useless before the event – yet afterwards it tends to be all but too late. Evidently Nostradamus is determined that nobody shall be able to use his prophecies to manipulate the future, but only as a guide to understanding and reacting to it appropriately when it comes – or subsequently, as apparently in the present case. Meanwhile there seems to be nothing particularly threatening about this particular prophecy at all, even if we collectively should choose subconsciously to reinvoke it in the future.

II.29 *Forth from his seat the Oriental goes,*
Crossing the Apennines fair France to see.
He'll pierce the sky, traverse the seas and snows
And strike all with his rod, whoe'er they be.

Following on immediately as it does from the quatrain above, commentators almost universally assume that this verse refers to the same figure – even though Nostradamus almost never seems to arrange his predictions in this way. Since the Antichrist is traditionally supposed (like the Messiah himself) to appear from the East and (again like the Messiah) to act as a kind of universal scourge, the would-be interpreters find in these details gratifying confirmation of their presupposition that the person being referred to is indeed the Antichrist in person. On the other hand, he seems to bear no real resemblance at all to the figure mentioned in the preceding stanza. In fact, since no specific timing or identification is offered, the present prediction could apply to almost any particularly aggressive or vengeful Eastern figure. One who immediately springs to mind is the former Ayatollah Khomeini, who indeed flew from the Middle East to exile in France, from where all kinds of threats were issued and aggressive acts initiated. Antichrist or no Antichrist, in other words (and the Imam was certainly a non-Christian, and violently opposed to the nominally Christian United States, which he persistently described as the 'Great Satan'), he has already fairly adequately defused this particular prediction, and there is thus no reason for it ever to be relit – unless in the foolhardiness of our imagination we choose to do so. Unfortunately, however, there seem to be all too many signs in later predictions that we shall do precisely that.

VI.33   *Through bloody Alus shall his final fight*
         Fail to ensure his status oversea.
         Between two rivers, fearful of armed might,
         The furious Black shall make him bend the knee.

This quatrain is included here mainly because, once again, the enigmatic 'he' is widely assumed to be a future Antichrist. On the other hand the text itself says nothing of the kind. By some it is even assumed that 'Alus' is his actual name. In fact, however, it seems more likely that 'Alus' – whose name, removing the Latinate ending, could well be 'Ali' – is merely a military ally of whoever is being referred to, and possibly one who lets him down either overseas or on the naval front. The familiar phrase 'between two rivers' immediately suggests the area of modern Iraq. Whether any of this, like VIII.70 above, is of relevance to the Gulf War of 1991 is thus rather dependent on whether Saddam Hussein had a senior military associate called Ali. *In the event, he did.* Alaa Hussein Ali Khafaaji, a formed senior officer in the particularly bloody Iran–Iraq war, and subsequently in charge of Iraq's antimissile programme, was appointed to head the puppet government in Kuwait following Iraq's invasion but, as predicted, was unable to hang on to the country on Saddam's behalf. Nostradamus could thus have picked up on either his first or his third name.

As for the 'furious Black' (*le noir l'ireux*) the curious construction makes it look almost as if the first two words were meant to be a name such as 'Lenoir' – hence my capital 'B' – unless, of course, the double article half-implies a double subject (i.e. 'the Black and [the] furious one'). As it happens, the 'avenging angel' whose furious assault forced Saddam to his knees during the course of what was specifically code-named 'Operation Desert Storm' was one General Schwarzkopf, the allied commander *whose German name actually means 'Blackhead'*, and who was nicknamed 'Stormin' Norman' for good measure. As if all this were not enough, behind the 'furious' Schwarzkopf stood his own commander-in-chief, General Colin Powell, who was indeed black in his own right.

It seems very likely, then, that this quatrain is merely a continuation of the earlier quatrain (see page 47). With black skies, black seas, black desert, a black commander-in-chief and a local commander whose very name incorporated the word for 'black', small wonder that Nostradamus should have picked up particularly on blackness in both stanzas. In short, it seems that the current prediction, too, has already been fulfilled in most if not all respects, and certainly needs to have no apocalyptic or future significance for us whatsoever.

V.92   *Once he for seventeen years has held the see*
            They'll change the papal term to five years' time,
            What time another shall elected be
            Who with the Romans not so well shall chime.

We now turn to unfolding events in the Vatican, in which Nostradamus always showed a keen interest, almost as though they were a kind of index of future world events. However, in his day the Vatican also exercised a tight control over European thought and opinion. Perhaps this is why the seer evidently felt that his original line two – and to some extent line three as well – was contentious enough to merit some fairly heavy scrambling *à la* Virgil, and duly did so effectively enough to fool whole generations of later interpreters who were prepared to skate over the rather odd resulting complexities (see 'Academic Notes'). Once the line is restored, however, the meaning becomes clear. After some seventeen years the reigning pope asks to resign. He is refused, but is offered a new law whereby popes, like many lay presidents, will in future reign for only five years at a time – with himself automatically appointed as the first of them. Thus, if the pope in question happened to be the present incumbent, John Paul II, he would (having been elected in 1978) tender his resignation in 1995, but be asked to continue for a futher five years. This would place the end of his pontificate in the year 2000, when he would be eighty – a fact which, as we shall see, would help to date various associated developments too. However, only actual events can possibly reveal the accuracy or otherwise either of Nostradamus's prediction or of its interpretation above, and the Vatican would not necessarily announce it anyway.

V.25   *Mars, Venus, sun in Leo: to Arab lord*
Shall Christendom at length by sea succumb.
Some million men Iran shall move toward:
To Nile and Istanbul coiled snake shall come.

At this point, though, we are brought face to face with something altogether more worrying. Some massive power is destined, it seems, to start moving towards Europe out of Asia via the Middle East, its armies counted in millions. True, this has happened before. As early as the fourteenth century the budding Ottoman empire started to expand westwards from Turkey, its sack of Constantinople in 1453 and the consequent flight of the Greek scholars resident there helping to spark the European Renaissance. It then moved steadily westwards into Europe, the Mediterranean and right across North Africa. Even a massive defeat at the celebrated battle of Lepanto of 1571 by a European naval confederacy comprising Spain, various Italian states and the Papacy failed to halt its progress, and it was 1683 before another confederacy – this time involving Poles, Germans, Spaniards, Portuguese and Italians – at last managed to turn back the Muslim tide before the very gates of Vienna.

Nostradamus was well aware of this Turkish threat: he lived with it all his life, after all. Might he then really be referring to this, rather than to events in our own future – much as he specifically does elsewhere? It is always possible. But if so, then (not for the first time) he is in error – and (less usually) in three important respects, at that. First, the Turks were not Arabs; second, Christianity did not succumb at the time – indeed, not even the Papacy did; and third, the Sunni Ottomans conspicuously failed to make any inroads into Shi'ite Persia.

Could it be, then, that Nostradamus is expecting another invasion from the East entirely, once again overrunning not merely Istanbul and Egypt, but this time Iran too, and in some way characterised by the image of what he describes as the 'coiled snake'?

V.27   *Near the Black Sea by fire and arms shall he*
From Persia come fair Trebizond to take.
With Arab blood the Adriatic Sea
Swims red: Paros and sunny Lesbos quake.

Once again it is clear that the campaign is quite different from that of the Ottomans – and consequently we can now start to see where Persia fits into the picture. Evidently the invasion itself has started either there or even further east, somewhere in the former Mongol empire. From there it beats a devastating path through Iran and northern Turkey. Then it will eventually take to the sea, threatening the Greek islands and the waters between Greece and Italy, where it is destined to run into stiff opposition. Once again Nostradamus uses the word 'Arab'. At first sight this may seem rather puzzling. As subsequent quatrains reveal, however, this is merely one of a number of alternative names that Nostradamus continually applies to the coming invaders – partly because (as we shall see) he has good reason for identifying them as Muslims, and partly because (as we shall also see shortly) one wing of the invasion force is about to swing into North Africa.

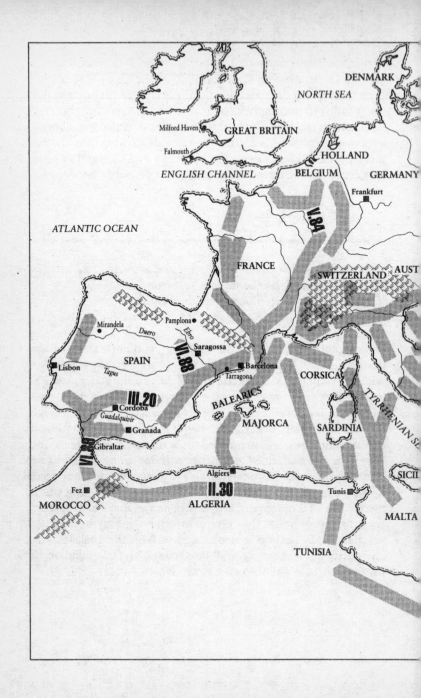

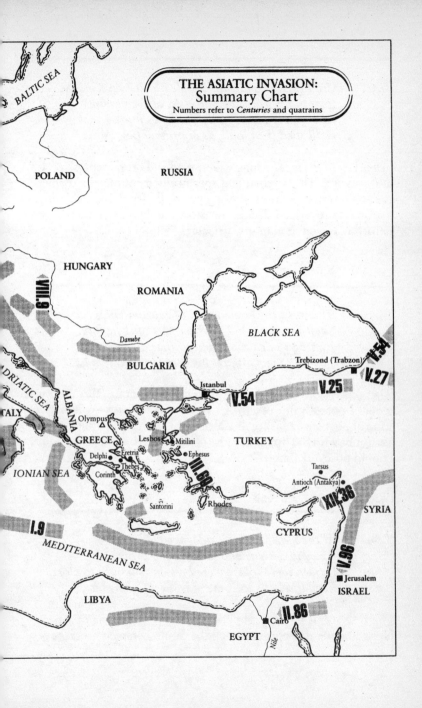

III.60   *Crowds are condemned to death all over Turkey,*
E'en to the utmost south-west of the nation.
Of a young black guilty of doings murky
He'll shed the blood, as in propitiation.

In Turkey itself, meanwhile, widespread and brutal repression is
in full swing. The original text specifically mentions the former
south-western regions of Mysia, Lycia and Pamphilia. Evidently
the oriental overlord decides to make a public example of one
unfortunate young man in particular.

III.59   *The third to seize control of Muslim lands*
Shall promptly kill the best part of their folk,
Putting to death one out of four old hands
For fear their folk on his should death invoke.

The repression continues. Apparently paranoid, the Asiatic
leader – possibly one of a *troika*, or three-man *junta* – conducts a
kind of pogrom to ensure the safety of his own occupying troops,
no doubt with the threat of more of the same to come if anybody
should pose any danger.

V.96   *At the world's centre rules the mighty rose,*
For new designs with state blood profligate.
If truth were told, t'were best one's mouth to close,
Even if what's to come must needs come late.

The rose seems to be symbolic of a long-lived regime of which
Nostradamus disapproves mightily. Some commentators have

identified it as the symbol of the French socialist party under President François Mitterrand. However, the first line seems to suggest that its fiefdom will include Palestine, and specifically Jerusalem, traditionally regarded as standing at the world's centre. Almost inevitably, therefore – unless it simply refers to the former Ottoman empire – this verse would seem to apply to the occupation-regime of the future oriental invaders already referred to. Nostradamus's reaction is to suggest that the less said, the better. Within the occupied lands at least, resistance will not be an issue, still less public unrest. Those aching for change will simply have to wait for their salvation to come from somewhere 'out there'. That having been said, though, one wonders whether François Mitterrand himself is aware of this prediction, and has understood line two in terms of mighty schemes of grandiose public works . . .

V.54   *From Black Sea's shores and greater Tartary*
To see fair France a monarch shall come nigh.
Alania and Armenia lanced, shall he
In Istanbul his bloody rod lay by.

Once again, this quatrain could conceivably be seen as relating not to modern times at all, but to the former Ottoman invasion of Europe. On the other hand, it suggests that the invaders will reach France, which the Turks never did. Moreover, it is so similar to II.29 (p. 63) – with its evident mention of air travel – as to suggest a specifically modern context. This time, though, there seems to be a good deal more to it than a mere errant Ayatollah. It looks suspiciously like some kind of military campaign, very much along the lines of that just adumbrated. Now, however, Nostradamus is starting to be more specific. Consequently we are able tentatively to identify it. What we seem to be faced with is nothing less than a great Asiatic invasion of the West, not unlike the long-expected one traditionally associated with the term 'the

Yellow Peril', and which – in line with the Bible's cryptic prediction of the advent of 'kings from the east' (Rev. 16:12) – looms so large in a good deal of independent psychic projection, too. The word 'Tartary', after all, is quite specific, and refers to the former Mongol empire which originally covered much of central Asia and northern China, and whose domains corresponded roughly to the geographical area of Muslim Turkish-speakers that is nowadays known as Turkestan, much of which has so recently emerged from under the yoke of the former Soviet Union. Clearly, too, whoever it is is very much on the war-path, invading both Armenia and the territory of the former Alani, which lay a little to the north-west, not far from the north-eastern shore of the Black Sea.

The only hope lies in the last two lines. By the time the invaders reach the borders of south-eastern Europe, it seems, their martial ardour will (for whatever reason) have started to cool somewhat. Perhaps this will merely be because they have run out of funds and equipment: alternatively, as the last line could perhaps suggest, the original overlord has possibly died. It is even conceivable that the warlike phase of the oriental invasion may finally have run out of steam and be about to give way to something much more like a simple migration – given half a chance, that is. Other psychics, certainly,[6, 14, 20] suggest that whole phases of the migration may turn out to be largely peaceful, if not actually benevolent, eventually petering out not far from the Franco-German border. Even quite staid observers, indeed, are coming to the view that Third World migrations of this type are increasingly likely in the future, as a direct result of population growth and shortage of resources. But then such things pose a threat only to those who believe in national borders and in keeping parts of the earth's riches exclusively for themselves – in which case the events (if events they indeed turn out to be) will merely be our judge. That they will turn out to correspond in any real sense to the *Last* Judgement, however, there is every reason to doubt, as subsequent quatrains make perfectly clear.

II.62   *When Mabus shortly dies, there shall ensue*
Of man and beast a laying waste most dread.
Then suddenly shall vengeance heave in view:
Thirst, famine, blood, with comet overhead.

Our third possible reason for the halting of the oriental campaign now seems to harden into something much more like a certainty: evidently the original oriental overlord has died. Moreover, Nostradamus even reveals to us his name. Discounting the Latinate ending, he sounds suspiciously like someone called Mab – or even Mao. Indeed, line two seems to offer a tolerably good description of the effects of Mao Tse-Tung's cultural revolution in China. On the other hand, the datings do not fit. The cultural revolution took place in 1966, whereas Mao did not die until ten years later. No significant comet appeared, either, until 1985/6 (Halley's). Thus, Mabus has to be somebody in the future. Immediately, of course, this encourages the professional doommongers to spring into action with predictions of the Antichrist under yet another name. Quite why he cannot stick to one name is not entirely clear, unless it should be that the multiplicity of names actually refers to a multiplicity of people, none of them necessarily true Antichrists in the biblical sense at all. The label unfortunately tends to be stuck by commentators upon anybody of any importance who is predicted as doing anything unorthodox at all: in effect, it is code for the unknown – which makes it totally unsurprising that all the unfulfilled predictions, and especially the scarcely intelligible ones, all of a sudden acquire an alarming apocalyptic tinge. In the present case, however, the reference is merely to a leader whose death precipitates disastrous war, followed by an equally violent backlash. The phenomenon is so familiar as to be almost commonplace. It is context alone that can narrow the possibilities down to something quite specific – and in this case that context seems to be the predicted Asiatic invasion. With the death of the original leader, it seems, things are likely to get not more peaceful, but a very great deal worse. The result is likely to be war on an almost unprecedented scale, leading to the almost inevitable 'heavenly vengeance' of famine and the whole catalogue of other familiar side-effects that tend to accompany military conflicts. The sign of that vengeance, suggests Nostradamus, will be the sudden appearance of a comet in the sky. But then again, *Raymond E. Mabus* was the US ambassador to Saudi Arabia until 1995.

X.72   *Let 1999's seventh month arrive,*
Then comes from heaven a great financing lord
The Mongols' mighty leader to revive.
War reigns before, then haply is restored.

This is possibly the most celebrated — and feared — of Nostradamus's predictions. No doubt this is partly because the date is so specific, and partly because in most translations the term *Roy deffraieur* ('defraying king') in line two — itself possibly a misprint for *Roy deffraieur* (see 'Academic Notes') — is rather dubiously rendered 'King of Terror' (almost as though it were printed *Roy d'effrayeur*). Possibly Nostradamus actually intended the ambiguity. Dark clouds are seldom without their silver linings, nor silver linings without their dark clouds, apocalyptic or otherwise. But then the prediction is quite likely, as usual, to turn out not to be truly apocalyptic at all: almost any rescuing (or threatening) world leader would quite easily fill the bill, and especially one with money in his pocket. In the present case, with the oriental invasion having ground to a halt somewhere in the Middle East on the death of its leader — possibly as a result of shortages of funds and equipment — a powerful world figure is destined to fly in as paymaster to finance the resumption of the mighty onward march, at the same time reinvigorating its leadership. (If so, then it would seem likely that the invasion campaign itself will have started well *before* 1999.) The fact that Nostradamus feels bound to break his usual silence and actually date the event, meanwhile, suggests not merely that he feels that it will offer a kind of *terminus a quo* for the whole sequence of predictions that follows, but that it will prove historically crucial for the future of Europe in general, and of his own homeland in particular. In the following quatrains we shall no doubt discover the reason why. Erika Cheetham sees fit to warn us, though, that the 'seven months' may well need to be counted, not from January, but from Nostradamus's contemporary New Year, which was the spring equinox of 20/21 March.

V.55   *A mighty Muslim chief shall come to birth*
In country fortunate of Araby.
He'll take Granada, trouble Spanish earth
And conquer the Italians from the sea.

At this critical point an important new player enters the game, taking over command of the Asiatic forces where Mabus left off. Thus, he is no doubt directly responsible for the dire events predicted by Nostradamus for the aftermath of Mabus's death. By 'Araby' Nostradamus may mean precisely that, or he may merely be referring to the whole, vast Muslim area stretching from North Africa far into central Asia. The new leader's projected military achievements look distinctly worrying, however.

V.84   *Of parentage obscure and shadowy,*
Born of the gulf and city measureless,
As far as Rouen and Evreux he'd see
That prince's power destroyed that all confess.

In this quatrain Nostradamus reveals the full extent of the new Muslim leader's disturbing ambitions. Born in a city that seems remarkably like Cairo (the 'gulf' may well be the Mediterranean, as in the case of Franco in Chapter 3), but which could equally well be Alexandria or Istanbul, he is determined to destroy what looks rather like the Pope's fiefdom – i.e. European Christendom – not merely in the south, but all the way to Normandy in northern France.

X.75   *So long awaited, never to return,*
        O'er Asia and o'er Europe he shall lour –
        A robber-Hermes who will trickster turn
        And o'er all eastern potentates shall tower.

Not only is the new leader destined to threaten Europe with all the god Hermes' most disquieting characteristics (which, unlike Nostradamus himself, I have actually outlined in line three): he also controls what Nostradamus calls 'Asia' – which in the seer's day normally meant what we today call Asia Minor or Turkey, but which could of course extend much further east, too. Perhaps the most disquieting feature of this quatrain is the first line, which rather suggests that he is a unique figure who has been known about for centuries. If Nostradamus is right, after all, this begs to mark him out – at last we are forced to face the possibility – as none other than the biblical Antichrist himself, red in tooth and claw. At this point, though, we should (as ever) be wary of attaching too grand or cosmic a significance to such concepts. Both the Bible and Nostradamus are prone to make what are essentially local events look much bigger than they really are. Heaven knows, the man looks likely to be quite awful enough – but he will still be, as Burns is sane enough to remind us, 'a man for a' that', and one who will have no more power than we are prepared to allow him. Moreover, as Nostradamus reminds us, he is destined – once survived by those who are lucky enough to do so – never to return.

X.10
With murder stained and malefactions vast,
He'll be the enemy of all men living.
Far worse than any like him in the past,
By sword, fire, water, bloody, unforgiving.

Nostradamus goes on to compare him unfavourably even with all his grim forebears – among whom we could presumably number either Hitler or Stalin, if not both – though in this case it is interesting to note that the seer does indeed admit that he will have *had* forebears, thus confirming our earlier suggestion that the word 'Antichrist' is not used by Nostradamus in any exclusive sense. However, in the present case he evidently cannot bring himself to use the term at all – thus suggesting once again, paradoxically enough, that he is face to terrifying face with the biblically genuine article. Still, it should be remembered that millions of us managed to survive both Hitler and Stalin. No doubt, then, the same will happen again, however unlikely that may seem at the time.

Présage 40
Seven kings in turn death's deadly hand shall
smite,
Hail, tempest, plague and furious desecrators:
The Eastern King shall put the West to flight
And subjugate his former subjugators.

The theme continues. Seven successive administrations (presumably of France – compare IV.50, p. 237) will be plagued by invaders from a part of the Orient that was formerly colonised or at very least subjugated by the West. Since there is virtually no part of the Orient that has not been, the information is not particularly helpful to us – except in that it tends to confirm that the subject is not the Ottoman empire, which was very much pre-colonial.

I.15   *With warlike force Mars threatens us amain.*
        Full seventy times he'll spill both blood and tears.
        The church first grows, then is destroyed again.
        So, too, are those who'd rather shut their ears.

Meanwhile, in a general quatrain, Nostradamus offers an overview of warlike events that seems to encompass both his times and ours. In the process, it would appear that Christianity, after a period of relative prosperity, will be virtually wiped out, in Europe at least. Atheists, suggests Nostradamus, will be no better off, either. For details of the precise how and where, however, we shall have to await subsequent developments.

III.27   *A Libyan leader in the West ascendant*
         Shall make the French against Islam irate.
         To literary scholars condescendent,
         The Arabs into French he shall translate.

In an effort to defuse the increasingly threatening situation in the Middle East, somebody who sounds remarkably like the present Moamar al-Gaddafi will, it seems, attempt to bypass the official interpreters and take upon himself the responsibility for representing Arab intentions to the Western world. Evidently he merely succeeds in stirring the pot.

I.51   *Saturn and Jupiter in Aries met:*
        Eternal God, what changes are in train!
        In France and Italy what stirrings yet
        As the slow round brings evil times again!

Here we may possibly have the first indications of the oriental invasion starting to affect the Mediterranean shores of Europe. The quatrain even seems to contain some kind of astrological dating. Following the publication of Nostradamus's predictions, the next astronomical conjunction of the type described occurred on 13 December 1702, when France under Louis XIV was deeply involved in the War of the Spanish Succession. According to Erika Cheetham,[3] it will next occur on 2 December 1995 (my own research suggests February 1999). Bear in mind that what is predicted is merely 'stirrings' (*emotions*) and 'evil times', and that Nostradamus sometimes tends rather to over-dramatise such ill tidings as he has for us. That having been said, though, it is not impossible that he is referring to the very start of a troublesome period during which both France and Italy will start to feel the effects of the oriental advance. Indeed, subsequent quatrains will, as we shall see, confirm this and elaborate on it in increasingly terrifying detail.

XII.36   *In Cyprus they the fierce assault prepare*
         (Weep now your coming ruin at the altar!).
         Arabs and Turks the evil deed shall share
         'Twixt separate fleets: huge ruin via Gibraltar.

In this supplementary quatrain the scene is now set for the ensuing action. Evidently the Eastern power is destined to make Cyprus its main base for what looks like a mass invasion of Europe, split into a northern and a southern wing – the latter, swinging through North Africa, being of a particularly brutal and violent kind.

X.58   *The Arab chief at time of mourning dark*
        Shall war declare upon the youthful Greek.
        France he shall shake, menace the papal barque:
        Westwards, Marseille with words to sway he'll seek.

Even while the Asiatics are still mourning the recent death of
Mabus (which may suggest a period of no more than forty days
or so), their great military campaign starts to swing into violent
action again. Their first assault is apparently on Greece. Since the
'young Macedonian' to whom Nostradamus refers also turns up
again during the later part of the conflict, *but this time as a
powerful leader on the Arab side*, it is possible that he is a Greek
or Balkan commander who at some point is persuaded to defect
to the invaders. The rest of the verse looks like a summary of
what is to come. France is to be shaken to its roots, the ship of the
papacy (i.e. the Vatican and the whole Catholic Church) put in
danger and Marseille subverted in some way.

II.39   *A year before war comes to Italy,*
        French, Germans, Spaniards shall think might
        *   is right.*
        When falls their infantile republic, see
        How right is mostly choked to death by might.

With large-scale war now in the offing, foreign might seems
destined to overwhelm some kind of administrative community
recently cobbled together by the three rather over-confident
powers mentioned – 'the schoolhouse republic', Nostradamus
calls it. This naturally begs tentative identification with the
present European Community. Evidently, then, the conflict is
likely to involve a good many more countries than merely France
and Italy. (I have to confess, however, that the play on the
expression 'might is right' is my invention, not Nostradamus's.)

II.84   *From Naples north as far as Florence falls*
No drop of rain for six months and nine days.
An alien tongue across Dalmatia calls
Ere running on, the land entire to raze.

Nostradamus now starts to give us what appear to be the first
details of the route of the mooted invasion. Possibly the first line
– which in the original actually specifies Campania, Siena,
Florence and Tuscany – is intended to serve as a kind of meteorological warning of things to come. It is after the temporary
drought that alien forces will, it seems, enter Dalmatia on the
former Yugoslavian west coast, prior to overrunning the whole
country. Whether Nostradamus intends this to mean Yugoslavia
or Italy is not at this point made clear.

IX.60   *Muslims at war, all clad in headdress black:*
'Midst bloodshed shall the great Dalmatia quake.
The mighty Arabs press home their attack:
When Lisbon helps, though, all their tongues
*   shall shake.*

Unless, once again, this verse merely refers to the former
Ottoman invasions, there seems to be some kind of western
European support for the former Yugoslavian forces as they fight
a desperate rearguard action. Evidently this is enough to cause
some agitated discussion among the invaders. The word 'ranes'
(from Latin *rana*, 'frog') in the last line poses all kinds of difficulties for the commentators, though. Why, after all, should the
frogs shake – other than to make it possible for Nostradamus to
get up to a favourite trick of his, namely to repeat an idea from
the first half of his verse (in this case, that of trembling) in the
second half as well? The answer lies in Nostradamus's own

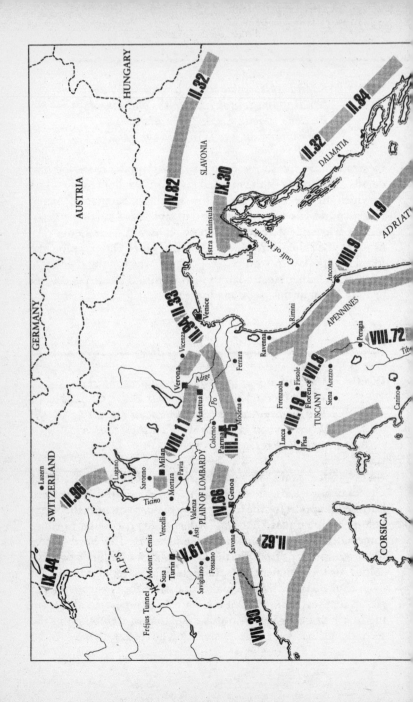

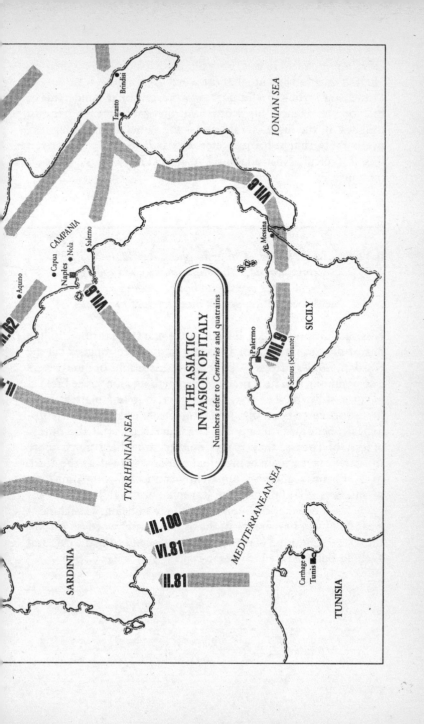

THE ASIATIC
INVASION OF ITALY

Numbers refer to *Centuries* and quatrains

curriculum vitae. He was, after all, a doctor of long experience. He was thus fully aware that the word's diminutive form *ranula* ('little frog') refers to a 'ranine' cyst – i.e. one on the underside of the tongue. Hence, his word *rane* inevitably means 'strange tongues' in the most literal sense – the same 'strange tongues', presumably, that he has just referred to in II.84 (p. 81). Clearly, if this is typical, Nostradamus had a healthy, if wry, sense of humour.

II.32 *Milk, blood, strange tongues over Dalmatia,*
    Contagion near Balennes, and joined the fight,
    Great is the cry throughout Slavonia
    When first Ravenna's monster sees the light.

Nostradamus now takes his grim joke one stage further. In line one of this stanza he actually refers to the alien tongues via the word *grenoilles* ('frogs') – so fooling generations of interpreters into assuming that he is predicting something akin to the biblical plagues of Egypt. The rest, however, is no joking matter. True, there do seem to be strange (but by no means unknown) meteorological phenomena along the Yugoslavian coast at the time – unless, of course, they really indicate something much more sinister – but the main point is that war now spreads to the north of the former federation, apparently connected with some kind of 'monster' that first arises in Ravenna, northern Italy. It is not made clear whether the monster is a human being, a machine, a weapon of war or merely – as the original Latin word *monstrum* suggests – some kind of omen. 'Balennes' seems to be the classical Trebula Balliensis, which lies in central Italy, near Capua.

IX.30 *On blessed Nicholas' and Pula's shore*
In Kvarner's Gulf shall northern fighters die.
The chief the Muslims' pillage shall deplore.
Cadiz and the Philippian stand by.

As the fighting spreads northwards, the retreating defenders are driven into the sea near the former Yugoslav port of Pula, not far from the Italian border, possibly as a result of being trapped on the Istra peninsula. Spain and Greece offer what help they can.

II.33 *As by Verona's torrent, rushing on*
Towards where great Po's deltaic courses end,
Wat'ry disaster strikes, so on Garonne
When force Genoan shall on them descend.

The hordes come ever nearer. There is to be great loss of life on the River Adige, which flows into the Adriatic just north of the Po. Evidently the invaders are sweeping in from the north-east and about to spread out over the Plain of Lombardy. There can thus no longer be any question of the text's referring to the former Ottoman invasion. This is for real, and it is for our own future. The text's use of the word *naufrage* ('shipwreck') suggests that there will be great loss of men and materials in the waters of the River Adige itself. Meanwhile, the considerable extent of the expected conflict is starting to become clear: Nostradamus expects virtually the same scenario to be repeated later on around the River Garonne, in south-western France, when forces from the area of Genoa cross that river in turn. This does not necessarily make them Italian, however: as we shall see, Nostradamus constantly names invading armies after the territories they are currently occupying. There can be little doubt, in other words, that it is the self-same Asiatic invasion force, by then in control of north-western Italy, that will eventually be responsible for the French disaster, too.

II.94   *Great Po for France great woes endures, alas!*
The British lion at sea no terrors bind.
A race unnumbered shall the ocean pass.
A quarter-million no escape shall find.

An immense conflict now ensues on the banks of the River Po, which is seemingly intended to provide Lombardy's last major line of defence. The invaders are being reinforced all the time by sea in massive numbers. Only the British, restricting their participation to naval operations, remain relatively secure.

I.9   *From Orient Afric hearts a passage beat*
To th' Adriatic, Italy to try,
Accompanied by all the Libyan fleet:
Emptied each Maltese church, each isle nearby.

Unless, once again, this is merely a reference to the former Ottoman empire, Nostradamus now suggests that the coming Asiatic invasion will have a sea-borne component, too, based somewhere in North Africa. Naturally, the Mediterranean islands will be among the first territories to be affected, offering as they do a convenient jumping-off point for further operations against southern Europe. Meanwhile, the enemy's naval activities in the Adriatic are likewise confirmed. It might of course be objected that no present-day Muslim countries in the Mediterranean area have the size of navy necessary to carry out the kind of operations referred to here and below in the face of the major western European fleets, any more than do those from central Asia: from the quotation at the head of this chapter, however, one gains the impression that the Asiatic invaders will have purchased a large number of surplus ships from their northern neighbour Russia, inheritor of most of the armaments of the former Soviet Union.

IV.48   *On Latin plains so fertile and so wide*
         So many flies and locusts shall have bred
         That the sun's light shall all but be denied
         And, eating all, great pestilence they'll spread.

Generally speaking, Nostradamus's quatrains can be interpreted surprisingly literally. In the present case, however, he seems to be talking about something a good deal more disturbing than mere locusts: after all, in V.85 (p. 176) he has them attacking the Swiss as well – whose land is hardly locust country at the best of times, even allowing for the fact that in the present case he merely refers to the insects as *sauterelles* ('grasshoppers'). Noticing this fact, various commentators have seen fit to interpret them in all kinds of weird and wonderful ways – principally in terms of enemy aircraft. This might even fit the description in line three (helicopters especially spring to mind – how else, after all, could Nostradamus possibly have described these strange, futuristic contraptions?). My own hunch, though, is that the clairaudient Nostradamus has somehow managed to 'hear' the oriental invaders described as 'swarming like locusts' across the plain of Lombardy and has then – not for the first time – translated the expression into an actual, visual image. The last line, similarly, could have resulted from his having 'heard' the expression 'plagues of locusts': on the other hand, in the light of subsequent quatrains it is just possible that this time he means what he says, and that as the invaders spread out, ravaging the country's food supplies as they advance, some kind of disease epidemic will indeed break out in their wake. We shall in due course see what dire results this will have.

III.33   *When in the city's heart the wolf shall call*
The enemy shall then be close at hand.
Friends, too, at hand upon the Alpine wall
As alien armies devastate the land.

Here Nostradamus seems to be referring to one of the far northern Italian cities such as Verona, Milan or Turin. The impression is given that, although Italy's allies are on the borders, they will decline to intervene. If the reference to wolves is to be taken literally, it is perhaps worth noting that wolves tend to move into towns in search of food mainly during the winter – a fact which could help date the events in question.

III.75   *Vicenza, Saragossa, Verona, Po*
Shall bloody swords from distant lands o'errun.
By foul disease shall massive swellings grow.
Help's near at hand, yet nothing can be done.

The assault continues in Lombardy, while once again the nearby allies fail to intervene. The surprise appearance of *Sarragousse* at the end of the original list of places affected suggests that Nostradamus may have misread his original notes, or indeed that it may be a late replacement, possibly for 'Saronno', inserted so as to rhyme with *gousse* in line three. This latter, meanwhile, is a puzzle. Normally it refers to something pod-like, shell-like, husk-like. One might suspect that it refers to the *bubons* of bubonic plague, but for the fact that the actual word was available to Nostradamus, who was himself a specialist on the disease. The word *ampoule*, similarly, was available had he been referring to blisters, as was *croûte* for scabs. Possibly we should think in terms of allergic swellings – which might conceivably suggest the effects on the skin of something akin to chemical warfare. The lack of clarity at this point is a pity, as this is almost the only description Nostradamus offers us of the symptoms of the 'plague' to which he will so often refer in the context of the fighting. However, see IV.58 (p. 104).

VIII.11   *A people numberless invades Vicenza –*
Though not by force – basilica aglow.
Near to Lugano falls he from Valenza,
While Venice from the sea shall face the foe.

Interestingly enough, Nostradamus reveals that the invasion will not always involve fighting. Sometimes the incoming hordes will simply be allowed to enter the towns and cities unopposed. Elsewhere, though, the defence will be fierce. One commander is forced to retreat from Valenza (which lies in the middle of the triangle formed by Turin, Milan and Genoa) into the mountains, where he is duly defeated on the route north between Lakes Maggiore and Como. Meanwhile, in the Adriatic, Venice is still resisting.

IV.66   *Secret explorers under colours fickle*
Shall be sent forth by seven with shaven pates.
In wells and fountains they shall poison trickle.
Man shall eat man within Genoa's gates.

The shaven-headed overlords presumably belong to the oriental invasion forces. Evidently they do not care over-much what measures they use to achieve their nefarious ends, as long as they are effective: Genoa is both poisoned and (eventually) starved.

Présage 31   *Up stormy Danube Muslim vessels fare.*
At sea, troop-carrying ships off Sicily.
Florence reduced, Siena passed, the pair
Whom friendship joined as good as dead shall be.

The invaders are appearing on the horizon in increasing numbers
– and not merely on land (both in Italy and further east), but on
the sea, too. Nostradamus specifically refers to them, both here
and elsewhere, as *Barbares* – a term which means not merely
'uncivilised', but 'Arabs' (by false association with the word
'Berber') and thus (for the Judaeo-Christian Nostradamus at
least) 'Muslims', 'infidels' or simply 'heathen'. As we have
already started to see, there are good reasons for assuming that
'Muslims' is the correct interpretation, though due allowance
needs to be made for Nostradamus's understandable religious
prejudice at the time. Moreover, here as elsewhere, the fact has
no objective implications whatever for the validity of the Islamic
faith. Religious affiliations may indeed (as so often) have a role in
sparking off the conflict, but thereafter the term 'Muslim' is used
mainly as a convenient label, a simple indication that the
invaders will come from a Muslim part of the world. Indeed,
their subsequent actions will turn out to be every bit as contrary
to Islamic teaching as they will be to its Christian counterpart.
The 'pair' to whom their advent eventually proves mortal would
seem to be France and Italy (see I.51, p. 78, and VIII.9 and II.72,
pp. 105 and 108).

V.47   *The mighty Arab ever onward goes,*
Yet is betrayed by Turks behind his back.
Then antique Rhodes confronts him, while
*   worse woes*
Follow the stern Hungarian's attack.

The invaders will not have it all their own way, however. Even while the European campaign is in progress, there will be troubles at home. The island of Rhodes will refuse to lie down, while the Hungarians will apparently manage to push the Asiatic forces back as in Ottoman times – or at least, perhaps, to restrict them to the area south and west of the Danube.

V.48   *After the setback to their rulership*
            Two enemies before their forces fall.
            To Hungary comes ship on Afric ship.
            By land and sea shall dreadful things befall.

The Asiatics are not about to give up, however, as this direct successor to V.47 above reveals. The Hungarian campaign is redoubled – though their 'two enemies' are not specified. Possibly they are Italy and France once again. At the same time there is no question of an Asiatic walk-over.

II.96   *A flaming torch aloft the evening sky*
            Near to the head and source of mighty Rhône.
            Famine and war: too late relief comes by.
            The Persian turns his troops on Macedon.

From northern Italy, meanwhile, the invaders are also infiltrating central Switzerland, where the Rhône has its source. Possibly Nostradamus is referring to Geneva. Evidently neighbouring countries are still slow to recognise or respond to the danger. A further spearhead thrusts southward from the former Yugoslavia into northern Greece. Perhaps taking the former David-and-Goliath situation of the ancient Graeco-Persian wars as his symbolic precedent, Nostradamus here describes the invaders as *la*

Perse – thus at the same time living up to his normal practice of naming them after the countries that they are currently occupying.

IX.44   *Flee! Flee Geneva, each and every one!*
Saturn shall pure gold into iron change.
Land of the rose wipes father out and son.
Before th' assault shall signs the sky derange.

As ever, there are warning signs, and consequently there is always an extent to which we are ourselves responsible for what happens to us. As we shall see, Nostradamus never tires of driving the point home. At the same time he refers here to the symbolic 'rose' already mentioned in V.96 (p. 70), this time making great play of the invaders' pinkness or even redness via the capitalised anagram RAYPOZ (*'pays rose'*). As we shall see later, the colour red will become a standardised feature of his description of them – though to assume on this basis (as many commentators do) that they are therefore necessarily Communists is perhaps to jump rather too hastily to conclusions.

II.100   *Among the isles so dread a tumult roars*
That nought is heard save gathering defiance:
So great the onslaught of the predators
That all shall rush to form a grand alliance.

Unless, once again, this is merely a reference to the attempted Ottoman invasions of the fifteenth and sixteenth centuries (which never in fact succeeded in taking over the islands of the western Mediterranean) the picture is of a gathering storm of invasion in the area which will prompt all those concerned to form defensive alliances – and not, it seems, before time.

II.43   *When into view shall swim the bearded star*
             The three great lords shall comrades be no more.
             Peace from the sky is shattered, earth a-jar;
             Po, Tiber seethe; snake lands upon the shore.

The approach of a comet is accompanied by discord and war, especially in Italy. The three great *princes* are unidentified, but later stanzas will suggest that they are the leaders of the three main wings of the oriental invasion, who are now about to fall out and go their separate ways, as though from now on in competition with one another. The *serpent* that is cast up on the beach seems to refer back to the 'coiled serpent' of V.25 (p. 66) – apparently a symbol for the oriental invader. Whatever it means, some kind of insinuation of newcomers into Italy by unexpected means is certainly hinted at, possibly via Albania (see V.46, p. 118).

II.5   *From out a fish where papers, arms are stowed*
            One shall emerge who then shall go to war.
            Across the sea he shall his fleet have rowed
            At length to appear off the Italian shore.

Possibly this quatrain explains the mechanics of the invasion, at least in part. Apparently at least one submarine is involved in the landing – if not of the invading forces as such, then at least of their high command. In line three Nostradamus indicates that he does not actually expect the fleet to come in under sail, yet is clearly at a loss to understand how his self-propelled fleet could possibly cross the sea other than under oars. As ever the picture is observed, in other words, through sixteenth-century eyes. Meanwhile, compare I.29 (p. 44), which could conceivably fit events at this juncture rather better than those of the Second World War.

V.62   *Blood falls like rain the very rocks upon:*
Sun rising, Saturn o'er the western lands.
Great evil seen in Rome, war near Orgon,
Ships sunk, Tridentine throne in hostile hands.

As Nostradamus now confirms in this further summary of the more immediately forthcoming events, the eastern invasion is destined to spread first into Italy and then into south-eastern France. The details are compressed, almost telegrammatic, but the initial event once again sounds suspiciously like a dawn assault by sea. Rome is eventually taken and the Vatican, seat of Peter the Fisherman, seized. Meanwhile, in France, the invaders will soon start to make inroads into the eastern fringes of the Rhône delta (the town of Orgon is a local administrative centre on the Durance).

VII.6   *Palermo, Sicily and Naples are*
Alike inhabited by heathen might.
Salerno, Corsica, Sardinia —
Death, plague and war, nor end to it in sight.

As already foreshadowed, the Mediterranean islands are soon engulfed at the start of what promises to be a long-drawn-out struggle, and the southern cities are not slow to follow.

VI.10   *Awhile shall all the Christian churches stay*
Commingled with the colours black and white.
Reds, yellows then their flocks shall steal away:
Blood, fire, fear, plague, hunger and water white.

Nostradamus now looks ahead to what is awaiting European Christianity itself. Precisely what he means by 'black and white' is unclear. He could be referring to skin colours, to a confusion of values, or to something of a political or sectarian nature. But then he is evidently determined to have fun with colours in this stanza anyway. At first sight the 'yellows' beg to be identified with the proverbial 'Yellow Peril' from the East, and the 'reds' with Communism, but the latter association in particular is, as we have seen, far from a foregone conclusion, and it would be far wiser to suspend judgement until it actually happens. The most that can be said is that the oriental influx is likely to remove large numbers of Christians from their parishes, whether through war, forced conversion, death or simple flight – which of course is no more than might be expected.

VI.20   *The holy union shall not long survive.*
Of those who change most shall change back again.
In churches then an army shall arrive
When over Rome a new lion comes to reign.

Certainly there are signs of some kind of new ecumenical initiative which falls apart as the invaders move in and Rome acquires an unnamed new overlord.

X.3   *After five years he'll fail his flock to feed.*
A fugitive he'll free for Poland's sake.
Of help false rumours here and there shall speed,
Until the pastor shall his see forsake.

This quatrain fails to define the identity of the *chef* – the leader whom, in the light of the first line, I have translated as 'pastor'. As subsequent stanzas suggest, however, it seems likely that the term refers to the reigning pope – in which case this verse would confirm very satisfactorily the proposed interpretation of V.92 (p. 65). Almost at the end of his new, five-year term, it seems, the pontiff is forced for some reason to relinquish his duties – possibly as a result of the growing eastern influx. Some kind of international difficulties ensue which are only resolved when he finally leaves Rome. The original word *Penelon* seems to be a pseudo-anagram for *Polonais* ('the Polish one' or 'the Poles') – possibly, then, a reference to the present incumbent. To arrive at the full significance of this quatrain, however, it is necessary to read it in conjunction with the other 'papal' predictions below.

VI.25   *Mars shall afflict the sacred monarchy:*
In trouble ruinous great Peter's barque.
Young monarch red shall seize the hierarchy.
Traitors shall act 'neath rain-clouds dank and dark.

The war duly has its dire effects on Rome and its Church. As we have already seen, Nostradamus constantly associates the invaders with the colour red. He also repeatedly refers to *bruine* ('drizzle') in connection with the various assaults, in a way which suggests some sinister connotation. The possibility of chemical or even biological attacks can therefore not be ruled out.

VI.30   *By one who feigns deep sanctity to keep*
The see's betrayed to enemy most arch,
E'en on that night when all thought safe to sleep.
Near Brabant, Liège's host is on the march.

However, betrayal from within is likely to prove a much more deadly weapon in the hands of the invaders. The last line, meanwhile, is interesting. It suggests that some of the northern powers, at least, are likely to prove more vigilant than those immediately threatened in the south. Evidently Belgium, foreseeing a more general invasion of Europe, is starting to rearm.

I.11   *The way in which sense, heart, feet, hands all tend*
        Is one in Naples, Lyon, Sicily.
        Sword, fire and water on Rome's lords descend:
        Killed, drowned and dead through addled idiocy.

Throughout the conflict, suggests Nostradamus, it will be the same old story over and over again. In the face of the Asiatic threat, what is likely to pose the chief danger is not the enemy, nor even betrayal and sedition, but the Europeans' own apathy and incompetence. The message, in other words, seems to be that the eventual outcome, far from being predestined, is at least partly in our own hands. Fatalism – unsurprisingly – is merely likely to prove fatal.

II.41   *Seven days the mighty star burns on its way –*
        A cloudy star, like two suns in the sky.
        The whole night shall the burly watchdog bay
        When the great Pope his former state shall fly.

This is another prediction that is often given an apocalyptic significance, mainly because the extraordinary star described in it is assumed to be the one called 'Wormwood' (curiously enough, *Chernobyl* in Russian) in the Revelation of St John (8: 10–11). However, Nostradamus does not mention any of its dire biblical effects, and so it seems safe to assume that this is merely the same particularly bright comet that has already been referred to, and that it probably has no particular relevance to the end of the age, unless at a very considerable remove. The last comet that was bright enough to be seen during the day in the northern hemisphere was Halley's in 1910, but neither this nor any other comet seems to have coincided with the removal of the papal base from one place to another – at least, so far as I have been able to ascertain. This in itself may well indicate, therefore, that the prophecy has yet to be fulfilled, quite possibly within the context of the oriental invasion of Italy – a fact which would then tie in with II.43 (p. 93). The signs to watch out for, then, are self-evident – though I have to confess that the precise significance of line three eludes me, unless it should be that (as a number of commentators have predictably suggested) the 'fat mastiff' in some way symbolises the so-called British bulldog. The comet in question is unlikely to be as late as Halley's of 2062, however (whose last appearance before Nostradamus's expected Apocalypse, incidentally, is due to occur in the year 2822), since psychic sources[6, 8, 12, 14] suggest that there will be only one or two more popes.

VIII.99   *By power of the three kings temporal*
           The Holy Seat shall elsewhere be removed,
           Where spirit's seat and substance corporal
           May be restored and for its truth approved.

Unless this quatrain refers to Pius VI's historical removal to Valence by Napoleon in 1799, it suggests that the pope in power at the time of the oriental invasion, too, will be forced to leave the Vatican, in his case by an alliance of three secular leaders. As we shall see later, this reference seems to be to the three heads of what is evidently the Asiatic confederacy itself.

V.75   *High in the property, rightward some way,*
          Above St Peter's Square he'll sit and look
          Beside the window at around midday,
          His mouth clamped shut, holding his twisted crook.

The picture here is unmistakably of the Pope at the window of his apartments at the time of his traditional Sunday noon blessing of the pilgrims below in St Peter's Square. Two points, however, are worthy of note. The first is that he is sitting, rather than (as is traditionally the case) standing – which might suggest that he is either ill or a very old man. The other is what Nostradamus actually calls his 'twisted staff' (oddly reminiscent of the present Pope's crucifix-staff, with its curiously distorted upper end): its presence possibly suggests that the pontiff is about to embark on some pastoral journey. Seen in the present context, then, the image is a moving one. It is of the old man appearing at his window for the last time before going into exile, and casting a final, wordless look on the beloved city over which he has ruled for so long.

IX.99   *The north wind shall the see oblige to quit,*
            As red-hot ash and dust blow o'er the walls.
            Through rain thereafter (much harm comes from it)
            Their last hope lies towards where the frontier calls.

Most commentators suggest that this quatrain really refers to Napoleon's retreat from Moscow in 1812. If it applies here, however, it suggests that, as the invaders close in and parts of Rome are already aflame, the Pope and his staff will hastily set out for the French border. As in VI.25 (p. 96), the 'rain' may or may not be natural.

VII.23   *The royal sceptre he'll be forced to take,*
As those before him had engaged to do,
Since with ringed Pope no contact they shall make
When to the palace comes that plundering crew.

At this point, with the Vatican no longer occupied by the reigning pontiff, and the latter not even contactable any more, somebody has to take over the administration of the Catholic Church pending the arrival of the invaders. It would seem that the task falls to one of the senior cardinals.

VIII.62   *When of all holy temples shall be seen*
Plundered Rome's greatest, and profaned its site,
On them shall fall a pestilence so keen,
No word of blame shall 'scape the king in flight.

Evidently the invaders' eventual sacking of Rome will be accompanied by an outbreak of disease in their ranks – possibly as a result of the chemical or biological attacks already mooted above – severe enough to evoke the fleeing Pope's pity and compassion. Certainly this somewhat surprising reaction squares with the known nature of the present Pope, having been in evidence once before when he forgave his former would-be assassin and visited him in prison. Whether it will also apply to his successors – or whether it will even need to – only time will tell. It has to be said, however, that Nostradamus actually writes *du rosne* rather than *de Rome*: it is just possible, in other words, that the temple whose sacking will be so significant is in fact Avignon cathedral.

VIII.72   *Upon Perugia's field what great defeat!*
            And all about Ravenna what affray!
            The victor's horse the loser's oats shall eat;
            Free passage granted on a holiday.

The invaders now move on northwards. As was ever the case, the conquering army commandeers all the local provisions and resources. There is more than a hint, meanwhile, that its success will be due at least as much to the defenders' incompetence and apathy as to its own military efforts. As we have already seen, this theme recurs repeatedly throughout the conflict – an apparent indication on Nostradamus's part that we have it within our own hands to mitigate, if not to prevent, much of what he predicts for us.

VI.36   *Nor good nor ill the battle shall instil*
            The limits of Perugia's lands inside.
            Pisa rebels: Florence's star bodes ill.
            Chief hurt at night shall muddy donkey ride.

The invaders continue to move on towards Pisa and Florence, largely ignoring Perugia itself. The detail in the last line is something that only contemporary light is likely to be able to elucidate.

VII.8   *Flee, Florence! Flee him who from Rome shall come.*
            At Fiesole battle is declared.
            Blood shall be shed, the mighty overcome.
            Nor church nor monastery shall be spared.

Line one of the original text apparently uses the expression 'the nearest Roman' to refer not to the original inhabitants of Rome themselves, but to the city's new occupiers. As we have already seen, Nostradamus uses this technique repeatedly throughout his quatrains. Once in any given city or country, the Asiatics are treated as being *of* it (or rather *from* it). Evidently Fiesole, near Florence (which Nostradamus often refers to as 'Flora'), is set to become the site of a major battle as the tide of invasion continues to sweep northwards.

VI.62
> *Both Florences are lost too late, too late.*
> *'Gainst holy law no act the snake shall try.*
> *The French stave off the force confederate.*
> *Martyrs from Monaco to Savona die.*

Nostradamus now predicts the late loss of two *fleurs*. Since he normally uses the word 'Flora' to refer to Florence, it seems likely that he is referring here not only to this city ('Firenze' in Italian), but also to Firenzuola, a few miles to the north. Only circumstances at the time can hope to explain how either could possibly be lost *too late*, however. Line two seems to suggest that the invaders will for the time being let the Vatican be, despite the apparent contradiction between this and the last line of the foregoing stanza (VII.8): subsequent stanzas may help to explain this. Meanwhile the French are not only starting to assist the beleaguered Italians, but are conducting an effective rearguard action, though there are now increasing signs of naval and/or amphibious attacks along the Mediterranean coasts of northern Italy and – for the first time – of southern France.

I.83   *The alien race shall share out all the spoils.*
             Angry-eyed Mars shall Saturn then affright.
             Latins and Tuscans caught in alien toils;
             Greeks too, though they be straitly charged to fight.

Nostradamus seems to link the next phase of the invasion with an astrological dating – whether merely involving the presence of Saturn in Aries or (as the decidedly ambiguous text actually suggests) an actual conjunction with Mars. For whatever reason the newly-attacked Greeks fail to keep the incoming hordes at bay. Note how Nostradamus once again takes up an idea (in this case the word 'alien') from the first half of the verse and reapplies it – rather after the style of the Hebrew psalms – in the second half.

III.19   *Shortly before the change of overlord*
              In Lucca blood and milk fall from the sky:
              Famine and thirst, great plague and war abhorred
              Far, far from where its rightful Prince shall die.

As the war continues to spread northwards, some worrying phenomena put in their appearance – worrying because, if not of natural origin, they could conceivably indicate some kind of chemical warfare, presumably designed to soften up the opposition before the invading troops actually move in. The chief local administrator is, it seems, abducted and eventually dies or is killed while in distant exile.

IV.58　　*In human throats shall stick the burning sun.*
　　　　On lands Etruscan human blood shall rain.
　　　　Water in pail, the chief leads off his son:
　　　　To Turkish lands his lady captive ta'en.

Here again, the first two lines may suggest the use of chemical weapons. There are indications that the effects on the human body will include semi-suffocation – unless Nostradamus merely means that, to the population, the attacks will prove the last straw. In addition, overpowering thirst seems to be indicated by line three. On the other hand, 'water in pail' could merely be a reference to Aquarius, and hence to the months of January or February. Whatever the means, however, this stanza certainly indicates the devastation of Tuscany and the direst of consequences for its leaders and inhabitants.

VI.67　　*To power shall quite another hand attain,*
　　　　Further from goodness than felicity:
　　　　Ruled is the realm by one whom vice shall stain
　　　　And realms condemn to mighty misery.

The new Asiatic overlord proceeds to impose a vicious regime on Italy, and will subsequently extend his sway to other lands as well.

V.61　　*Son of the chief who was not at his birth*
　　　　The Apennines subdues. Nor shall he stop:
　　　　With fear he'll fill the trading lands of earth,
　　　　And fire the mountains up to Cenis' top.

Apparently born out of wedlock, he pursues his campaign with great vigour over the Apennines as far as the Alpine border with France. This causes great trepidation among 'those of the balance' – i.e. the great trading nations of Western Europe.

V.57   *From Roman hill towards Cisalpine height,*
Then through the tunnel he his army steers.
Between two rocks they'll catch the prey in flight.
Fugitive Paul's great name then disappears.

This quatrain seems to suggest that the Pope, leaving his flight until the last moment before his escape is cut off by the invading forces in the north, will be pursued by armed troops across the Alps into France. Nostradamus describes them as turning through what he calls a *trou* ('hole') – presumably one of the modern road or rail tunnels that to Nostradamus in the sixteenth century necessarily made no sense at all. Line three seems to refer to the pass of Tarascon on the Rhône, where in VIII.46 (p. 111) the Pope is predicted as being finally captured. In the same prediction he is also dubbed *Pol mensolee*, a title to which the current quatrain likewise refers specifically in line four. Note how important, though, the overall context is to interpreting this or any other quatrain: *by itself* it is not necessarily either of popes, or of oriental invaders, or even necessarily of the future at all.

VIII.9   *While Cock and Eagle fight around Savona,*
To Hungary the Eastern fleet sails in.
Troops at Palermo, Naples and Ancona.
In Rome and Venice calls the dread muezzin.

The symbolic terms 'Cock' and 'Eagle' presumably refer to the French and Italian forces respectively. Even while they are still making a last effort at resisting the invaders around Savona, a further incursion is being made up the Danube to the north. In Sicily and southern Italy the invaders are by now securely ensconced, while new, Islamic regimes are, it seems, already in place in Rome and Venice. Nostradamus is obviously horrified at the prospect of the Muslim call to prayer being broadcast across the rooftops of Western European cities, familiar (and totally unthreatening) though neighbourhood mosques have nowadays become.

IX.67   *Upon the mountains all about Isère*
They gather at Valence's rocky gate
From Châteauneuf, Pierrelatte and Donzère:
There shall Rome's flock the Muslim force await.

This quatrain helps us to narrow down the expected route considerably. 'Valence's rocky gate' identifies itself as the valley of the River Isère, a fact which in turn suggests that the invaders will have crossed the Alps between Turin and Grenoble, in part possibly via the Fréjus tunnel – which indeed lies quite close to Mount Cenis (see V.61, p. 104). Once again, meanwhile, Nostradamus refers to them as Muslims – in this case in terms of the word 'crescent'. This serves to remind us that their original heartlands may well lie mainly in the southern part of the former Soviet Empire and the western borderlands of China, much as Nostradamus's terms 'Mongol' and 'Tartar' specifically hint.

VII.7 *After the combat 'twixt the horses light*
Great Islam they shall claim at bay to keep.
Death, shepherd-dressed, shall stalk the hills at
   night:
The clefts flow red in all the chasms deep.

We do not have to take too literally Nostradamus's reference to
light horses, which may refer to a battle between light armoured
vehicles. What certainly seems to occur is a series of night-time
commando-type operations that have extremely bloody consequences.

V.15 *The Pope is captured while* en route *conveyed:*
The outraged, thwarted clerics waste their breath.
Absent, the next elected's star shall fade:
His bastard favourite be done to death.

As though to confirm our interpretation above, this verse pursues
the theme of the Pope's capture and looks ahead to the unpromising prospects of his successor.

VII.22 *The people from Iraq shall, furious, fall*
Upon the friends of Spanish Catalonia.
With games, rites, feasts, none of them wakes at all.
Pope by the Rhône; Rome taken, and Ausonia.

From the papal flight and capture we turn aside for a moment for
a brief *résumé* of the broader picture. The invasion, it seems, has
already reached south-eastern Europe: now it is about to spread

to the south-west, apparently via the south-eastern part of Spain (Nostradamus's singling out of the Catalonian trading city of Tarragona in line two seems to spring purely from his need for an appropriate word to rhyme with *Ausone* in the last line, and so I have returned the compliment). Nor is the campaign without its own special kind of violence in this quarter. Meanwhile, Nostradamus seems to identify the invaders from the east as 'citizens from Mesopotamia' – i.e. Iraq – thus suggesting that they are neither serfs nor conscripts, but autonomous members of a possibly republican state. Since it seems unlikely that Iraq could ever pose such a serious threat on its own, the true significance of the phrase may well be that the incoming hordes are, as previously indicated, from much further east. *En route*, it seems, they will have *passed through* Iraq, possibly even staying in the Middle East for a while before resuming their westward march. This temporary halt may in fact correspond to the mooted pause for replenishment already referred to in X.72 (p. 74). Whoever they are, then, this will certainly be no mere second Gulf War. The unprepared Italians, in particular, intent on the usual 'bread and circuses' that are by now so familiar to the Western world, will already have woken up to find their country ('Ausonia') under the heel of the invaders, who (as we have seen) may well have crossed unexpectedly from Albania. The fact that the Pope has apparently fled, finishing up like his fourteenth-century predecessors somewhere beside the River Rhône (line four makes it quite clear, incidentally, that this is no mere disguise-word for 'Rome') is also well established by now. Line four is a marvellous example of Nostradamus's *penchant* for telegrammese, especially when pushed for space in the final lines of his quatrains.

II.72   *Hard-pressed in Italy is France's might;*
          Great loss and heavy fighting many-sided.
          Rome fleeing, France repulsed. Ticino's fight –
          Or that of Rubicon – is undecided.

Evidently France, sensing the imminent threat to its own borders, has belatedly sent an expeditionary force to Italy to help resist the invaders. In the event, however, it is not up to the task. Forced back into north-western Italy, it makes its final stand on the River Ticino near Pavia in order to prevent what promises to be a kind of crossing of the Rubicon in reverse. For a while at least, stalemate is achieved.

IV.90   *The walls can neither fighting force regain.*
Trembling and fear Milan, Pavia sap.
Hunger, thirst, doubt shall pierce them all amain.
No bread, no food: of rations not a scrap.

Two different defending armies – possibly the French and Italian – now find their retreat cut off. One has the impression that the nearby cities have been encircled and possibly besieged. With their normal supply-routes disrupted, they start to suffer severe famine.

VII.39   *The leader of the fighting force from France*
Shall think his principal formation trapped.
Doubts over food and shelter he'll advance.
By Genoa's aliens he shall be sapped.

Apparently demoralised, the commander of the last French forces still in Italy starts to invent good reasons for withdrawing, as invading troops from around Genoa continue to press him hard.

IX.95   *The new-made chief the host leads where he can,*
Almost cut off, towards the river-bank,
Helped by a force of shock-troops from Milan:
Milan's chief blinded, barred in prison dank.

The remaining defenders in northern Italy now straggle towards one of their last defence-lines, probably the River Ticino (see II.72, p. 108).

II.15   *Shortly before the king shall meet his end,*
O'er Twins and Ship the comet shall come in.
State funds by land and sea they shall expend;
The lands cut off from Pisa to Turin.

The Pope's exile in France is not likely to last long, for the same comet that marks his flight also presages his death – or so, at least, it seems. That it could be a *second* comet, after all, seems rather unlikely. Nostradamus actually seems to trace its path. It will, he suggests, pass through the constellations of Gemini and Argo (unless what Nostradamus really means is that there will be two popes attempting to rule the 'ship' of the church at once, as happened once before in connection with the papal flight to France in the fourteenth century: in fact the French text makes this interpretation seem marginally more likely). By this time, it seems, the invaders will have consolidated their grip on northern Italy (the original text, which I have been forced to summarise somewhat, mentions Asti and Ferrara as well), to the point of turning it into forbidden territory.

VI.6   *Near Cancer's claws and the Septentrion*
            Of famed Great Bear, the bearded star appears
            To Susa, Siena, Thebes, Eretrion.
            Great Rome shall die the night it disappears.

Here Nostradamus becomes even more specific, once again link-
ing the death of the Pope to the expected comet, and casting even
more light on its likely track (whether this information is com-
patible with that offered in II.15, opposite, I have no idea, but –
as I have pointed out – the latter may not really be astronomical
at all). Just as its appearance marks his flight from Rome, its
disappearance will, it seems, mark his death. Line three suggests
that the comet will be most easily visible in Italy and Greece –
unless these are merely the areas where its astrological significance will be most dire. The word that I have rendered as
'Thebes' is in fact 'Boetia': 'Eretrion' is a Nostradamian coinage
for 'Eretria' based on the Latin *Eretriensis*, and presumably
forced upon him by the need to rhyme with 'Septentrion'.

VIII.46 *Three leagues from Rhône shall die Paul* main-soleil
            Fleeing of nearby Tarascon the strait.
            Of Eagle and French Cock, dread Mars's sway
            Shall then the worst of brothers three instate.

This extraordinarily obtuse quatrain is one of a number that
include the intriguing expression '*Pol mensolee/mansole/mansol/
mausol*' – evidently the key to identifying the latter-day pope to
whom so many of the predictions refer at around this juncture. It
looks suspiciously like one of those geographical puns on which,
as we shall see, Nostradamus is so keen – as in the case of VIII.16
(p. 126), where he impishly disguises the word *fessan* ('broad of
bottom') as a classical place-name – for St Paul-de-Mausole is a

former Priory just to the south of his own birthplace of St Rémy-de-Provence. Yet the whole point about such puns is precisely that they have a double meaning. 'Pol', clearly, is merely a version of 'Paul', but the word following it begs to be interpreted as a version of the French *main-de-soleil*, or rather the Latin *manus solis*. The word *manus* normally means 'hand', but in Virgil particularly its meaning is often extended to include 'work', and particularly 'handiwork'.

'Hand-of-the-sun', then, or 'work of the sun' – what can Nostradamus possibly be driving at? In the event, it turns out to be something quite specific – namely the celebrated and often remarkably accurate twelfth-century forecast by the Irish St Malachy of all the popes from his own day until the end of the Vatican.[8, 13, 14] Each is given a Latin tag which in some way describes his pontificate, and the last figure but two is described as *De Labore Solis* ('Of the work of the sun'). Evidently, then, Nostradamus is referring specifically to this figure. Since, however, the papal succession and St Malachy's list have long since been matched up with each other, that individual's identity is widely known, even in the Vatican. *He is none other than the present Pope*, who in his youth at least had the grace to fit Malachy's Latin tag by working in the open air with his bare hands, having been assigned to the Polish stone-quarries by the Nazi invaders. (The last two on Malachy's list, incidentally, are *Gloria Olivae* ['Of the glory of the olive'] – here apparently seen by Nostradamus as the worst of three monkish candidates – and *Petrus Romanus* ['Peter the Roman' or 'the Roman rock'], during whose reign the Vatican will allegedly be destroyed.)

The prophecy, in consequence, suggests that it is the by-then very aged John Paul II (no less) who will be the fleeing pope described in the foregoing quatrains – *in which case V.92 (p. 65) clearly indicates that his flight, in common with all the events described above, will occur by the year 2000 at the latest*. He it is, too, who will eventually die six miles from the Rhône (presumably just outside Lyon, if the foregoing stanzas are not only relevant, but to be believed), after being captured at the pass of Tarascon. This scenario, then, suggests that his intended new headquarters will be at Avignon, to which the popes fled once before, between 1309 and 1377, and whose papal palace is consequently still available – though quite what he will be doing to the south of it at Tarascon Nostradamus does not deign to explain. Could it possibly be that our northern scenario involving his flight via the Alps is in error, and based on quatrains that in fact refer to other circumstances entirely? Could it be that he will after all have taken the southern route? Or could he indeed have reached Avignon via the northern route, but be chased southwards out of it again by forces representing either or both of his two expected successors? Can it in any case be that Nostradamus is really expecting fourteenth-century papal history to repeat itself in the extraordinary way indicated – or is he merely allowing his imagination to run away with him, deluding himself with half-remembered scraps of history and memories of his own university days in the city? Could it even be that, despite all the suggestions to the contrary, he is talking about another pope entirely? In respect of all five questions we should perhaps remember at this point the apparently seditious operation, despite all our best intentions, of prophetic Law 8 (see page 20).

X.93   *Much travel shall the new-found vessel know.*
         Here, there and everywhere they'll move the see.
         To Arles, Beaucaire the hostages shall go,
         Near two shafts, newly found, in porphyry.

This quatrain makes it seem that, following their capture at Tarascon, the crew of the papal 'barque' of 'Peter the Fisherman' – i.e. the Pope and his party – will initially be treated as hostages and constantly moved about the Rhône delta to foil any possible rescue attempt. The area just to the south of the towns mentioned – as well as of Nostradamus's own birthplace of St Rémy – is particularly rich in Roman remains.

I.43   *Before the mighty empire changed shall be*
A thing miraculous shall come to light.
The soil removed, a shaft of porphyry
Shifted to stand upon a rocky height.

Nostradamus seems fascinated by the new archaeological discovery, though he fails to explain what is so miraculous about the stone-carved relic. Clearly, though, he sees it as presaging a change of regime – possibly, in this case, the demise of the authority of the Roman Church in Europe in favour of that of the invaders.

IX.32   *A tall shaft found, of porphyry the best:*
Imperial documents beneath the base,
Bones Roman, plaited hair to force attest.
At Mitilini ships stir up the place.

Even as the invaders are about to ship further forces to Europe from the Turkish west coast, with a fleet waiting in high anticipation off the isle of Lesbos, the ever-curious Nostradamus cannot resist delving further into the details of the discovery.

VII.2   *Exposed to Mars, Arles shall refuse to fight.*
Black, white and blue are hidden in the ground.
The soldiers all shall be surprised at night.
In the false shadows traitors shall be found.

This verse is almost as shadowy as its subject, but there seem to be hints that the military group guarding the captive Pope (still on the archaeological site), though not attacked openly, will suddenly be overwhelmed at night by resistance guerillas. Presumably, then, he is rescued – though there are also hints that watching eyes will be secretly recording everything that happens.

II.97   *O Roman Pope, beware lest you come near*
            The city that is washed by rivers two!
            When blooms the rose, those who to you are dear
            Nearby shall spit their blood – and so shall you.

The Pope now flees north towards the city of Lyon, watered as it is by the two rivers Saône and Rhône (both of which Nostradamus actually names in this connection in IX.68, p. 116), where he presumably hopes to find safe haven. It has to be said, though, that the death of a pope in the area of the Rhône occurred once before: Pius VI, imprisoned by Napoleon at Valence along with thirty-two of his priestly entourage, died there of acute gastro-enteritis on 29 August 1799 ('when blooms the rose'). Erika Cheetham therefore suggests, quite naturally, that the current prediction, far from applying to the future, has already been fulfilled – not that the fact would necessarily have carried any weight with Nostradamus himself, who clearly believed that history (and no doubt especially predicted history) was quite happy to repeat itself *ad infinitum*. On the other hand, Valence is not Lyon – indeed, it lies all of sixty miles south of it – and gastro-enteritis is not a respiratory ailment such as one normally associates with the coughing up of blood. Nor, for that matter, did death strike the papal entourage itself. Consequently the prediction seems still to be waiting for a modern Pope – apparently the present one – to fulfil it. The 'rose' reference may indeed be to the time of year, but elsewhere (V.96, p. 70) Nostradamus seems to refer to the rose as symbolic of some future regime that he regards with particular unease – probably that of the invaders themselves.

Note, meanwhile, the important suggestion in the first line that it is actually possible for us to *take warning* from Nostradamus's predictions for our future and to act in some measure to defuse them. In other words, they are not irrevocable: thanks to their inherent vagueness, many of them can be interpreted on a much less dramatic level than first impressions may seem to indicate (indeed, we have already noted Nostradamus's occasional tendency to over-dramatise those with an apocalyptic content), while others can – if at a considerable linguistic and conceptual pinch – be held to have been fulfilled already, as Erika Cheetham's efforts amply demonstrate in respect of the current quatrain.

IX.68   *Obscured shall be Montélimar's great light.*
Where Saône runs into Rhône shall evil strike.
On Lucy's day, troops hid in woods from sight
Horror commit. None ever saw the like.

Shorn of context, this quatrain could refer to almost anybody at almost any time. While the word *throfne* in the original last line suggests a ruler either religious or temporal, line one merely refers to a 'noble one'. Nevertheless, the expected papal flight immediately gives the prediction a possible meaning. The fugitive Pope, it seems, will be ambushed by troops somewhere in the Rhône valley, apparently after passing through Montélimar. This event, though, does not seem to be the same as his initial capture at the pass of Tarascon, just south of Avignon, as described in VIII.46 (p. 111). As previously indicated, one has the impression that after that incident he is destined to escape to Lyon, and that it is during an attempt to leave that city in turn that some kind of further evil awaits him. Nostradamus even offers a date: the final capture will take place on St Lucy's day, 13 December.

V.17   *The princely Cypriot the king shall spy*
As he pursues a narrow track at night.
King stricken, up the Rhône the soldiers fly,
Conspiring him to kill as best they might.

This quatrain, too, may well refer to the capture of the Pope –
here described as 'king' rather than 'noble' – though the Cypriot
is unidentified. The fact that the pontiff's capturers flee along the
Rhône suggests not only that he may have been attempting to
return to Avignon from Lyon, but that the soldiers in question
are not yet a truly occupying force, but rather a roaming band in
what is still basically unconquered country.

VIII.34   *Leo at Lyon shall triumphant be:*
Betrayal and slaughter then on Jura's slope
Of thousand easterners seven score and three.
At Lyon falls down dead the slippered Pope.

Coded though its language is (see 'Academic Notes') this quatrain could hardly be more specific. True, 'Leo' is not identified:
the word could refer to somebody of that name, or whose device
is a lion (England, for example), or even to matters astrological –
in which case the battle may well be timed for late summer. In
view of Nostradamus's known predilection for puns and double
meanings, indeed, any combination of all three could apply. The
'Leo' in question could even be John Paul II's papal rival and/or
successor.

Certainly, though, up in the Jura there will be a bloody battle,
presumably with the invaders, as they try to press down into the
Rhône valley via Haute Savoie. For the Pope – whether currently
triumphant or imprisoned – it is of little consequence. By accident or design, he dies either at or not far from Lyon (Nostra-

117

damus the versifier constantly switches between the two possibilities, mainly because the one – *à* – gives him one syllable, while the other – *près de* – offers him two to play with.)

V.46   *When Sabine candidate shall be elected*
          The cardinals shall feud and disagree.
          Great theses shall against him be erected
          And Rome by force Albanian injured be.

Having no obvious historical fulfilment, this quatrain begs at first sight to be interpreted as applying to a future pope who hails from the north-eastern quarter of Rome. However, V.49 (p. 120) suggests that he will actually come from Sabinar or Sabiñánigo in Spain, or even from Sabinas in Mexico or Sabine in Texas. The *Albanois* could be either singular or plural, and could equally well come from Alba, Albens or even Britain (Albion). 'Rome', similarly, could mean either the city, the Roman Church, the Vatican or even the Pope himself. (Nostradamus, clearly, is quite good at hedging his bets.) The present Pope, John Paul II, was certainly injured in office, but by a Turk: moreover, the other details seem not to be a particularly good fit, despite the controversy which has long reigned within the church over his policy on birth-control.

   Possibly, then, the quatrain indicates the controversial election of a new Pope at a time of great turbulence, during the course of which Rome is asssiled from the direction of Albania. The circumstances of the oriental invasion immediately spring to mind once again. But if so, then we need to refer to the various other quatrains on the same subject (see above and below).

X.65 *O mighty Rome, dread ruin comes again*
Not to your walls, but to your living part.
Hurt you shall be by words of harsh disdain,
Whose sword shall pierce you to the very heart.

In view of the clarity and directness of this quatrain, it seems quite possible that Nostradamus himself interpreted it as applying, not to the Church of Rome but to the city itself – and with it, possibly, the entire Holy Roman Empire (*vaste Romme*) – even though, in the nature of things, this would be likely to include the Vatican as well. The 'sword' in the last line, similarly, he would probably have understood in literal, physical terms. But then, no more than anybody else was he necessarily a reliable interpreter of his own visions. We have already noted his tendency, in particular, to translate mere words and phrases into concrete images that can all too easily lead the interpreter astray. My own hunch is that the prophecy probably indicates the eventual end of the papacy as a major religious force, mainly as a result of severe criticism in books and the media – whether political, moral or theological (possibly the 'great theses' mentioned above). Other sources of prediction[6, 8] suggest a date not too far after the turn of the present century for this event. This, in turn, could indicate that the last two popes could have quite brief reigns.

VIII.19 *The mighty Pope to help, in trouble sore,*
The reds are on the march (or so they say).
His family, o'erwhelmed, are at death's door.
The reddest reds his Redness wipe away.

We now start to see the reason for the disrepute into which the Vatican has evidently fallen. The invaders, it seems, have allowed one of the cardinals to ascend St Peter's throne as Pope but only on condition that their own candidate be elected, and that all effective power be in fact devolved to them. Putting it about that the College of Cardinals itself has asked for their aid, they then march openly into the Vatican. His 'family' is presumably the shocked and oppressed Church. And so it is that one group of 'reds' (the Asiatic occupying power) is about to put paid to another (the cardinals, and this cardinal in particular).

VIII.20 *Of rigged elections rumours false shall flood*
The city through: broken, the pact's unpacted.
Votes bought, the holy chapel stained in blood,
The empire to another is contracted.

This verse makes it clear that something of the kind has indeed happened. But events do not go according to plan. In the Sistine chapel, consequently, a mixture of bribery and brute force is brought to bear to produce a new result, thus breaking the secret agreement and destroying even the last pretence of legality.

V.49 *Not from old Spain; instead, from ancient France*
Elected o'er the trembling church to rule,
Promises to the foe he shall advance
Who in his reign shall prove a plague so cruel.

The original choice, it seems, came of Spanish stock. Now, however, it is a French cardinal more sympathetic to the invaders who is substituted – or at least one with ancient French ancestry – and then only after having offered them some pretty scandalous guarantees.

Note, meanwhile, Nostradamus's use of the word 'plague' to

describe the invaders. Since, as we shall see, he will go on to use this word repeatedly in connection with them during the course of the predictions that follow, it is as well to take due note of the fact that he does not necessarily always mean plague in the literal, medical sense.

VI.78   *To vaunt the lunar crescent's victory*
The folk of Rome the Eagle high shall raise.
Milan, Pavia, Genoa disagree,
So by themselves the great king they must praise.

Evidently the inhabitants of Rome have by now settled into the new occupation regime, and are persuaded to stage a public celebration of their 'liberation' by the invaders – or even of the new Pope's election. The regions in the north, however, having only recently been conquered, see through the whole charade, and are not inclined to join in.

VI.38   *The beaten shall the foes of peace behold,*
Once prostrate Italy lies dead and still.
The bloody Moor and red shall then make bold
Fires to ignite, blood in the waves to spill.

Whether or not because of the new allegations against the Church, the leader of the occupying forces now decides – promises or not – to expunge from the face of the earth all trace of the former regime (both secular and ecclesiastical) that he apparently finds so objectionable. Deliberate conflagrations and persecutions result.

V.73   *Sorely the Church of God shall be oppressed,*
         The holy temples looted of their store,
         The naked child by mother but half-dressed,
         Arabs and Poles allied as ne'er before.

As the church is pillaged, social conditions deteriorate, and widespread social privations are experienced throughout the occupied lands. The rather surprising last line suggests either an alliance between the invasion's furthest southern and northern flanks or (more likely) a 'forced marriage' between the invading Muslims and the followers of *Pol* ('Paul'), the former Polish Pope. On the other hand, the word *Polons* could conceivably be a front for *Polois* ('inhabitants of St Pol'), which might then refer to the town of St Paul just north of Avignon. In this case, in other words, the quatrain merely confirms that groups of invaders will by now be firmly ensconced in the Rhône delta.

IV.82   *Out of Slavonia the horde draws near:*
         The ancient city's sacked by vandals' ire.
         Desolate shall his Rome to him appear,
         Nor shall he then know how to douse the fire.

Whether Nostradamus is referring at this point to a second wave of invaders from the north-east is not entirely clear. At all events, massed troops duly descend on Rome itself. The 'he' of the last two lines may refer to the last, beleaguered Pope, who is powerless to defend his city. Alternatively, it could refer to the oriental commander who, once having set the invasion in motion, eventually finds that it has acquired an uncontrollable momentum of its own which actually destroys what it was intended to grasp – in this case the power and riches of Rome.

III.84   *The Mighty City shall be desolated:*
Of its inhabitants shall none remain.
Walls, temples, women, virgins violated;
By sword, fire, plague and gun they shall be slain.

The results are inevitable, and need no elaboration from me.

VIII.80   *With innocents bleed maids and widowed dames –*
So many ills the Great Red shall commit.
The holy icons dipped in candle-flames:
For fear and dread all motionless shall sit.

Nostradamus's description is graphic. He is evidently so pious as to see the violation of religious monuments on much the same level as that of women and children – not a view, I suspect, that would be shared by many nowadays.

II.81   *Fire near consumes the city from the sky.*
Noah's flood shall loom anew ere winter's done.
Sardinia's coast shall Afric vessels try
Once from the Scales has passed the autumn sun.

Nostradamus seems to foresee the use of artillery and/or incendiaries during the new attack on Rome – unless he is referring to the much more sinister thermal weapon referred to in later predictions as being deployed in the south-west of France. For whatever reason, a great flood then follows. Nostradamus associates this with that of the Greek Deucalion, thus apparently suggesting that it will in some way originate in Greece: for metrical reasons, I have substituted the biblical one of Noah. Meanwhile, Sardinia's resistance is likely to continue until new attacks descend on it from the African coast, along which the invaders are now about to spread (see II.86, II.30, pp. 128, 140). If the last line's original reference to *Phaëton* refers to Jupiter, then it may be possible to assign this prediction to a particular year and month: if, as seems more likely, it refers to the sun whose son and *alter ego* Phaëthon was in Greek mythology, then it appears to date the events described to late October or early November.

III.6 *The lightning deep within the temple falls.*
The citizens behind their doors shall shrink;
Their cattle too, as water laps the walls.
E'en weak ones take to arms for food and drink.

This quatrain seems to suggest, in fact, that the attacks will continue until the expected great flood itself puts a stop to them. To this extent, then, the latter could be seen as something of a saving event, for all the resultant shortages of provisions.

II.93 *Death comes apace hard by the Tiber's flow*
Shortly before the mighty inundation.
The vessel's captain's taken, sent below:
Castle and palace in full conflagration.

This prediction is highly reminiscent of the kind of scenario envisaged by a number of other psychics, too.[6, 8, 12, 23] It appears to refer to the end of the Vatican and the death of the last Pope, often dated to not long after the end of the present century. The 'vessel's captain' who is taken captive into the cellars begs identification with the then Pope himself. Both Angelo and Vatican, it seems, will be set ablaze shortly before – to cap it all – the great flood already referred to descends on the city.

I.52   *Saturn and Mars in Scorpio are met:*
        The mighty lord is murdered in his hall.
        To plague the Church a monarch new is set
        In southern Europe and the north withal.

If this quatrain is relevant at this juncture, the last Pope is now destined to be murdered on his own premises. The 'new king' is presumably the oriental overlord, and his advent spells the doom of the Catholic Church throughout Europe.

II.52   *For several nights the earth shall quake amain.*
        Springtime shall two successive spasms see.
        War shall be waged by doughty champions twain.
        Ephesus, Corinth drowned by either sea.

While the ding-dong battle continues in the Mediterranean and Aegean, matters are suddenly complicated by two massive earthquakes which bring enormous tidal waves crashing down upon the coastal cities of Greece and Turkey.

III.3   *Mars, Hermes, silver shall conjunction make:*
        Towards the south a great drought shall ensue.
        In central Turkey, Earth is said to shake.
        In Ephesus confusion, Corinth too.

Here Nostradamus widens the picture somewhat. At the same time as the seismic disturbances in the Mediterranean there are further ones in central Asia Minor, as well as droughts in Africa (or possibly merely in southern France). The first line suggests some kind of astrological dating, though the significance of the word *argent* ('silver' or 'money') is unclear: it could refer to the moon.

VIII.16 *There where great Jason built his famous boat*
    So huge a flood shall burst old Ocean's banks
    That hearth and homeland out of reach shall float
    And waves shall climb broad-based Olympus'
     flanks.

Once again, consequently, the great flood already mentioned looms into view, but this time more explicitly. One is tempted to wonder whether the mighty volcano of Santorini has perhaps exploded once more, as it did back in Minoan times to such catastrophic effect.

I.69 *The mighty mountain near a mile in girth*
   Shall – after peace, war, hunger – floods beset.
   Far they shall roll to countries of the earth,
   However old, however mighty yet.

Nostradamus pursues the theme, confirming the present mountain's Olympian identity by giving its girth (evidently a prominent feature to which he also refers in the previous quatrain) as seven Greek *stadia*, or about 1400 metres. Despite the rhyme-influenced wording of my third line, the original is in fact innocent of any specific suggestion that the floods will affect countries outside the Mediterranean area. Meanwhile line two confirms that war and famine will already have swept Greece during the earlier stages of the oriental advance.

V.31   *That Attic land, in wisdom first of all,*
Which still remains the flower of the world
The sea shall ruin: its eminence shall fall,
By waves sucked down and to perdition hurled.

But it is inevitably Greece itself that will be most severely affected. Virtually the whole country – or at least its lower-lying portion – is destined to be laid waste by the sea, and no doubt a good many of its artistic and monumental achievements with it.

V.63   *Too much they'll plead vain enterprise's glory.*
Among th' Italians boats, cold, hunger, water:
Not far from Tiber all the land is gory:
All kinds of plagues shall human beings slaughter.

The tidal waves duly reach Italy, bringing their usual dire effects to add to the existing catalogue of woes. Possibly line one suggests that it was some kind of local rebellion that served as the final trigger for the burning of Rome and the Vatican.

X.60   *Weep, Nice, Savona, Monaco, Siena,*
For bloody war your New Year's gift shall be!
In Malta, Pisa, Genoa, Capua, Modena
Fire, earthquake, flood and dire necessity.

By this stage the oriental invasion is evidently spreading from Italy into south-eastern France, as well as affecting the Mediterranean islands. Nostradamus even seems to date this phase of the conflict to a particular time of year. Although I have split the quatrain into two, the original French ascribes *all* the calamities listed to *all* the places named. Fire and desperate reactions are of course the natural consequence of war, but the earthquake and flood once again suggest that a seismic catastrophe of some kind will also occur at about this time in the Mediterranean area.

II.86   *A fleet is wrecked near Adriatic sea*
           Lifted by earthquake, dropped upon the land.
           Egypt, a-quake the Muslims' spread to see,
           An envoy sends, surrender in his hand.

The earthquake in the eastern Mediterranean has a familiar consequence: the resulting tidal waves bear boats and even large ships inland – in this case what looks suspiciously like an entire Muslim invasion fleet, at anchor off the eastern shores of Italy. Meanwhile, Nostradamus uses his familiar technique of repeating an idea from the first half of his verse in the second half – in this case the notion of 'quaking' – to give us our first direct indication that the invasion is also about to spread across North Africa. The Egyptians, naturally, are not over-inclined to resist.

IX.31   *The earth shall quake Mortara all around.*
           Drowsy with peace, by war roused up again,
           Saint George's isles of tin shall be half-drowned.
           At Easter schisms rend the church in twain.

Evidently Britain is affected by the Mediterranean earthquake after all – or at least by its marine after-effects. Here Nostradamus associates it with Mortara, some thirty miles south-west of Milan. Meanwhile the destruction of the Vatican is also having its after-effects within the Church itself. Once again, in other words, Nostradamus achieves a kind of echo-effect within his four-line verse: a physical earthquake in one place is reflected in a doctrinal one somewhere else.

III.70 *Great Britain – England in another age –*
Shall be by water flooded to great height.
The new Italian league such war shall wage
That they against them shall combine to fight.

Even while still partially inundated, however, Britain – no doubt sensing the danger to itself if the invasion spreads – agrees to support France in its struggle against the invaders (note that the term 'Great Britain' had not even been invented in Nostradamus's day). The exact form or extent of that support is not clear at this stage, however. The main British involvement seems to be reserved for the later stages of the hostilities.

X.66 *Through power American the British head*
Shall lay an icy slab on Scotland's isle.
An Antichrist they'll find and leader red
Who'll draw them all into the fight awhile.

In this quatrain we seem to have a mixture of history and futurology. The context of the last two lines seems clear enough, with the future invaders being associated (neither for the first nor for the last time) with the colour red. It is the first two lines that pose the problem. The 'icy slab' seems mysterious in the extreme – until one realises the difficulties that Nostradamus would have

129

been faced with had he ever 'seen' or 'heard' a modern media report to the effect that 'the first *Polaris submarine* has been laid down in Scotland'. Even more amazing, however, is the suggestion by Nostradamus (in the mid sixteenth century, remember!) that newly-colonised America would at some future date actually be able to wield a measure of power in Europe. The last line seems to suggest that not only Britain, but at some stage America too, is likely to become involved in the conflict.

IX.42   *The plague sweeps Barcelona, Monaco,*
         Genoa, Venice, Sicily and more;
         Yet to the Muslim fleet their teeth they'll show
         And chase them all the way to Tunis' shore.

Whether the 'plague' in line one refers to actual pestilence or to the incoming swarms of what Nostradamus elsewhere describes as 'locusts' (i.e. the oriental invaders) is not made clear. At all events, there seems to be some spirited resistance by sea, to start with at least. Monaco, as we saw above, is among the places to bear the brunt of the foreign onslaught.

I.37   *Shortly before the setting sun goes down*
         Battle shall start, a mighty race unsure.
         Defeated, no response from harbour town:
         Burial at sea twice over they'll endure.

In the event, however, the outcome is disastrous. The hard-pressed European navies, possibly expecting reinforcements from Marseille or Toulon, are disappointed. The last line seems to hint that at least one crew will go down with its ship.

IX.100   *When night o'ertakes the battle on the sea*
Fire shall destroy the occidental fleets.
Red new-bedecked shall then the flagship be.
Wrath to the vanquished: rain the victors greets.

The curious detail in line three suggests that the European flagship may be captured and placed under new colours – the colour red is constantly associated by Nostradamus with the invaders – unless, of course, it is merely stained with blood. The original text's 'drizzle' in the last line may not be as innocuous as it sounds: later predictions seem to see such phenomena as noxious in some way, almost as though indicative of chemical or bacteriological warfare. This in turn may even tie in with Nostradamus's frequent references to 'plague' in connection with the fighting.

II.78   *The British power beneath th' abysmal flood*
With Afric blood and French shall mingled be.
Neptune being late, the Isles shall swim in blood.
E'en secrets told shall harm far less than he.

In line one Nostradamus seems to use 'Neptune' – presumably complete with trident – to refer to a British submarine force (compare II.59, p. 156). As a result of the disastrous sea-battle, the invaders' southern forces are enabled to carry out sea-borne landings from Africa on the Mediterranean islands off the coast of southern France. Nostradamus seems to suggest that the British will leave their intervention until far too late, while further harm will be done on the intelligence front. As ever, the European defeat will owe almost as much to the Europeans themselves as to the enemy.

VI.90 *Stinking, outrageous, and a rank disgrace:*
Yet after it they'll praise him to the skies –
The chief excused who turned away his face –
Lest Neptune tempted be peace to devise.

The accusations go further. Evidently the failure of the British to come to the rescue was some sort of deliberate act of policy. Nevertheless the French are not inclined to make too much of it, lest the British use it as an excuse to withdraw from the fray altogether.

III.1 *After the fight and battle under sail*
Great Neptune shall attain his apogee.
Once red, though, shall the foe for fear grow pale
And terror spread across the mighty sea.

Moreover, the disastrous outcome of the battle does the British navy no harm at all. Possibly its new-found confidence has arisen because, as a direct result, it has received authorisation to use the full might of its nuclear weapons in future if necessary. Certainly this could explain the enemy's corresponding loss of confidence at a time when by rights it should be feeling cock-a-hoop – as well as providing Nostradamus with the chance for a piece of engaging colour-play.

VII.37 *Ten sent by one the captain's life to strip*
'Midst fleet in mutiny find him alert.
Murderous chaos reigns: ship attacks ship
Off Lerins, Hyères: but he is in la Nerthe.

Once again we are at sea among the Mediterranean islands – in this case the Îles de Lerins, off Cannes, and the Îles d'Hyères, off the town of Hyères between Toulon and St Tropez. In the wake of the naval defeat, there is fighting within the allied fleet itself, conceivably in connection with the British let-down. Possibly it is the British commander who, forewarned, arranges to be safely ashore in la Nerthe at the time, just to the north-west of Marseille.

II.40   *Shortly thereafter, not too long delayed,*
Yet greater shall the naval conflict swell.
By land and sea great tumult shall be made,
Fires and strange creatures leaping up as well.

Even now, however, the naval conflict is not at an end. Both naval and shore-based installations seem to be involved in a further battle involving what sound curiously like guided missiles. One wonders whether the British contingent has finally felt moved to deploy its ultimate weapon.

VI.81   *Hearts cold as ice, cruel, black and hard as stone*
Bring tears, wails, cries of fear and screams
    appalling,
Bloodshed, great famine, mercy never shown,
Leman and Genoa's greater isles befalling.

Nevertheless, the Muslim fleets evidently once again win the day. On the lands from Switzerland in the north to Corsica and Sardinia in the south, consequently, a regime of almost unprecedented cruelty and terror is about to descend.

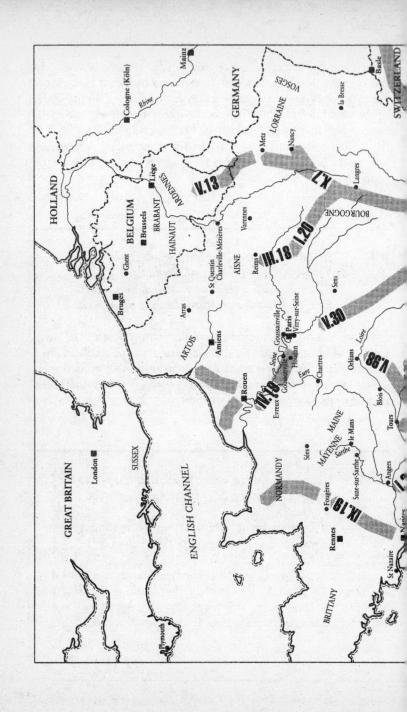

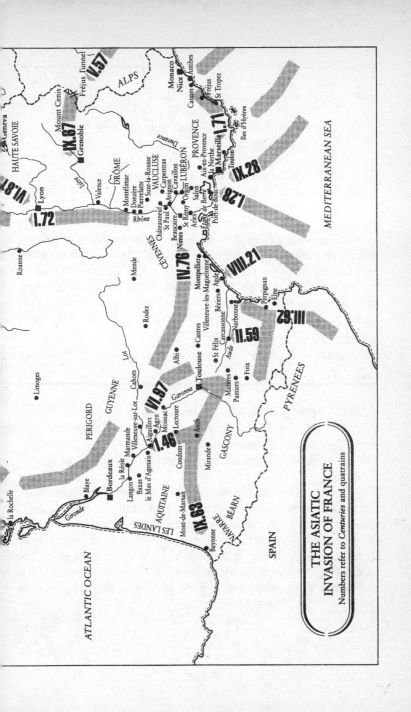

THE ASIATIC
INVASION OF FRANCE
Numbers refer to *Centuries* and quatrains

II.4   *From Monaco almost to Sicily*
The coast entire shall be of folk bereft.
No city, town nor suburb shall there be
But has not suffered heathen sack and theft.

The results for the French and Italian coastal towns and cities, similarly, are catastrophic. Note, meanwhile, that Nostradamus once again uses the term *Barbares*, meaning not so much 'barbarian' as 'Berber', and thus (erroneously) 'Arab'. For reasons that we have already examined, he tends throughout to associate the Asiatic invasion with the Muslim faith; later on, as we shall see, he will have the additional justification that the attacks in question have come specifically from North Africa. Moreover, the characters in Nostradamus's prophetic drama always tend, as we have seen, to take on the nationality of the places through which they are currently passing.

IX.61   *Pillaged shall be the shores along the sea,*
Naples and nearby towns threatened, assaulted.
Many Maltese Messina shall decree
A poor reward – to be tight locked and bolted.

The theme continues. Nostradamus's *cita nova* could be any one of the numerous small Villeneuves that litter the French south coast, from Villeneuve-Loubet just south of Cagnes-sur-mer to Villeneuve-les-Maguelonne just south of Montpellier. Naples (from Greek *Neapolis*) is perhaps an even better candidate. The occupying regime in Sicily, meanwhile, is proving particularly repressive to the inhabitants of the Mediterranean islands.

VII.30 *Shortly a force of peasants sacks and harries*
Po's burning lands as streams all bloody course.
For Turin and Fossano Genoa tarries,
Then Nice from Savigliano takes by force.

Not that events go all the invaders' way. In particular, there seems to be a good deal of unrest behind their backs, as well as dissension within their own ranks, as the various occupying armies vie for the various highly desirable prizes now within range in southern France. The forces occupying Genoa, it seems, are proving particularly powerful.

III.10 *Seven times of blood and famine shall occur*
Growing calamities along the ocean strand:
Monaco starved, all taken prisoner,
Their lord encaged, borne off by hostile hand.

The whole Mediterranean coast, in fact, is in for a whole succession of hostilities and other disasters. Monaco, in particular, is destined to suffer all kinds of horrors.

III.13 *Lightnings shall melt all metals soft on board.*
Both captives shall the other sore assail.
Upon the deck is stretched the city's lord
When 'neath the waves the mighty fleet sets sail.

This quatrain is very difficult to decode precisely. One has the impression that some kind of high-level kidnapping has been attempted by submarine in the very midst of an aerial bombardment, during which the governor of a city has been either wounded or killed, while VIP prisoners have also been removed. The allegiance of the submarine is thus presumably to the orientals – though both sides, it will be remembered, have submarines at their disposal. The soft metals referred to are in fact listed as gold and silver – which could even indicate some kind of military bullion robbery.

VII.19   *Over the fort at Nice no fight shall rage:*
It shall be overcome by metal red.
Long time its fate shall people's tongues engage:
The citizens shall find it strange and dread.

Possibly the town in question is Nice, the aerial bombardment duly reflected in line two. The weapon in question seems to be more than a mere naval shell, though. 'Red-hot metal' seems more reminiscent of napalm.

III.82   *Fréjus, Antibes, Nice and the rest shall be*
By land and sea despoiled along the shore.
Locusts shall ride the wind by land and sea:
Captives trussed up, raped, killed 'spite laws of war.

The theme of war continues as the invaders advance into France with the aid of amphibious landings from the Mediterranean. Note how Nostradamus once again describes the invaders in terms of a swarm of grasshoppers – whether because of their vast numbers or because he has 'seen' (but been unable adequately to interpret) whole squadrons of helicopters descending from the sky.

II.65   *Thrift once abandoned, great calamity*
           Milan's environs and the West assaults.
           The church aflame, plague and captivity.
           In Archer Mercury, and Saturn halts.

As the church is put to the torch, the cost of rearmament will, it seems, bring economic catastrophe to both northern Italy and Western Europe – i.e. all those lands now either affected or threatened by the Asiatic advance (compare II.15, p. 110). The last line appears to offer us an astronomical dating. According to Erika Cheetham,[3] Wöllner tracks down the events predicted to December 2044. Later predictions, though, will suggest that this is much too late for the events in question.

VII.15   *The mighty city of Milan before*
            For seven long years their dreadful siege they'll lay.
            The mighty King shall enter through its door
            And all its enemies shall flee away.

This interesting quatrain suggests (if I have placed it correctly) that the northern city of Milan, already besieged (see IV.90, p. 109), will somehow manage to hold out for seven years. It would be distinctly unwise, however, to assume that from the end of the invasion of Italy no more than seven years will elapse until the start of its eventual liberation. As quite often happens in Nostradamus's verses, the two halves of the quatrain may admittedly be linked by a single theme (in this case, the city of Milan), but they could well apply to two separate events that lie many years apart.

VI.24   *When Mars and Jupiter are in conjunction,*
            'Neath Cancer ghastly war shall be at hand.
            Later a priest anoints with royal unction
            A king who brings long peace to all the land.

Once again we have the two halves of a quatrain applying to events widely spread in time. Erika Cheetham reports, on apparently good authority, that the astrological conjunction in the first line will occur at midsummer 2002. The dating seems apt, for it seems to mark the point at which mere naval assaults and amphibious raids along France's south coast escalate into a full-scale land-war. Nobody should be fooled, however, by Nostradamus's use of the phrase *un peu apres* at the start of line three: the projected coronation of a royal saviour-figure is destined to occur (as we shall see) not 'a little after' 2002, but a little after the end of the conflict itself – and that auspicious, if surprising, event still lies an almost unbearably long time in the future.

II.30   *One who the hellish gods of Hannibal*
            Restores to life again shall men affright:
            Nothing more dread shall records ere recall
            Since chanced to Rome what comes by Babel's
                might.

At this point a new variable enters the equation. The great Asiatic invasion, as we saw earlier, will not be confined to southern Europe. It will have a southern wing, too, which will have been advancing along the North African coast (the great Hannibal mounted his own invasion of Rome from Carthage, in what is now Tunisia), from where it will eventually mount its own threat to the southern coastline of Europe. Nostradamus foresees that events in this particular theatre of operations are likely to prove especially horrific. 'Babel' is in fact simply the standard Hebrew word for 'Babylon' (the Bible's Greek equivalent), and refers back to the invaders' occupancy of the Middle East and their consequent association in Nostradamus's mind with 'Babylon the Great' in St John's Revelation.

V.68　　*To drink he comes by Rhine's and Danube's shore:*
　　　　　The Mighty Camel no remorse shall show.
　　　　　Quake, you of Rhône; of Loire quake even more.
　　　　　Yet near the Alps the Cock shall lay him low.

Nostradamus now turns his attention specifically to this new, south-western theatre of operations. The African invader is described in terms of the Arab 'ship of the desert' using Europe as his distant oasis. In naming the Rhine and the Danube, Nostradamus seems to define the eventual limits of his advance, while suggesting (by his references to the Rhône and Loire) that the devastation he causes will tend to become worse the further north he goes. Finally he foresees his eventual defeat by the 'Cock' – the familiar symbolic bird of France. As previously, however, the beginning and end of the stanza are not necessarily connected: that propitious event could still lie many years in the future.

VI.80　　*From Fez shall rulership to Europe spread,*
　　　　　Firing its cities, slashing with the sword.
　　　　　O'er land and sea, by Asia's Great One led,
　　　　　Christians, blues, greens fall prey to his vast horde.

Yet again the mention of a 'Great One from the East' presses the 'Antichrist' button in the minds of most orthodox commentators, even though several features of this quatrain are rather more suggestive of Franco's return to Spain via Morocco at the start of the Spanish Civil War. If this prediction *does* have a future fulfilment, however, it once again seems more likely to refer to the great Asiatic invasion's southern, or African wing, which will by now evidently have reached Morocco, and be threatening south-western Europe with an unusual degree of violence. The 'blues' and 'greens', though, are unlikely to be identifiable until nearer the time in question.

XII.59   *Accords and pacts broken on every side,*
         Friendships by discords horrid are corrupted,
         Hatred stirred up, all faith decayed, denied
         All hope; Marseille disquieted, disrupted.

The former agreements apparently made between the Asiatics and Marseille (X.58, p. 80) are now peremptorily torn up, and the city (or perhaps it is France itself) starts to fear the worst.

XII.56   *Chief against chief and head 'gainst warring head,*
         Fury and rage shall reach the furthest border.
         Hatred shall reign, dissension rule most dread:
         In France great war, great change and great
              disorder.

The prospects are gloomy. The whole of France looks likely to be torn apart.

IX.28   *Confederate ships shall put in at Marseille;*
         At Venice, too, to march on Hungary.
         From out the Gulf and the Dalmatian Bay
         Others blast Sicily and Italy.

It does not have long to wait. But then France is not alone in its extremity. This originally somewhat obtuse and telegrammatic verse serves to summarise a whole range of hostile naval operations that Nostradamus foresees for the early stages of the war.

III.90   *The Caspian's mighty Tiger-Satyr shall*
         To those at sea a welcome gift award:
         A Persian shall come forth as admiral
         To seize the land from Marseille's overlord.

At this point there is an interesting link-up between the orientals' main invasion-campaign via Italy and south-eastern France, and what looks like its southern, or African wing. The invaders' supreme commander in the north – here described as from the former Hyrcania, which lay in what is now eastern Iran, bordering the south-eastern coast of the Caspian Sea –evidently allows the seaborne forces to take Marseille, rather than his own troops, who are possibly encountering stiffer resistance than expected as they attempt to advance into France over the Alps and along the Mediterranean coast. According to Nostradamus, the sea-borne commander will hail from Carmania, in what is now Iran.

I.28   *Port-de-Bouc's fort a while for craft shall quake*
        From Muslim lands then, later, from the west.
        Great toll shall both of beasts, men, chattels take.
        What deadly strife at Bull's and Scales' behest!

Port-de-Bouc is a fortified port at the entrance to the Étang de Berre, an enormous inland lagoon some twenty miles long and up to ten across, lying only a few miles to the north-west of Marseille, and offering immediate access to the city's hinterland. Apparently the sea-borne invaders will cannily choose this slightly roundabout invasion-route in preference to a frontal attack on Marseille itself. Nostradamus does not reveal whether the initial landings will be successful, but he does suggest that the episode will be repeated at a much later date – the words *longtemps après* could even mean some *years* later, though this seems unlikely – by a similar invasion force from somewhere further west. The first attack will occur in April/May, the second in September/October.

II.37   *Out of the host that shall be sent to take*
        Assistance to the fort so sore beset
        Famine and plague shall all of them o'ertake
        Save only seventy who are murdered yet.

If I have identified the right fort in the right war, it would seem that all attempts at relieving Port-de-Bouc's besieged fort will prove unsuccessful.

I.71   *Thrice is the sea-fort stormed, then taken back*
           By Spanish, Arab and Italian thunder.
           Marseille, Aix, Arles shall troops from Pisa sack,
           While Turin's forces Avignon shall plunder.

As the ding-dong battle for Port-de-Bouc goes on, Nostradamus
is not optimistic about the outcome. He even details which
foreign forces will meanwhile take various of the towns on the
Rhône delta, here identified in terms of which Italian towns they
are currently occupying (as we have already seen, this is a
favourite trick of the seer's).

I.16   *Scythe joined to pool as Archer of the Night*
           Draws near his highest point of exaltation:
           Plague, famine, death by military might –
           The cycle nears its mighty renovation.

At first sight this prediction seems to speak of some significant
astrological conjunction. After all, Sagittarius is clearly present,
and the 'scythe' seems to indicate Saturn – yet, if so, the 'pool'
hardly fits. The commentators' desperate efforts to associate it
with Aquarius are frankly unconvincing, not least because Aquarius and Sagittarius are simply not adjacent. Consequently, one
has to conclude that the quatrain is not primarily astrological at
all. Instead, the *estang*, or 'pool', has to be the self-same Étang de
Berre as is referred to in I.28 opposite (there can be virtually no
doubt about this: the Étang is not only by far the largest stretch of
inland water in France, but lies only some ten miles or so to the
south of Nostradamus's own home at Salon – which inevitably
means that the simple, unidentified term *l'étang* would have been
his normal way of referring to it). In the light of this, the 'scythe'
begs to be identified in turn with the lunar 'sickle' that is the
Muslim invaders' emblem.

Taken as a whole, in other words, the verse constitutes a warning that they will eventually succeed in penetrating the Étang de Berre, probably during the Sagittarian month of December – thus opening up the entire hinterland of Marseille to their sea-borne invasion. This prompts Nostradamus to trot out all his familiar, well-worn themes of war, famine and plague – which might be impressive, were it not for the fact that they are recognisable as three of the four horsemen of the biblical Apocalypse (Rev. 6: 3–8). This fact in itself should put us on our guard against taking them either too literally or too universally – even though the plague, far from having been wiped out as is generally assumed, is still lurking virtually world-wide in the shellfish of our apparently innocent coastal waters, only awaiting its chance to break out again just as soon as we are prepared to let it. Perhaps it is because of the seemingly apocalyptic nature of these phenomena that Nostradamus thinks he knows when. It will occur during the run-up to the Millennium, which he elsewhere dates at the year 2827/8 (see I.48, p. 270). On the other hand, the expression 'during the run-up to' has a good deal of elasticity about it. The fact that Nostradamus sees the events in question as signs that the Millennium is approaching does not necessarily mean that he sees it as imminent. The events described, in other words, are merely 'signs of the times', premonitory birth-pangs of the new world order. Consequently they could occur at almost any time between now and the twenty-ninth century. In the light of the associated events described above and below, some time early in the twenty-first century still seems the most likely date.

I.18   *Through French discord and negligence shall be*
        To Muslim forces free access allowed:
        Siena's lands blood-soaked by land and sea,
        And ships and boats shall Marseille's harbour
            crowd.

Thus it is that, through sheer incompetence, the invasion-force is allowed to break in and occupy Marseille. Nostradamus is not specific about the nature of the French negligence, but there is a distinct suggestion here that events such as this could well be mitigated, if not actually avoided, were the peoples of Western Europe to be more alert and determined to defend themselves. As ever, in other words, the answers lie in our own hands.

III.79 *Law's constant chain, from age to age imparted*
Another order suddenly denies.
The chain of Marseille's harbour shall be parted,
The city taken, foes as thick as flies.

In describing Marseille's takeover by the new, Muslim regime, Nostradamus once again resorts to a familar stylistic trick: rather like the Hebrew psalms that were so familiar to him from his Jewish childhood, he takes a theme mentioned in the first half of his verse and reapplies it in the second, albeit in an entirely different sense.

X.88 *At second watch, mounted and foot alike*
Shall force an entry, wasting all by sea.
Within Marseille's defences they shall strike.
Tears, screams and blood: ne'er worse times shall
*   there be.*

The details are now graphically spelt out, and need no explanation from me.

I.41   *The town, besieged, by night shall be assailed.*
        Few 'scape: fierce battle rages near the sea.
        Mother exults to find her son bewailed:
        Poison in letters' folds concealed shall be.

This quatrain, too, seems to describe the attack on Marseille. If so, then the last two lines seem to offer both a personal touch and a specific detail whose veracity is only ever likely to be confirmed by those directly concerned.

VIII.17 *At once the well-to-do put down shall be:*
         By federates three the world is sorely troubled.
         The foes shall take the city of the sea.
         Famine, fire, blood and plague – all ills redoubled.

Somewhat gleefully echoing the biblical 'He hath put down the mighty from their seat', to say nothing of Virgil's celebrated equivalent phrase *debellare superbos*, Nostradamus seems to foretell the fate of Marseille – and especially of its élite – at the hands of the invaders. Apparently he anticipates that the latter will in fact constitute an alliance of three leaders, or powers – possibly those advancing along the coast, those invading from the sea and those who have been advancing from further westwards via north Africa.

I.72   *Chased and pursued, towards Lyon they shall go:*
        Marseille of its inhabitants is bled.
        Narbonne, Toulouse by forces from Bordeaux
        Outraged. Of captives near a million dead.

As Marseille is invaded, the inevitable happens: the inhabitants flee northwards up the Rhône valley towards Lyon. At the same time there are further alarming developments in the south-west, which subsequent quatrains will now go on to elaborate. As we shall see, however, a south-eastward attack up the Garonne valley from the direction of Bordeaux actually seems unlikely (unless, of course, the reference is to some kind of counter-attack by the northern defenders): possibly, in other words, Nostradamus is merely using the expression 'from Bordeaux' as a code-version of 'from the seashore' (*du bord de l'eau*). Nevertheless, it would be unwise to be too definite about this, as there are hints later of the establishment of what seem to be particularly brutal puppet-regimes in the areas of Bordeaux and Toulouse.

VII.21   *While Languedoc is racked with plague most dread,*
Veiled enmity the tyrant shall pursue.
At bridge of Sorgues the thing comes to a head:
He shall be put to death – his henchman too.

As ever, invasion and war bring disease in their wake. For a while at least, however, underground popular resistance persists in the south of France, eventually resulting in the assassination of a commander of the occupying forces and one of his staff at Sorgues, just north of Avignon.

III.46   *By fixèd stars and signs both bright and clear*
The sky, O Lyon, does to us foretell
That of your change the time is drawing near,
Whether for ill or yet for good and well.

So portentous and pompous is this quatrain as to tell us virtually nothing at all – except, possibly, that it was deliberately concocted by Nostradamus in full consciousness, rather than as the result of one of his nocturnal visions, possibly after a rather fruitless night.

II.85 *By order strict the old, full-bearded man*
At Lyon of French troops is made the head.
The little chief too far pursues his plan.
Arms sound in heaven: th' Italian seas are red.

The southern invasion now achieves what, thanks to the barrier of the Alps, the forces from Italy have so far been unable to manage – a full-scale invasion of the French heartlands. Whether the full-bearded leader whose appointment as military governor of Lyon seems to be rather unpopular is the same as the 'little chief' is unclear, but the latter's defensive measures are unsuccessful, possibly because he fails to recognise when to call it a day. While sea-battles rage off Italy, air-battles are clearly much in evidence, too.

V.81 *Seven months each night o'er solar city's walls*
The royal bird its warning promulgates.
Midst thunderbolts the eastern bastion falls.
Seven days, no more, and foes are at the gates.

I take the 'solar city' to be Lyon, largely because the lion is traditionally the solar beast *par excellence*. The 'royal bird' is presumably an eagle, though the possibility cannot be ruled out that it is some kind of aircraft engaged in reconnaissance – or even in propaganda calling upon the city to surrender. At all events, with the southern forces preoccupied with the invasion via Marseille, there is a tremendous clash of arms in the Alps resulting in the final collapse of the eastern defences, too, and within a week the enemy are at the gates.

VIII.6   *A blazing light at Lyon seen shall be.*
Malta is quickly taken, blown away.
Sardinia treats the Moors deceitfully.
The Swiss in London feign France to betray.

As Lyon is attacked, developments elsewhere are no more propitious, either. The Mediterranean islands have either been laid waste or have made shady deals with the enemy – whom for the first time Nostradamus seems to describe, quite understandably, as 'Moors' (see 'Academic Notes'). Meanwhile the Swiss seem to be engaged in some kind of double game on the diplomatic front – possibly putting it about that, despite being themselves invaded, they propose to maintain their traditional neutrality, while covertly planning defence action in France in co-operation with the British.

III.7   *Then all shall flee as fire falls from the sky.*
Of fighting crows the battle shall draw near.
From earth to heaven goes up the plaintive cry
When near the wall the combatants appear.

I have placed this quatrain here partly because it seems to fit, and partly because the aerial combat in line two seems to reflect that in the last line of II.85 opposite. Otherwise the details could apply to any beleaguered city, and not merely to the imminent fall of Lyon.

II.74 *From Sens and from Autun the Rhône they'll reach,*
Then head on out towards the Pyrenees.
The hordes advancing from Ancona's beach
Shall chase them in long files o'er land and seas.

In an effort to hold the line, the French now send reinforcements
from further north. Having reached the Rhône, though, they
realise that they are too late to help Lyon, and head westwards
instead — for reasons that will become clear shortly. They are
pursued, however. Line three meanwhile confirms what we
assumed earlier: at least part of the invasion-force originally
came ashore on the western Italian coast (the Marches of Ancona
comprise a long strip of coastline lying opposite Dalmatia, in the
former Yugoslavia).

IV.99 *Of princely daughter shall brave eldest son*
So far push back the fighting French hard-pressed,
That he'll send lightnings flashing like the sun
First near, then far, then deep into the west.

The slightly odd construction of this stanza seems to suggest that
the French defenders will, in the event, retreat even faster than
the invaders can pursue them, almost as though the oriental
armies are no longer quite as keen as they were to give chase.
Perhaps it is because of this that the latter's commander resorts
either to long-range artillery or to tactical guided missiles — or
possibly even to the mysterious fire-weapon to which subsequent
stanzas will start to refer.

V.11   *The solar powers the sea no longer sweep.*
        Who Venice holds, holds Africa as well.
        Saturn nor sun o'er them his rule shall keep.
        On Asia, not on them, the change shall tell.

At this point, it seems, the 'solar' powers – i.e. the northern
Europeans opposed to the lunar crescent – make the mistake of
withdrawing their naval forces. This allows the African wing of
the invasion to cross the sea unhindered, thus taking over where
the Asiatic assault via Turkey is about to leave off. Indeed, there
are increasing hints that (whether or not for astrological reasons)
the ground forces advancing from Italy will indeed be starting to
run out of steam by this juncture.

VIII.21   *Infidels bringing foul disease along*
           At Agde from three assault-craft start their rout.
           From overseas they'll mass a million strong,
           At the third try their beach-head breaking out.

Possibly we now see the reason for the defenders' hasty westward
flight. For now, in harmony with the foregoing stanza, Nostradamus sees further invaders coming ashore in droves at the port
of Agde on France's south-western coast. Evidently they pose an
even greater threat than the incursion into the south-east. Despite
valiant efforts, the European defenders are unable to contain
them. The 'pestilence' mentioned in line one may be either literal
or figurative: the reference could be merely to the 'plague' of
invaders. As often happens in Nostradamus's predictions, an
idea mentioned in the first half of the verse is repeated in the
second, almost as though he were using the one as a kind of
symbol for the other: in the present case, the theme in question is
the number three.

III.81 *The great loud-mouth, shameless and just as daring,*
Shall of the army be elected head.
So bold his fight is and so proud his bearing,
The beach-head bursts. The city faints with dread.

Thus it is, at all events, that the invaders break out of their beach-head and start to fan out over town and country under a charismatic new leader.

IV.56 *When once the Rabid-Tongue has won the battle*
The spirit's tempted tranquil rest to seek.
All through the bloody war he'll crow and prattle
Enough to roast flesh, bones and tongue (in-cheek!).

He is, it seems, a leader who never stops boasting about his achievements both past and proposed. Nostradamus is far from impressed, but glad of the opportunity to play his usual repetition-trick with the word 'tongue'.

III.20 *Through all the country of Guadalquivir,*
From Ebro to Granada far away,
Muslims the Christians from the lands shall clear:
Of Cordoba shall one the land betray.

Meanwhile the Muslims are busy reoccupying the Spanish lands from which they were last driven out only a few years before Nostradamus's birth. The European defenders are expelled from most of the south-eastern half of the country, with Cordoba in particular succumbing as the result of an individual act of treachery.

VI.88   *A mighty kingdom desolate shall remain.*
Near to the Ebro they shall all assemble.
In Pyrenees he'll consolation gain
When in the month of May the earth shall tremble.

Most of Spain is accordingly laid waste, and the invading hordes then muster in the valley of the Ebro, prior to attempting to extend their conquests over the Pyrenees. Their leader, meanwhile, takes a mountain holiday a few miles to the east.

VIII.51   *Peace-offerings the Turkish chief shall make*
Once Cordoba resumes its captured state:
Long journey past, Pamplonan rest he'll take.
Prey captured crossing by Gibraltar's strait.

This extremely obtuse quatrain once again refers to the invaders' campaign in Spain. Cordoba, it seems, is initially captured, but somehow manages to free itself again before finally succumbing, possibly as a result of the piece of treachery referred to above. At this point, the invaders' commander (here described as 'the Byzantine') sues for a truce to allow him to recuperate his forces' strength. If my interpretation of line three is correct, he then travels to the region of Pamplona in the north-east, in harmony with the foregoing stanza, in an effort to recuperate his own as well – which would suggest once again that much of the rest of Spain is already under foreign control. The 'prey' in line four is not identified, but seems to be some rather important would-be escapee.

III.68 *Leaderless folk in Spain and Italy,*
Dying, their two peninsulas shall flood,
Their laws betrayed by crass stupidity
And every crossroads swimming with their blood.

Nostradamus paints a sickening picture of the consequences of the conflict as it continues to spread through Europe. At the same time he once again presses home his point that the Europeans are themselves largely to blame. Rather more wisdom rather earlier, in fact, could yet help to avert much of what he predicts.

III.62 *By Duero and the land-girt Inland Sea*
Through the high Pyrenees a path he'll seek.
The shortest route and crossing noted, he
On Carcassonne his stratagems shall wreak.

The geography of this quatrain seems decidedly odd. The invasion force now occupying Spain is described as taking a route from the River Duero, in northern Spain, via the Mediterranean coast to the Pyrenees and thence into south-western France. (Well might it seek the 'shortest crossing' as described in line three!)

II.59 *Supported is the French fleet by the hand*
Of Neptune and his warriors' tridents tall.
To feed the horde Provence lays waste its land.
War at Narbonne, with missiles large and small.

It is commonly assumed by the commentators that 'Neptune' refers, here as elsewhere, to Britain. In this case it is intriguing to note that Nostradamus specifically describes its sailors, who have clearly still not given up the fight, as wielding *tridents*. Possibly this development represents the arrival, rather late in the day, of better-equipped British reinforcements in an attempt to disrupt the invasion from the south-west. One trusts, though, that neither these nor the missiles in line four ('javelins' and 'darts' in the original) will involve a nuclear component. The reference to Narbonne will be taken up again in subsequent stanzas.

IV.94   *Two brothers out of Spain shall harried be,*
           The elder vanquished in the Pyrenees.
           From Agde, Narbonne, Béziers; from Germany,
           Rhône and Leman infected: bloody the seas.

Written in Nostradamus's best telegrammatic style, this prediction reveals specifically that the main invasion will have both a south-western and an eastern wing. The former will, as indicated above, come in not only via Spain, but also via the port of Agde in south-western France, the latter via southern Germany and western Switzerland into the Rhône valley. The identity of the 'two brothers' is not made clear – but it seems that they are on the side of the invaders who, in Spain at least, will not be having it all their own way.

V.78   *Not long allied the duo shall remain*
           With Arab land – some thirteen years or less.
           On either side such losses they'll sustain,
           That one the cassock of the Church shall bless.

This stanza throws some interesting light on the timescale involved. The invading partnership – or rather its alliance with the Asiatics in the south-east – seems destined to last only until around 2018 or so (compare IX.73, p. 163), at which point one of the leaders involved will apparently change sides. This in turn suggests, first that there will still be a different side to change to (which at least is encouraging), and second that the 'two brothers out of Spain' will not themselves be of Asiatic or African origin. One of them, indeed, could conceivably be the Macedonian, or 'man from Greece' mentioned in IX.64 (p. 161).

I.5   *Harried they'll be as fight leads on to fight:*
The country districts shall be most oppressed.
City and town put up a better fight.
Carcassonne and Narbonne put to the test.

It is not clear from the text which of the invaders' two south-western spearheads will be involved here, though IV.94 (p. 157) suggests that it will probably be the sea-borne one.

Sixain 27   *Out of the west shall fire burn in the sky:*
Out of the south, too, eastwards running by.
For lack of food shall worms die in the earth.
A third time shall the warlike Mars return.
With eerie light the carbuncles shall burn:
An age of carbuncles – and then great dearth.

Here Nostradamus sets the scene for continuing developments in the south-west of France. Some extraordinary celestial phenomenon will bring fire from the sky and widespread famine, while strange, luminous fires burn all over the landscape. The invaders, it seems, are likely to get hold of some ghastly new aerial weapon whose effects will sear the very landscape and blight it for a very long time to come: the 'carbuncles' – originally mythical, self-luminous jewels – seem curiously reminiscent of modern laser technology, though of course it would be unwise to draw any definite inferences.

Commentators hitherto have been extraordinarily keen to use line four as an excuse to jump on the Third World War band-wagon, but nothing so grandiose is in fact suggested. Certainly it will be the third time since 1900 that France will have experienced war on its home territory, but the stanza could equally well mean that the Asiatic invasion will have three main military phases, of which the 'fire in the sky' phase moving in from the south-west will merely be the last. It could even suggest nothing more general than a triple exchange of missiles. The final dearth, or famine, seems to be the direct result: evidently the attack burns up all the crops.

II.3 *Like sun the heat shall sear the shining sea:*
The Black Sea's living fish shall all but boil.
When Rhodes and Genoa half-starved shall be
The local folk to cut them up shall toil.

This simple quatrain needs little explaining. Picking up on line two of the foregoing stanza, it suggests that the 'fire from the sky' phenomenon will even be felt as far east as the Black Sea. Whether this once again indicates an exchange of thermal missiles between East and West, or merely that the orientals will have first tested their new fire-weapon in their own home area, is by no means clear. The self-same scenario is re-echoed in V.98 (p. 174).

V.100   *The firebrand shall be burnt by his own fire,*
Carcassonne and Comminges, Foix, Auch, Mazères
Burnt from the sky: away the old grandsire
The troops from western Germany shall bear.

Evidently the enemy, as yet inexperienced in its use on the battlefield, deploys his new fire-weapon much too near his own lines to start with. Nevertheless it is devastatingly effective. One old leader, however, manages to escape, thanks to the intervention of troops from Hessen, Saxony and Thuringia — which at least suggests that the Germans, anticipating an eventual threat to their own country, are starting to involve themselves on the Mediterranean front, as well as defending their own southern borders against the Asiatic forces advancing through Switzerland.

II.6   *Of ne'er-seen scourge shall fall the double stroke*
Each city deep within and at its portal.
Famine and plague within, expelled their folk,
Calling for help upon their God immortal.

Nostradamus does not give the names of the two cities concerned. Past commentators have been keen to identify them as Hiroshima and Nagasaki. In the present context the most likely targets, however, are Carcassonne and Narbonne. The unprecedented scourges may be the new fire-weapon, but could as easily be some kind of bacteriological attack.

III.85 *Taken the town shall be by ruse and fraud,*
Yet by one young and fair he'll cornered be:
Midst fighting by the Robine, near the Aude,
He and all his die for their treachery.

Nostradamus does not state which of the two towns mentioned is
involved here. However, since the attack in question is met by an
effective counter-attack beside the Robine – nowadays a canal
that joins the River Aude near Narbonne – the latter seems the
more likely. For a brief moment, then, the invaders' advance is
stemmed. The leader who dies is possibly one of the two
'brothers from Spain' mentioned above.

IX.71 *With sheep is seen about the holy place*
One who to face the daylight does not dare.
To Carcassonne by way of meet disgrace
He shall be brought, to serve his sentence there.

This is one of those predictions whose true meaning can only be
determined at the time in question. The person concerned seems
to be one of Narbonne's leading defenders who is flushed out
from his hiding-place in a former church or temple amidst nearby
sheep-country and brought into Carcassonne to confront his
fate.

IX.64 *The man from Greece shall cross the Pyrenees.*
No armed resistance shall Narbonne present.
Such schemes he'll hatch by land and on the seas
The chief shall know not where to pitch his tent.

Literally in the light of the fire-weapon, Narbonne finally capitulates to the second wave of invaders advancing from Spain. We do not have to take too seriously Nostradamus's apparently Hellenic term *Aemathion* ('Macedonian') in the first line. The figure concerned may indeed come from Macedonia. On the other hand, he could merely be the commander of the Asiatic force that is currently *occupying* Greece or the southern Balkans. It may even be that Nostradamus is using the term to suggest that he is a mighty conqueror of the stature of Alexander the Great of Macedon. As we have already seen, Nostradamus endlessly rings the changes on his names for the invaders, often using their current habitat as a kind of pseudonym. At all events, this particular leader, whom we seem to have met much earlier in the campaign as a young commander on the European side (X.58, p. 80), seems especially powerful and his influence especially wide-ranging. We shall meet him again later, too.

IX.63   *Wailing and tears and screams shall rend the air*
         Near to Narbonne, in Foix and at Bayonne.
         What dread calamities, what changes, ere
         Mars round his track shall many times have gone!

Catastrophe now follows for the people living in the south-west. Since Mars takes nearly two years to revolve about the sun, Nostradamus seems to envisage that the conflict is likely to last a good many years – not less than six, say, though possibly not much longer than ten or so. If Nostradamus seems particularly sensitive to coming events in the south-west and south-east of France, this is of course only to be expected: the Rhône delta was, after all, where he was born, grew up and first went to university, while it was in the south-west that he spent much of his professional life.

IX.73   *Blue-turbaned chief in Foix himself shall find.*
E'er Saturn's back he'll no more rule the land.
White-turbaned chief wipes Turkey from his mind.
Sun, Mars and Mercury near Aquarius stand.

With the aid of a rough astrological dating, which so far as I know has not yet been satisfactorily decoded, Nostradamus suggests that the invaders' occupation of the south-west will last no more than the orbital period of the ill-omened planet Saturn – i.e. some twenty-nine-and-a-half years. Since Nostradamus seems elsewhere to date the end of the Asiatic conflict to no later than the year 2044, this reference in itself could conceivably offer us a tentative dating for the invasion of the south-west of 2014 at the latest, and possibly a good deal earlier. The two chiefs seem to be the local commanders of the two opposing sides.

II.2   *Blue-head shall white-head harm in such degree*
As France's good to both shall e'er amount.
Hanged shall the Great One from the yard-arm be
Once the King of his captives gives account.

In this oddly convoluted quatrain, Nostradamus adds a few further details to the struggle between them – though which of them (if either) is the 'Great One' and which the 'King' is something that it will doubtless take contemporary eyes to figure out. The 'captives' seem to be prisoners taken from the Great One by the King.

IX.10 *Child of a monk and nun exposed to die*
       Killed by a she-bear, taken by a boar.
       Near Foix and Pamiers shall the army lie;
       Against Toulouse Carcassonne's levies war.

The curious detail of the first two lines seems to be of purely local significance. In the last two, however, the war continues as the invaders seemingly recruit local troops from the Carcassonne area to attack Toulouse.

III.92 *As the world's final age draws near apace*
        Saturn comes late once more his ill to wreak.
        Empire shall be transferred to th' eastern race;
        Narbonne's bright eye plucked out by goshawk's
          beak.

Here Nostradamus seems to suggest that the invasion of France from the south-west will serve as advance warning of the approach of the eventual Millennium in the twenty-ninth century. He sees it, in other words, as a 'sign of the times', or as one of the inevitable birth-pangs of the Millennium, however remote in time. But then the same could be said about most of his predictions for our future. In the present case, he foresees eventual victory for the invaders, whom he calls *'Brodes'* – a double-edged term which is both a derogatory Old French expression for 'unworthy, dark-skinned people' and the Provençal for the former Allobroges, an Alpine (and thus 'eastern') tribe vanquished in classical times by Fabius Maximus in the area of the River Isère (as Nostradamus's own son, César, points out in his *History of Provence*). As ever, in other words, Nostradamus invests the incoming invaders with the name of the territory they have just conquered. Narbonne appears to have been made by the defenders into some kind of regional headquarters during the initial stages of the campaign: the 'eye' does not have to be anything so specific as a radar installation – merely, perhaps, the supervision and surveillance that any headquarters necessarily operates.

VI.56   *The dreaded hostile army from Narbonne*
         Shall daunt those in the west. Emptied shall be
         Perpignan by the blinding of Narbonne.
         Then Barcelona shall attack by sea.

Narbonne once taken, it seems, the invaders will start to run riot in the south-west. Once again Nostradamus refers to the 'blinding' of Narbonne, almost as if its communications links have been cut. More likely, perhaps, he is simply referring to its having been 'taken out'. The precise role of Barcelona is unclear, but it seems to have been turned by the invaders into some kind of primary attack-base.

VI.64   *They shall not hold to what they shall agree.*
         All who accept them shall be duped at will
         By pact and truce. Fighting by land and sea,
         Shall Barcelona seize the fleet by skill.

Indeed, Barcelonan forces now manage to capture what is left of the French fleet, using any kind of treachery to achieve their ends. Possibly they surprise it at its moorings.

VIII.22   *Coursan, Narbonne's revolt use all your wit*
To warn; for Perpignan betrayed shall be.
The red regime shall not put up with it.
High-flying, grey, beflagged, your killer see.

There now seem to be revolts in three of the captured towns. In the spirit of V.96 (p. 70) Nostradamus goes out of his way to discourage this, even – in an extraordinary last line – apparently describing the missile that is likely to be launched against them in retaliation. Meanwhile line three offers us a familiar interpretational clue. In the French original, Nostradamus refers to the occupying authorities as operating from the 'red city': in the absence of any corresponding place name, accordingly, it seems reasonable to assume that he is once more associating the invaders not merely with the Muslim religion, but with the colour red. This does not necessarily mean, though, that they are Communists (as commentators have blithely assumed for years): it could merely be a reference back to the 'rose' with which Nostradamus also seems to associate them (see V.96, II.97, pp. 70, 115).

I.73   *Negligent France on five fronts to assail*
Shall Persia Tunis, Algiers urge from distance.
Leon, Seville and Barcelona fail
To keep the fleet, at Italy's insistence.

While the Asiatics' supreme command continues to direct the overall campaign from the Middle East, its theatre-commanders become increasingly prone to squabble among themselves. The occupying regime in Italy is jealous of Barcelona's recent naval success, and demands its share of the spoils. Meanwhile, the 'five fronts' mentioned in line one serve as helpful confirmation of our analysis thus far: France, it seems, has been attacked along the

Riviera coast, across the Alps, across the Pyrenees and, from the sea, via the ports of Marseille and Agde. Interestingly enough, no separate invasion from the north-east seems to be indicated.

IX.52   *Peace shall approach from one side, war the other.*
         Ne'er did such persecution e'er advance.
         Blood on the ground: moan, parents, sister, brother!
         What goes for one shall go for all of France.

Thus it is that France is, as it were, squeezed between two sets of forces – on the one hand those in the east and south-east, who are by now tending to settle down into some kind of peaceful occupation of the land, and on the other those in the south-west, who are ever more brutally on the warpath. The last line suggests that it is the latter who will now spread throughout the whole of France.

VI.98   *Woe to the Languedocians, terror-racked,*
         Their mighty town stained with contagion rank.
         By night and day their temples shall be sacked,
         Their rivers red with blood from bank to bank.

The terror duly starts to spread out northwards and westwards. Since the text specifically mentions *two* rivers, the city begs to be identified as Toulouse (which lies at the confluence of the Canal du Midi and the River Garonne), thus suggesting a continuing emphasis on the south-west. Meanwhile, the invaders, no doubt heartened and strengthened by their new aerial weapon, are endeavouring to push across the various rivers which the defenders from the north have hitherto been using as defence-lines.

XII.71   *Rivers and streams may slow the evil tide,*
           But anger's ancient flame will not be checked.
           Through France as fast as rumour it shall ride:
           House, manor, church and palace shall be wrecked.

Nostradamus duly confirms both the defensive strategy and its relative lack of success.

IV.43   *The noise of war is heard aloft the skies,*
           Made by the foes of all the priestly caste.
           Their aim of holy edicts the demise.
           Lightning and fatal war the faithful blast.

A particular aim of the south-western invaders, it seems, will be the destruction of the Christian Church and all that pertains to it.

VI.9   *In holy churches scandals shall be done*
           That shall be counted honours fit for praising
           By striking precious medals for each one.
           The end shall come 'midst torments most amazing.

Indeed, the anti-religious campaign will be continued with almost sadistic relish.

I.96   *He who was charged with putting to the torch*
Churches and sects shall change upon a whim.
The stones more than the people he shall scorch,
By beauteous speech sense being restored to him.

At least, however, one of the leading invaders is not totally deaf
to pleading. The Asiatic equivalent of Henry VIII's Thomas
Cromwell is persuaded to restrict his destructive activities ('burning' is merely my own selection from them) to the religious
buildings, rather than immolating the people within them too.

I.46   *Near Auch, Lectoure, Mirande, with scarce a pause*
Three nights shall mighty fire from heaven rain –
Stupendous and miraculous the cause –
Then shortly earth shall quake with might and main.

This prediction clearly applies mainly to the Département of
Gers in south-western France. Whether the earthquake (natural
or otherwise) is likely to be a purely local one, however, is not
entirely clear. The 'stupendous and miraculous' cause of the
aerial fire once again suggests some human agency at work,
whether military, scientific or technological. The most obvious
candidate, clearly, is the African invasion-force, as it continues to
spread into south-western France from Spain.

IX.51   *Groups of resisters shall the reds assail*
By fire, iron, water, rope throughout the land.
About to die, the plotters shall not quail –
Save only one who shall destroy their band.

Nevertheless, widespread resistance continues, albeit now driven underground. As so often happens in such resistance networks, though, there is always somebody who is prepared to betray his or her fellow-conspirators. Note how Nostradamus once again describes the occupying authorities in the south-west as 'reds'.

VIII.2   *At Condom, Auch and all around Mirande*
Fire do I see that from the sky shall fall.
Sun, Mars in Leo: lightning at Marmande
With hail: then falls Garonne's defensive wall.

This seems to be a further elaboration of I.46 (p. 169). This time an astrological timing is added. Once again the towns targeted are all in or near the Département of Gers in the south-west, and the Asian invaders may well thus have a hand in the phenomena mentioned. The strange detail concerning a wall falling in the Garonne area may refer to the final collapse of the local French defences: apparently the defenders will indeed have attempted to turn the river or one of its tributaries into a major defence-line, as suggested in XII.71 (p. 168).

II.91   *At sunrise shall a mighty fire appear,*
Its roar and glare towards the north extending:
Within the circle death and screams they'll hear,
Famine and death the flames of war attending.

Once again the 'fire from the sky' phenomenon all too easily presses the 'nuclear attack' button in the minds of a good many commentators, as the foreign assault extends steadily northwards. The 'circle', however, seems well enough defined to suggest something much more surgical and precise. Once again, in other words, what is involved could be something more akin to the laser – though all such conjectures are, of course, extremely risky, as Prophetic Laws 1 and 2 make clear (see page 20).

VI.97   *Latitude forty-five, the sky shall burn:*
To greater Villeneuve shall the fire draw nigh.
For a long moment flames shall chase and churn
When with the North conclusions they shall try.

Yet again Nostradamus returns to the horrific phenomenon of fire from the sky. This time he suggests that it has now moved north to the area of the forty-fifth parallel, as well as specifying that an unnamed *grand cité neufue* will be a main target of it. Commentators apparently prepared to scare the public with a picture of world-wide nuclear devastation as a result of a Third World War are only too prone to ensure that the 'new city' (thus, in all probability, a town with 'new' in its title) *is* named. It is, they suggest, Geneva,[7] New York,[3] even the determinedly un-'new' Paris.[19] In fact, however, Geneva is close to the forty-sixth, not the forty-fifth parallel, while neither New York nor Paris are anywhere near either. The various Villanuevas in Spain lie even further away. The Villeneuve just north-west of Avignon is a better candidate, but on the wrong parallel (the forty-fourth) – and clearly Nostradamus lived close enough to it to know what he was talking about. Villanova d'Asti, just south of Turin, is on the right latitude, but more likely to be subject to an east–west battle than a north–south one. Villeneuve-sur-Lot in south-western France, on the other hand, fits the case perfectly. It is well within the forty-fifth degree (lying about forty-four-and-a-half degrees north) and just north of the Garonne. True, it is not particularly 'great', but it is a good deal bigger than Villanova d'Asti: moreover Nostradamus does tend to fling the word *grand* around rather liberally, more or less as a form of poetic padding – in fact, there are remarkably few quatrains without at least one example of it. Evidently the town is a focal point for the battle between the invaders from the south and the defending northerners, or *Normans*, as Nostradamus calls them here.

VI.34   *Of flying fire th' ingenious machine*
The great beleaguered captain sore shall bruise.
Within, there shall be such sedition seen
That those it touches every hope shall lose.

Although this prediction is not specific as to time or place, it does seem to fit in at this point. The celestial fire, it seems, is indeed of human origin, though the consequent loss of morale among the defenders will prove at least as damaging as the ghastly weapon itself.

I.87   *Earth-shaking fires from the world's centre roar:*
About Villeneuve the earth shall be a-quiver.
Two mighty rocks long time shall be at war,
Till Arethusa reddens a new river.

The battle continues around Villeneuve, with both sides remaining rock-like and virtually immovable for a while. However, with the aid of their fire-weapon – apparently directed in some way *from the Middle East* – the invaders eventually succeed in pressing northwards across the River Lot, like the Garonne before it, its waters now reddened with their blood. Arethusa, one of the Hesperides, or Daughters of Night, was also the goddess of natural springs. Once again, meanwhile, Nostradamus takes an idea from the first half of the verse (the 'new' of 'New City', i.e. Villeneuve) and reapplies it in the second.

III.12   *By Ebro, Tagus, Tiber, Rhône and Po*
       And by Geneva's and Arezzo's lakes
       From Bordeaux and Toulouse shall leaders go
       Captive, drowned, killed, as war its booty takes.

The war in south-western France has by now become the main theatre of operations. The captured leaders of the cities on the Garonne are taken prisoner and transported as 'human booty' to Portugal, Spain, south-eastern France, Italy or Switzerland, where they are shamefully treated.

IV.47   *Once the fierce Moor his bloody hand has tried*
       And the whole land to fire, sword, bow has put,
       The people shall be shocked and terrified
       To see their leaders hanged by neck and foot.

Others, it seems, are publicly hanged as an example. The specific weapons in line two do not have to be taken too literally: they were merely the standard weapons of Nostradamus's day, just as automatic rifles and machine-guns are of ours.

IV.76   *Those at Agen by Perigordians later*
       Are harried all the way to flowing Rhône.
       The Gascons' friend, Bigorre's collaborator
       The church betrays ere yet the sermon's done.

Thus it is that the invaders from Africa (albeit continually harassed by European forces from further north) start to break out of the south-west, first occupying the whole of France's

Mediterranean littoral as far as the Rhône, where their Asiatic counterparts seem to have come to a halt some time previously. It is difficult to decode the last two lines, though, other than to suggest that they indicate a quick campaign.

V.98   *At forty-eight degrees of latitude*
As Cancer ends shall come a drought so dire
That fish-filled sea, rivers and lakes are stewed,
Béarn, Bigorre seared from the sky with fire.

The fire-scenario continues, this time stretching as far north as the River Loire at Orléans. Possibly the defenders have made the river into their fall-back defence-line as the invaders now press further northwards. To the south, in the Pyrenean foothills, the environmental effects are already horrific. Nostradamus seems to date this new development to the end of July.

IV.46   *Your good defences being your crowning virtue,*
Beware, O Tours, your imminent demise.
London through Nantes and Rennes shall not
*   desert you.*
Do not go out when rain drifts from the skies.

Further down the Loire valley, Tours, too, is attacked, but being protected on all sides apart from the east by the Rivers Loire and Cher, has a good chance of resisting the assault. Apparently the city of Rennes, to the north-west, is serving as the defenders' area headquarters, while Nantes has its own forces in the field. The British, too, sensing the increasing threat to their own shores, are at last starting to play a more active role in the fighting. Line four, however, hints at a rather sinister development: evidently the attackers, in their frustration, will once more resort locally to something that looks remarkably like chemical or bacteriological warfare.

VI.44   *By night near Nantes a rainbow shall be seen.*
Maritime arts raise rain out of thin air.
Fleet sunk off Araby: monster obscene
In Saxony is born from sow and bear.

One of Nostradamus's more fantastic quatrains, this one is no doubt just as rationally explicable as all the others. Some kind of worrying technological wizardry is displayed by the enemy navy as the invaders attempt to cross the Loire. The same noxious 'rain' seems to be referred to as in the last stanza. I cannot begin to suggest who or what the 'monster' might be: some commentators suspect that it may have something to do with the rebirth of a united Germany as a result of co-operation between Russia and the West – but just who that would make the sow I would not care to suggest.

IV.74   *From Lake Leman, from Rivers Eure and Sarthe,*
All meet to face the threat from Aquitaine.
Even more Swiss than Germans shall take part,
Yet shall be beaten, as shall those from Maine.

The signs are that even the more northerly defensive line is destined to fall. All the defenders except the Swiss, after all, appear to come from north of the Loire.

V.85   *Among the Swabians and the Swiss shall they*
        Against the swarms prepare themselves to fight.
        Like sea-borne locusts they'll the camp assay:
        Exposed shall be Geneva's failings quite.

Clearly, neither naval activities nor locusts fit south-east Germany or Switzerland itself particularly well. Since the foregoing stanza describes the Swiss as fighting alongside their allies in northern France – presumably to defend the Loire defence-line – the 'camp' would seem to be in the area of St Nazaire, which lies on the northern shore of its estuary. Evidently, though, they will not prove very effective. As for the 'locusts and the like' to which the original line three refers, it seems once again as though Nostradamus has adopted the image as a code-word for the swarming invaders (or possibly for their helicopters), along much the same lines as in IV.48 (p. 87).

II.64   *Genevans shall for thirst and hunger cower*
        When once their last and brightest hope recedes.
        At near collapse shall be Cévennian power:
        To put in at the port no fleet succeeds.

Once again the mention of fleets and ports suggests that the Swiss are fighting well outside their own homeland. As previously, then, the River Loire suggests itself. Troops from the Cévennes, in the south of France, are also evidently making what is virtually their last stand there. Indeed, the geography rather suggests that the two armies will be responsible for defending the river's lower reaches. The impression is strong that they are expecting to be supplied via Nantes, but that the invaders' blockade of the port has reduced them virtually to impotence.

I.20   *Tours, Blois, Reims, Angers shall a change intense*
Like Orléans and Nantes soon overtake:
About them foreigners shall pitch their tents.
Missiles scourge Rennes: both land and sea shall
        quake.

So it is that the northern defence-line falls, like the southern one
before it, and the whole of northern France is opened up to the
swarming invaders. Rennes, as a regional defence headquarters,
comes in for special treatment, and both there and near St
Nazaire massive bombardments ensue involving what the
sixteenth-century Nostradamus can inevitably only call 'darts' or
'arrows'.

X.7   *When mighty war at Nancy he prepares,*
The Greek shall say, 'I am the conqueror, I.'
Or drunk or sober, Britain's full of cares.
Metz shall not long continue to defy.

Presumably joining up with the invading forces still advancing
northwards towards Belgium out of Switzerland via the west
bank of the Rhine, the Asiatics' eastern flank is likewise rapidly
pressing northwards via Nancy and Metz. It is headed by the
same, powerful Macedonian commander whom we have
encountered on several occasions before. Seeing the tide of invasion sweeping towards the English Channel, the British are
naturally starting to become alarmed: neither reason nor drink, it
seems, is able to make things look much rosier for them.

IX.19   *Amidst the leafy forest of Mayenne,*
With sun in Leo, lightning shall descend.
The mighty bastard of the lord of Maine
That day a weapon shall at Fougères rend.

The summer sees alien forces pressing into north-western France, too, and nearing the borders of Brittany – while still deploying their aerial fire-weapon. Still the defenders are hard-pressed and one of their commanders is killed (whatever his family pedigree).

III.18   *After long rain, milk falls upon the ground:*
Such is what Reims shall garner from the sky.
What bloody conflict shall the place surround!
Fathers, nor sons, nor kings dare venture nigh.

At Reims, meanwhile, something more sinister seems to be in play – what looks remarkably like a renewed outbreak of chemical or bacteriological warfare. No wonder the actual fighting takes place exclusively *outside* the city, and that nobody dares venture near.

V.30   *About the mighty city there shall roam*
Troops billeted in every town and farm
To strike at Paris on behalf of Rome.
There on the bridge great ravages, great harm.

With Paris now surrounded on three sides, it inevitably becomes the invaders' next target. Possibly they regard it almost as their ultimate prize. The French, naturally, are determined to resist to the utmost, and the bridges over the Seine are liable to see heavy fighting, especially if some of the defenders attempt a symbolic last-ditch stand at the city's heart on the Île de la Cité.

IX.56 *Past Goussonville is Houdan's host diverted,*
Leaving its standard to the Scythian host.
At once, more than a thousand are converted,
Lest chiefs be chained to pillar and to post.

With the army in full retreat past Paris, the oppressed French people (such as still remain, that is) are forced to swear instant allegiance to Islam: Both Goussonville and Houdan lie just west of the city.

V.43 *The ruin of the priesthood's next in line*
Throughout Provence, Spain, Italy and France.
In Germany, Cologne beside the Rhine
Harassed to death as Mainz's hordes advance.

As the campaign continues, the invaders make a new attempt to wipe out organised Christianity throughout the occupied lands. Apart from Provence, the French text specifically mentions Naples, Sicily, Sées and Pons – symbolic respectively of mainland Italy, island Italy, France and Spain. At the same time their eastern flank continues to move northwards from Mainz along the west bank of the Rhine, apparently without, at this stage, crossing it and making inroads into the heart of Germany.

IV.19   *To Rouen troops from Italy lay siege,*
By land and sea all access having barred.
Of Hainaut, Flanders, Ghent and of Liège
They'll waste the borders, merciless and hard.

As the central front moves northwards to Rouen, the assault's right flank presses on towards the Belgian frontier. There is just a hint in the last line, though, that the advance may not persist very far beyond this point, especially in the rather more easily defended terrain of the Ardennes.

V.13   *The lord from Rome in furious anger black*
Shall send his Arab horde Belgium to rape:
But just as furious they shall chase them back
From Hungary to stern Gibraltar's cape.

Indeed, light even starts to show at the end of the long tunnel. Eventually, it seems, the defending forces are destined to stage a break-out from Belgium which will end in the reversal of all the invaders' successes and their ultimate expulsion from Europe.

III.49   *O France, what changes lie in wait for you!*
To foreign lands your government shall pass.
You shall be ruled by laws and customs new.
Rouen and Chartres shall hurt you sore, alas!

That, however, is for the future. The darkness has to be lived through first. Virtually the whole of France, after all, has fallen into the hands of the invaders, who have promptly imposed an entirely new system of government. Under the terms of it, the country is no longer run from Paris – possibly because the city is no longer available to exercise that function. Instead, regional centres such as Rouen and Chartres take over all administration. Indeed, in these two cases, the occupation regimes turn out to be of a particularly repressive and brutal kind.

VII.34   *In grief the land of France shall mope and pine,*
Lightheartedness be foolishness decreed.
No bread, salt, water, beer, medicine nor wine:
Their leaders captive: hunger, cold and need.

Abject deprivation and misery result. War and occupation have their customary results all over France.

IX.55   *After dread war that westward is prepared*
Contagion comes with but a year's demur.
In France nor old nor young nor beast is spared,
No, not by Hermes, Mars nor Jupiter.

This quatrain is commonly applied by commentators to the First World War and the devastating influenza epidemic that killed some twenty million people during the final stages of the conflict. On the other hand, both the geography and the chronology are wrong. From Nostradamus's point of view, the war was in the east, not the west, and the epidemic occurred during the final year of the war, not after it. Consequently the prediction begs to be associated instead with the future Asiatic campaign starting in the south-west of France. France, it suggests, will be not only subject to deprivation, but overrun by disease as well, to the point of becoming all but depopulated. The final line could be taken as suggesting that neither medical intervention (Hermes) nor military action – whether by land (Mars) or from the air (Jupiter) – will succeed in mitigating the consequences. Whether the 'contagion' is natural, or the result of deliberate chemical or biological warfare, is not made clear.

VI.43   *Long time unpeopled shall the country lie*
That's watered by the Rivers Marne and Seine.
Tempted the armies England are to try:
Folly to think to beat them back again!

The invaders having now moved north into Normandy and left it desolate, England lies open before them. Nostradamus warns its defenders (*les gardes*) against assuming that they can push back the Asiatic hordes once they have been allowed to land. Taking their lesson from the earlier saga of Italian and French apathy and incompetence, the British would, it seems, be well advised to use their air- and sea-power to fight off the attackers well before they come ashore, perhaps taking urgent steps in the mean time to seek powerful allies from abroad, much as they did in the Second World War. For obvious reasons, the Channel Tunnel will need to be flooded or even blown up. In some respects, meanwhile, Sixain 54 (p. 42), seems potentially more applicable to this situation than to the Second World War to which it is generally applied. Both England and Flanders, in other words, could now be subject to a long period of aerial bombardment.

V.71   *With the great rage of one who waits the tide,*
            With such great rage the whole host seethes
                and hums.
            Loaded on boats seventeen commanders ride:
            Too late along the Rhône the message comes.

Unless this stanza refers to earlier invasion attempts such as those of Napoleon or Hitler, it seems that the Asiatics in northern France will indeed prepare an invasion-fleet, only awaiting the order to attack the English south coast. Unfortunately for them, this is too slow to arrive from the south, and the vital moment is missed.

II.68   *Throughout the north their efforts shall be great,*
            Upon the sea the door be open wide.
            The island power shall all reintegrate.
            London shall quake when first the fleet's espied.

In consequence, the British defenders and their allies are given both a salutary shock, and a golden opportunity to rally and consolidate their forces.

III.71   *Those in the Isles besieged shall by and by*
            Their strength build up against the foreign foe.
            Abroad, the beaten peoples starve and die,
            And famine worse than ever they shall know.

This quatrain – equally reminiscent in some way of the Second World War – suggests that a pattern similar to the previous one will now be followed, and history consequently repeat itself, as Nostradamus himself was always convinced that it does. Once again, in fact, Britain seems to be destined to serve as the eventual jumping-off point for some kind of massive counter-attack.

5

THE GREAT RETURN

The Holy Sepulchre, so long revered, shall long remain exposed . . . to sun, moon, sky and stars. The sacred place shall be turned into a stable for livestock small and large, and put to other profane uses . . . The tongues of the Latin nations shall be mingled with Arabic and North African forms of speech (but) . . . the said reign of the Antichrist shall not last . . . The third northern leader shall raise a greater army than any of his predecessors to restore everybody to their original estate . . . A new incursion shall be made from the sea-coasts by those who ever since the Muslim occupation have been anxious to act as liberators . . . All the oriental leaders shall be driven away, overthrown and reduced to nothing, not entirely by the strength of the Northern leaders . . . but by the three members of the secret confederacy itself who shall attempt to trap, ambush and kill one another . . . The great Vicar of the church shall be restored to his former state, now desolate and totally abandoned following its destruction by the pagans and the rejection and burning of Old and New Testaments alike . . . Then shall two Northern leaders overcome the orientals and such shall be the noise and tumult of their campaign that all the East shall quake at the name of these two northern brothers

who are nevertheless not brothers . . . Afterwards the
French Ogmion* shall pass the Mountain of Jove,†
accompanied by so great a number as to permit distant
powers to impose on the Empire its own, greater law . . .
For then the oriental overlord shall be vanquished,
mostly under pressure from those from the North and
West, who shall kill him, defeat him and put all the rest to
flight . . .

Extracted from the *Letter to Henri King of France the Second*

THUS IT IS THAT, if Nostradamus is to be believed, the mighty
pendulum of war is destined finally to reach its furthest
extent in Europe. As is ever the case with pendulums, all that can
now possibly follow is a mighty reverse swing, for it is in the
nature of reality as we know it that neither good nor evil can ever
lord it for ever over the other. The one, indeed, depends for its
very life upon the other, and so events always tend towards some
kind of uneasy equilibrium. Whether this state of affairs might
eventually change is, of course, entirely dependent on whether
we ourselves can learn to change our consciousness, our very way
of knowing. Nostradamus and those with similar views might
well associate that ultimate human achievement with the coming
of the Millennium. But between that event and the current crisis
there is, it seems, a very great deal still to happen. . .

VI.12   *Against the Empire armies he shall raise:*
             Loyal to the Vatican the prince shall be.
             Belgium and England (Spain can only gaze)
             Prepare to fight both France and Italy.

---

* *Ogmios* was the eloquent, ancient Gallic version of Hercules.
† The Capitol Hill in Rome, ancient seat of government and site of the temple of
Jupiter Capitolinus.

France's ruler in exile – evidently a keen Catholic – now starts to co-ordinate the armed build-up that must necessarily precede any attempt to win back the conquered lands.

III.53 *When greater strength its mark begins to make*
    From Nürnberg, Augsburg, Basle they shall advance,
    Led by Cologne's chief, Frankfurt to retake.
    Then, crossing Flanders, they'll re-enter France.

Certainly such a counter-attack is what now follows in continental Europe itself. European forces start to advance once more from southern Germany towards the Rhine, while further north a push through Belgium succeeded in re-entering France. This, in turn, would tend to confirm that the oriental invasion will never have succeeded in penetrating very far into Germany or the Low Countries.

VIII.49 *When Saturn's in the Bull, Mars th' Archer eyes*
    And Jupiter reigns o'er Aquarian skies,
    February sixth brings death upon its heels.
    At Bruges the men of Aisne shall make a breach
    So deep that by the distant Red Sea's beach
    The Muslim chief death's dreaded sickle feels.

So dense and detailed is the astrological content of this originally four-lined stanza that I have been forced to render it as a *sixain*. That having been said, nobody seems to have been able to nail down the future date in question, even though a number of possible *past* dates have been suggested. Possibly the commentators have simply not been looking far enough ahead. At all events, the French, attacking via France's north-eastern border-

187

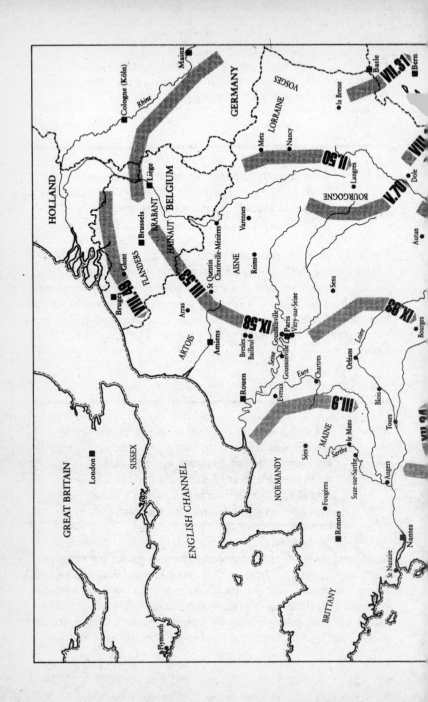

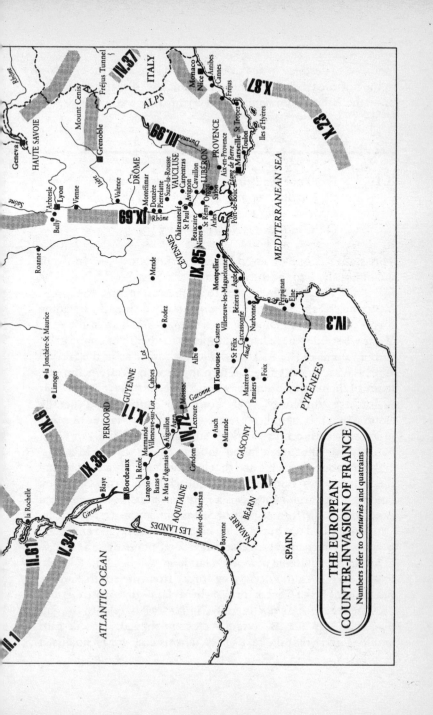

THE EUROPEAN
COUNTER-INVASION OF FRANCE
Numbers refer to *Centuries* and quatrains

lands, seem destined to achieve great success against the invaders in the north-east – with results that somehow threaten to undermine the Asiatic command at its very heart.

II.1 *From out the British Isles towards Aquitaine*
Of English troops great movements there shall be:
Dreadful the lands are made by icy rain.
On Genoa fall great assaults by sea.

This stanza is one of several that commentators – even if not unanimously – confidently assign to the First World War. The first three lines certainly seem to fit the case in some respects. Nevertheless, the text quite unambiguously defines the invading forces' goal as Aquitaine in the west, not Flanders in the east. What we seem to have here, in short, is further light on the great turning-point of the Asiatic conflict as, rather as in the Second World War, the defenders return in force to Western Europe, many of them using Britain as a base. True, *Port Selyn* in line four is not easy to identify. First World War enthusiasts generally assume that it is an indirect reference to Turkey via one or other of the sixteenth-century Turkish Sultans called Selim – or alternatively, via the Greek moon-goddess Selene, to the Muslims' crescent moon emblem – and that it is consequently a reference to the Dardanelles campaign and Churchill's abortive Gallipoli landings. The argument seems a mite *recherché*. A more natural candidate is the former port of Selinus in south-western Sicily, long since silted up, but offering miles of remote, sandy invasion beaches – which might suggest that at some point after the British invasion of Aquitaine new allied landings will be undertaken to attack Italy's Asiatic occupying forces from the south. On the other hand, Erika Cheetham elsewhere claims that Nostradamus uses the term *mer Seline* (literally, 'lunar sea') to refer to the gulf of Genoa – which is certainly crescent-shaped. This in turn would suggest that the text's *port Selyn* is code for Genoa itself (possibly Nostradamus is concerned not to reveal the invasion-site to the enemy in advance). The identification would certainly seem to fit in rather better than Sicily with what will come to emerge as the overall invasion-strategy in Italy, which (as we shall see) is to sweep the country from north to south.

V.34   *From out the heart of England's farthest west*
Where of the British Isles the chief's residing
A fleet invades Gironde at Blois's behest
By luck or judgement, fire in barrels hiding.

The first invasion-target, however, is France's west coast, and specifically the protected waters of the Gironde estuary. The massive fleet may well have been assembled in a large port such as Plymouth, Falmouth or Milford Haven. *Blois* seems to refer to the prospective French leader who, as we shall see in due course, seems to have royal blood which he traces back to that city.

II.61   *Hail, England, in Gironde and Rochelle's port!*
Wail the blood royal shot dead on the beach!
Beyond the river, ladders scale the fort.
Flashes of fire, great slaughter in the breach.

The invasion fleet arrives, and the British assault on the western coast duly commences. The initial target is indeed La Rochelle and the vast, protected estuary of the Gironde. In the course of the attack a member of the former French royal family is killed — here described, not for the last time, as *Troyen* after the old tradition that the kings of France were descended via the Merovingians from Priam of Troy. One wonders whether he is the very figure mentioned in the foregoing stanza and in VI.12 (p. 186). If so, his death could prove a grave, if temporary, setback to French morale.

III.83   *The long-haired warriors of Celtic Gaul*
Accompanied by troops from overseas
In Aquitaine take captive one and all,
Subjecting them to all their own decrees.

Once again Nostradamus confirms the participation of French forces in the attack, describing them in terms highly reminiscent of the ancient Gauls as well as of the former Merovingian kings.

III.9   *Bordeaux, Rouen and la Rochelle shall fight*
To hold the lands that border on the sea.
But English, Bretons, Flemings shall unite
And force them to the River Loire to flee.

Despite determined resistance by the occupiers of western and northern France, the liberation forces succeed in pushing them back at least as far as the Loire. Indeed, the last line of the French text specifically mentions the town of Roanne which, though on the Loire, is actually only a few miles to the north-west of Lyon. It is interesting to note that Nostradamus lists the liberators as coming from England, Brittany and Belgium – a fairly clear indication that all three lands have somehow managed to escape the worst of the Asiatic invasion. The Belgians' involvement, meanwhile, also suggests that the counter-attack's north-eastern spearhead will in due course join up with its central and western counterparts.

IX.38 *English attacks on la Rochelle and Blaye*
The Macedonian shall soon outflank.
The Gaul waits, from Agen not far away,
Then helps Narbonne, deceived by falsehoods rank.

After confirming that the British forces have landed not only at la Rochelle, but also at Blaye, deep within the Gironde estuary, this verse once again mentions the mighty Greek who had proved so effective an invading commander in the earlier stages of the war. In the south-west, meanwhile, a commander who looks suspiciously like some kind of powerful resistance leader is waiting to join up with the liberators, prior to freeing Narbonne, which is half-inclined to side with the retreating Asiatic invaders.

IX.85 *They'll pass Guyenne, the Languedoc and Rhône,*
Thanks to Agen, Marmande and la Réole.
Walls partly smashed, Marseille resumes its throne.
Battles shall rage near St Paul-de-Mausole.

The victorious invasion-forces now sweep westwards across the south of France, fighting a number of set-piece battles along the way at places such as those named in the second line. Marseilles is recaptured, and a battle is fought at the very place whose name Nostradamus has previously used as a geographical pun on the Latin tag awarded by the twelfth-century St Malachy to the by then deceased Pope John Paul II.

IX.58 *On the left bank at Vitry-upon-Seine*
They shall keep watch o'er France's red ones three:
All reds are killed, no blacks to gibbet ta'en.
By Bretons they shall all enheartened be.

In the north-east, meanwhile, the counter-invasion via Flanders continues. Evidently three of the fleeing Asiatic overlords are captured and lynched. If the Vitry mentioned is indeed Vitry-sur-Seine, it lies just to the south-east of Paris. The essentially non-political soldiery, however, are spared the worst.

V.70 *Some of the Libran lands at very least*
With mighty war the mountains shall assail.
Captives of either sex throughout the East
From land to land each dawn they shall bewail.

The forces in the north-east move to expel the invaders from the uplands of central Europe, presumably approaching Italy via southern Germany, eastern France and Switzerland. Continual daily progress will be made. The precise identity of the 'regions subject to the Scales' is not entirely clear. Erika Cheetham suggests a reference to Austria and Savoy, but the latter especially seems an unlikely candidate, as it will presumably still be occupied by the Asiatics. Her other suggestion seems more likely: the Scales are to be seen as symbolic rather than as specifically astrological, and so refer to the Western world's great trading nations – especially, perhaps, Britain, the Netherlands and Germany. It is even possible, as we shall see, that the United States, too, will at some stage become involved in the European conflict – though rather late in the day.

II.50　　*When those from Hainaut, Brussels and from Ghent*
　　　　　Their siege of Langres duly laid shall see,
　　　　　Behind their lines shall lands by wars be rent:
　　　　　The ancient wound worse than the foe shall be.

Military success is not all, however. The unaccustomed luxury of peace and freedom always brings its own problems. Behind the north-eastern front, what sound suspiciously like ethnic or religious squabbles break out – or possibly revenge killings – if anything, even more hateful than anything that has gone before. The first line once again makes it clear, meanwhile, that the Belgians, too, will be deeply involved in the great counter-attack from the north-east.

IV.98　　*Th' Albanians into Rome shall straightway fare:*
　　　　　Because of Langres the people are decked out.
　　　　　Those in control no living soul shall spare.
　　　　　Fire, smallpox, blood, crop-failures, widespread
　　　　　　drought.

Nevertheless, Langres evidently falls, and the citizens of Rome openly celebrate the fact. The occupying forces rush in post-haste to suppress the celebrations. One has the feeling, though, that their morale and authority are steadily weakening, or the demonstration would not have occurred in the first place. Perhaps the phenomena listed in the last line – many of them possibly direct results of their own military action during the invasion – will have more than a little to do with it.

VIII.10 *From Lausanne shall a mighty stench arise*
Whose origin no one alive shall know.
Expelled the foreigners 'neath fiery skies:
The aliens they at last shall overthrow.

The country around Lake Geneva in Switzerland is among the next territories to be liberated, despite the invaders' apparent continued use of their airborne fire-weapon.

VIII.73 *An Arab soldier shall assail his lord*
Almost to death, yet without reason due.
Ambitious mother is the cause abhorred.
That day both plotter and regime shall rue.

The connection with the earlier stanza describing the threatened death of the oriental leader now seems to be explained. The depressing news from abroad apparently sparks some kind of attempted palace coup. (The details are such as to suggest that this is no mere reference to the historical assassination of Anwar Sadat of Egypt.) The leader seems not to die at once, but may still be removed (in more ways than one) from the firing-line. If, therefore, despite everything, the 'twenty-seven-year war' of VIII.77 continues to apply in spite of the prior attentions of both Hitler and Stalin (and especially if *l'antechrist trois* should, after all, be read as 'the third Antichrist'), then this event could conceivably be dated to around the year 2026.

II.47   *The mighty foe, long-wailed, of poison dies,*
His generals overcome by numbers vast.
Stones from the skies or deeply hidden spies
He vainly blames, as death comes on at last.

Eventually, it seems, the oriental leader is 'helped' to die, as his cause goes from bad to worse and, in customary human fashion, he seeks to lay the blame on everything and everybody but himself.

IX.93   *Far from the fort the foes are driven back:*
Tanks shall a wall defensive constitute.
Above, the crumbling walls of Bourges shall crack
When Hercules the Grecian shall confute.

This quatrain describes a great victory at Bourges, which suggests that the counter-attack has now reached a point well south of Orléans and the River Loire. Nostradamus describes the use of *chariots*: the equivalent word *chars* nowadays means 'tanks'. 'Aemathion', the apparently Greek-born commander in line four, seems to be the same enemy leader who originally invaded France via the Pyrenees (see IX.64, p. 161). Evidently he has become a particularly powerful military overlord in the interim, possibly taking over control of much of occupied France. 'Hercules' is worth watching. As subsequent quatrains will reveal, he is a strong man who will eventually loom especially large, not merely in the campaign itself, but in subsequent French history.

VIII.60   *The first in France, the first in Italy,*
          That noble house shall wondrous things attain
          For England – Paris, too – by land and sea.
          Violent monster, though, shall lose Lorraine.

Already, in fact, it looks as though Nostradamus is referring to 'Hercules' almost as if he were destined to be a member of a dynasty of conquerors. There are hints of future successes stretching far down into the Mediterranean. There is, though, to be some kind of violent setback on the eastern front, apparently at the hands of some leader who totally loses control of himself. Further details of this may follow . . .

V.51   *Romanians, English, Poles and Czechs alike*
        A new alliance shall together knot
        To pass Gibraltar's narrow strait and strike
        The Arab tyrants with a fiendish plot.

At the same time a western strategy is devised to attack the invaders in the Mediterranean via what Churchill once called 'the soft underbelly of Europe'. This is clearly by way of a surprise attack. It is particularly interesting, meanwhile, to note the involvement of the peoples of Eastern Europe. This suggests that they will never have been overrun by the orientals in the first place – a fact which in turn confirms that the latter's attack will have taken an almost exclusively southern route. In view of this, it is now possible to understand in a surprising new light Mario de Sabato's prediction that the invasion (which he, too, foresees) will come to a halt in eastern France,[20] and Jeane Dixon's that it will reach the German border:[6] it will indeed reach the Franco–German border, but – ignoring all our logical preconceptions – *from the west.*

VII.10   *A mighty force from France and all the north*
            By land and sea past stern Gibraltar's cape
            For Maine's great lord shall valiantly go forth –
            Their leader's task Majorca's isle to rape.

This stanza (whose lines I have been forced for poetic reasons to recast completely) offers more details of the projected western sea-borne strategy. In the first place it is organised by a doughty commander from the area of Maine in France – possibly the same 'Hercules' as is mentioned in IX.93 (p. 197) – and with French participation. This suggests once again either that inroads will already have been made into northern France via Normandy, or that escaped free French forces will have spent some time in England in the interim, much as they did during the Second World War – probably, indeed, both. Unlike that former occasion, however, the aim now is apparently to turn the Balearics (or 'Barcelona's isle', as Nostradamus puts it) into a staging-post and possible marshalling area for large-scale landings in the Mediterranean, much as the Asiatics themselves may have done previously. (A mere raid over such a distance would, after all, be a rather pointless operation.)

III.78   *The Scottish chief, with six from Germany*
            By Eastern seamen shall be captive led:
            Crossing Iberia via Gibraltar, he
            Shall come in fear before Iran's new head.

At this juncture there is an unhelpful development. Somehow one of the British commanders manages to get himself captured at sea, along with six German colleagues, and is taken back to be brought before the new Asiatic supremo in his Iranian headquarters. Well may the prisoner quake in his boots.

V.14   *In Leo, Saturn, Mars. Poor, captive Spain,*
Trapped by the Libyan chief through act of war!
Near Malta shall the heir alive be ta'en
While France shall strike the Roman rulers sore.

Once again Nostradamus gets up to his usual trick of repeating an identical idea in both halves of his verse, even at the distinct risk of rendering the overall sense much more difficult to get at. Just as bypassed Spain remains in abject captivity, for the moment at least, so the 'heir' — possibly the same Scottish chief as in III.78 (p. 199), who looks as though he is none other than the deputy-commander of the task force — is likewise captured somewhere between Gibraltar and Malta. On the other hand, Nostradamus treats the 'heir' as *feminine*: either, consequently, he has to be referring to somebody else altogether, or women's rights will have made remarkable strides in the mean time.

X.87   *Near Nice the mighty chief shall shoreward ride,*
To stab to death the far-flung empire's heart.
At Antibes he shall lay his broom aside.
At sea all pillage shall at last depart.

The Mediterranean task force duly comes ashore on the French Riviera. His task of sweeping the invaders from the seas finally accomplished, the European commander sets up his initial headquarters on the coast at Antibes.

X.23   *Th' ungrateful people shall be argued with:*
          The force shall seize Antibes, make it its fee.
          'Board ship shall Monaco complain forthwith,
          While Fréjus shall be taken from the sea.

Curiously enough, not everybody welcomes the liberation, however. Some people have evidently profited from the long occupation.

V.76   *In open land he his encampment makes,*
          Nor will in any city have his base –
          Carpentras, Cavaillon, Vaucluse or Aix:
          Where'er he goes he'll leave no single trace.

The task force commander now starts to play a cat-and-mouse game all across Provence. Always on the move, he starts to harry the enemy from every side.

III.99   *From Alleins' fields and Vernègues' pastures green*
          To Lubéron's mount not far from the Durance,
          Bitter on both sides though the fight has been,
          Iraq at last shall lose its hold on France.

Nostradamus foresees that, following a bitter struggle around his own home area in the Rhône delta, the tide will at last start to turn in favour of the European defenders. Once again he associates the occupying invaders with the biblical – if not also the geographical – Babylon.

I.32
> *Transferred shall be the Empire's power entire*
> *To a small spot which soon shall grow apace –*
> *A tiny spot within a tiny shire –*
> *And at its heart his sceptre he shall place.*

Once the south-eastern corner of France is secured, 'Hercules' (if he it is) transfers control of all the liberating forces – and seemingly of France itself, too – to some hitherto relatively unimportant centre somewhere in that area.

III.93
> *In Avignon the lord of France entire*
> *Shall come to rest, Paris being desolate,*
> *While Tricastin fends off the Afric ire.*
> *Lyon shall at the change bewail its fate.*

The riddle is solved. Paris having been virtually destroyed earlier in the campaign, Avignon becomes the new French capital. Possibly the former papal palace is turned into the new centre of administration. Evidently Lyon had hoped to win the honour, and is disappointed. Meanwhile, hostilities are still continuing in the mountains to the east – Tricastin being the area now occupied by the *départements* of Drôme and Vaucluse.

IV.21
> *Most difficult the change is bound to be,*
> *Yet town and country both from it shall gain.*
> *High-placed, wise-hearted, cunning hunter, he*
> *Shall change their state by land and watery main.*

There are hints in this verse, meanwhile, that 'Hercules' will in some way be a cut above his fellows, as well as being the cunning tactician that we have already supposed him to be.

VIII.38   *In Avignon Blois's king shall set his throne,*
           Once more a ruler o'er a single land.
           Up to four residences by the Rhône
           He'll have, in Nola yet another planned.

Nostradamus seems to suggest that 'Hercules' has some ancestral connection with Blois, on the River Loire, former alternative capital of the French kings. It is a similar role, indeed, that Avignon too has now started to play as alternative capital of the whole of France. Evidently 'Hercules' himself is starting to show a certain regal resplendence and even extravagance. The mention of Nola, near Naples, suggests that his power is about to extend far into Italy as well.

VIII.4   *In Monaco the French Cock is received.*
          The cardinal of France then to him comes.
          By embassies the Romans are deceived.
          Weaker the Eagle, stronger the Cock becomes.

The impression is strengthened. Apparently some plot is being hatched between the Church and 'Hercules' – here represented by the traditional French cockerel – to hoodwink the occupying regime in Italy. Possibly the Church decides to support 'Hercules' actively, rather than merely standing on the sidelines. This might perhaps involve inciting its flock in Italy to passive resistance. At all events, Italy (if Italy is indeed what the Eagle represents) is about to lose power to France (the Cockerel).

IX.6   *Unnumbered English occupiers bestow*
            On fair Guyenne the name 'Anglaquitaine';
            From Languedoc to honey-bee'd Bordeaux
            Dubbed Ahenobarbus' Occitan domain.

British troops are now moving in huge numbers into depopulated western France, while leaving the area to the south of the Garonne to a local French commander to whom Nostradamus repeatedly assigns the name 'Ahenobarbus'. This is evidently a historical reference – not to the Emperor Nero, whose name it certainly was, but to his earlier namesake Lucius Domitius Ahenobarbus (d. 48 BC). This prominent Roman politician and general is best remembered for his passionate opposition to the rise of Julius Caesar and his clique. It was after the Senate had appointed Ahenobarbus to replace Caesar as commander in Gaul that Caesar carried out his celebrated crossing of the Rubicon and marched on Rome itself. Captured after confronting him in Italy, Ahenobarbus was released, but immediately raised a new revolt in Marseille, only to be killed in battle. By referring to the new southern governor as 'Ahenobarbus', Nostradamus thus tells us a great deal about him. His prime aim in life is evidently to free his fiefdom from an overweening conqueror and dictator – in this case the Asiatic one, presumably – while his main power-base lies in Provence, and probably in Marseille. Hence the word *Occitan* – a local word, popular among separatists, that refers to anything pertaining to the Languedoc, and especially to Provence and its language.

I.79   *Bazas, Lectoure, Condom, Agen, Auch know*
            Stormy disputes and fights o'er legal right:
            Carcassonne and Toulouse, Bayonne, Bordeaux
            Ruined by trying to resume their fight.

Not everybody is pleased with the new allocation of provinces, however. There is even armed resistance, however poorly organised at first. Especially in the south-west, the would-be liberators discover that the local town halls are extremely reluctant to surrender their ill-won power. Possibly they are influenced by large numbers of former Afro-oriental invasion-troops, who have put down roots locally. There are constant arguments and revolts. The results, though, are always catastrophic.

IV.79   *Flee, O blood royal! Montheurt, Aiguillon, Mas,*
The Landes are all with Bordelais replete,
Navarre, Bigorre with warriors armed. They are
So hungry that cork acorns they shall eat.

The rebellion spreads, centring on Bordeaux. The last line suggests that famine may lie at the basis of the unrest – unless Nostradamus really means that the dissidents are hungry for battle. Once again, meanwhile, he suggests that the former French royal line will somehow be involved.

IV.44   *For the two chiefs of Mende, Rodez, Milhaud,*
Cahors, Limoges and Castres the week bodes ill.
With night-attacks Bordeaux to war shall go.
Through Perigord the tocsin's sound shall thrill.

In this extraordinary quatrain, written (appropriately) in a mixture of French and Provençal, Nostradamus suggests that in little more than a week much of south-western and central southern France is likely to be up in arms again.

I.90   *When sounds the tocsin, Poitiers and Bordeaux*
        Shall send a mighty force to near Langon.
        Against the French their great north wind shall blow
        When hideous monster issues from Orgon.

Thus it is that the disparate revolts run together to produce a
bloody civil war between the dissidents and their own compatriots in the newly-resettled south. Possibly the attackers see
the newcomers almost as invaders in their turn. The true nature
and/or identity of the 'monster from Orgon' – which lies in the
south-east, near Nostradamus's birthplace of St Rémy – is prob-
lematical.

XII.65   *Furious, he shall constrain them to hang on.*
         Faint hearts! At Langon, advents dread ensue.
         One kick begets a thousand. The Garonne
         And the Gironde never worse horror knew.

Naturally, those attacked do their best to defend themselves.
Massive casualties result.

III.45   *Five foreigners who in their church appear*
         Shall see their blood profane its holy ground –
         To all Toulouse an earnest most severe
         Of one who comes its customs to confound.

There are signs that representatives from foreign lands will
hurriedly intervene and attempt to negotiate a truce in Toulouse
cathedral. However, their diplomatic immunity is cruelly
violated by the city's new overlord.

X.5   *Albi and Castres conclude a new-born league*
              Led by a soldier-statesman Portuguese.
              Toulouse and Carcassonne scotch their intrigue
              Once their new chief lours from the Pyrenees.

Two local towns at least decide to resist the rebels, even calling in a foreign allied general to help. Nevertheless, they are overwhelmed.

IX.46   *Away! Flee now the red ones of Toulouse*
              And make your sacrificial expiation.
              The evil lord, feigning his wits to lose
              Lies strangled as foretells the divination.

Once again Nostradamus describes what appear to be the new puppet-regimes of the south-west as 'reds'. Only actual events, though, can hope fully to explain lines three and four. Meanwhile, it is worth remembering that in Nostradamus's day Toulouse did indeed have a senate, or parliament, as in IX.72 (below), and that its members wore red into the bargain. It is always possible, in other words, that Nostradamus is being influenced in his predictions by the events and characteristics of his own time – though it is just as possible that history, as he himself firmly believed, is quite liable to repeat itself.

IX.72   *Once more to holy temples comes pollution,*
              Their ransack by Toulouse's senate passed.
              Two or three rounds of Saturn's revolution
              In spring bring people of a different cast.

Certainly the new, local regimes in the south-west seem to be anti-Christian. Moreover, Nostradamus expects them to last a good long time. Since Saturn has a sidereal period of twenty-nine-and-a-half years, after all, it will apparently take between sixty and ninety years before things change significantly for the better with the ousting of the local rulers by unspecified outsiders – in all probability, then, around the end of the twenty-first century (unbelievably late though this may seem).

XII.24   *The mighty succour coming from Guyenne*
          Near Poitiers shall its furthest limit find.
          Lyon shall yield to Montleul and Vienne
          And plundered be by folk of every kind.

Meanwhile, the more general advance of the liberators is continuing. In the west, the British invasion of western France has its clear limits. In the south-east Lyon is finally taken by a pincer movement mounted from Montleul (just to the north-east) and Vienne (in the Rhône valley to the south).

IX.69   *On Bully's mountain and l'Arbresle's high top*
          The proud ones of Grenoble shall be in hiding.
          At Vienne, beyond Lyon, hail shall not stop,
          Of locusts in the land no third abiding.

Evidently a kind of resistance *maquis* has been operating in the mountains north-west of Lyon throughout the occupation. For obvious reasons, Nostradamus is at pains to disguise the name of their hideout, ostensibly indicating in his original verse some unspecified hilltop near Bresle and Bailleul in northern France (he actually writes *Bailly*, which is in the Paris area). The 'hail' in line three may, of course, refer to a continuing hail of bullets and projectiles, rather than to their natural equivalent. By this stage of the campaign, meanwhile, less than a third of the original Asiatic occupiers (to whom Nostradamus once again refers by the name of 'grasshoppers') still remain in France.

IV.12 *The greater army routed, put to flight,*
Hardly much further shall the hunt advance.
Their host unhosted, and reduced their might,
They shall be chased completely out of France.

So it is that France is finally freed of the invaders, and the liberating forces begin a short period of well-earned rest.

VII.4 *Langres' great general is at Dole beset –*
Colleagues from Autun and Lyon he'll boast –
Geneva, Augsburg, Mirandela set
To cross the Alps against Ancona's host.

The coalition continues to build up its strength. Despite a local setback at Dole, in the foothills of the Alps, a coalition of Swiss, Germans and Portuguese is only awaiting the signal to cross into Italy and chase the invaders all the way back to their original beach-head on the Adriatic shores of Italy.

VII.31   *Ten thousand come from Languedoc, Guyenne*
Once more across the Alps to trace their tracks.
Towards Brindisi and Aquino then
Come Savoyards, and Bresse shall break their backs.

Not only French forces from Ahenobarbus's domains, but also British ones from the far west, now prepare to join those from nearer at hand to cross the Alps back into Italy and chase the foe the whole length of the peninsula.

IV.23   *The warriors of the task force maritime*
Long rest at anchorage secure shall earn:
Then, using pitch, magnesium, sulphur, lime,
With fire shall Hercules Genoa burn.

The commander of the Mediterranean task force (here confirmed as being the self-same 'Hercules' as was referred to earlier) now springs into action once more. As though attempting to emulate the oriental forces' original 'fire from the sky', he proceeds to attack the Genoan coast (if my tentative identification of the target-port in II.1, p. 190, is correct) with what appears to be some kind of incendiary weapon – which Nostradamus describes chemically in terms of 'Greek fire', the original 'secret weapon' used by both Greeks and Byzantines.

V.35   *The stone lies heavy on the stomach thin*
Of the free city of the crescent sea.
Through misty rain the British fleet sails in
To seize its chance: its lord at war shall be.

As elsewhere, however, the 'misty rain' suggests that the Genoan occupying forces will attempt to fend off the attacking fleet with chemical or biological weapons.

IV.37   *In bounds the French shall pass the mountains o'er,*
            Milan's own heartland soon to occupy.
            The mighty host shall reach its furthest shore.
            From Genoa, Monaco the red ships fly.

Ashore, the fight is meanwhile continued over the Alps and into northern Italy. Line one may foreshadow the use of paratroops. Looking ahead, Nostradamus foresees the success of this campaign too. So, apparently, do the Asiatics, who are hurriedly starting to pull their forces out by sea.

VI.79   *Near the Ticino, warriors from the Seine,*
            From Loire, Tain and Gironde, Saône and Garonne
            Beyond the Alps a bridgehead soon shall gain.
            Fight joined and Po secured, their wave rolls on.

Once the River Ticino has been successfully crossed, the plain of Lombardy lies open before the liberating forces.

II.26   *Because the city shall a favour show*
            To the great lord who'll later lose the fight,
            Ticino's troops shall flee towards the Po,
            Hacked to death, bleeding, drowned or set alight.

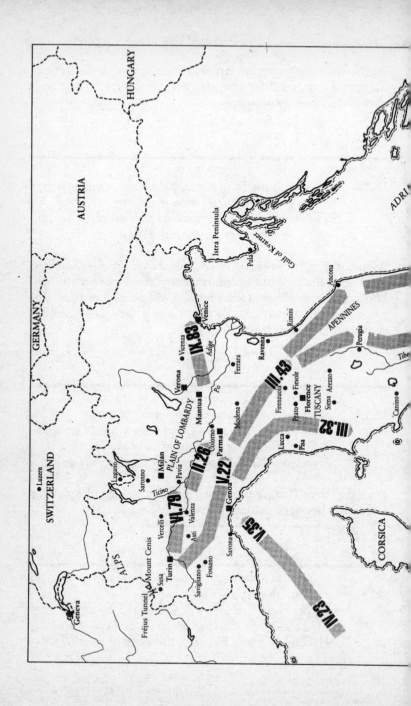

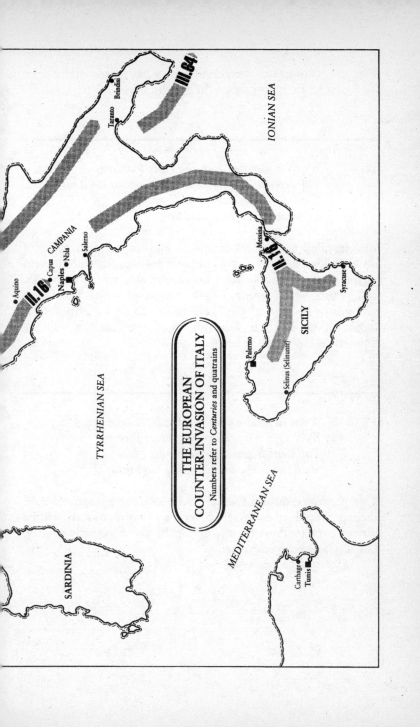

THE EUROPEAN
COUNTER-INVASION OF ITALY

Numbers refer to *Centuries* and quatrains

The rout is complete, compounded by what appears to be some kind of internal bickering on the Asiatic side.

VI.3   *When new-come Celt the river shall assay,*
        Throughout the Empire discord great shall reign.
        For help ecclesiastical he'll pray.
        Of peace the crown and sceptre he'll disdain.

As 'Hercules' pursues his campaign into Italy, there is news of unrest behind his back, which he attempts to pacify with the help of the newly re-established Church. Possibly strong voices are being raised against continuing the campaign, whether on moral grounds or because of the likelihood of heavy casualties. Certainly, though, he has no intention of calling off the attack merely in order to buy peace at home.

VI.16   *What from the youthful Hawk is taken back*
         By troops from Normandy and Picardy
         The Benedictines of the Forest Black
         Shall make the hostelry of Lombardy.

This quatrain is rather obscure, but it seems to suggest that one of the strongholds of the Arab governor of northern Italy will be turned over to the Church for use by the Benedictine order, possibly as a refugee centre.

214

V.22   *Before the lord of Rome gives up the ghost*
             Squadrons near Parma spring a deadly trap.
             Terror is great among the alien host.
             Then the two reds eat in each other's lap.

There follows what looks like a massive tank-battle that causes further panic among the enemy defending the southern borders of the plain of Lombardy. As a result of it, the enemy commander of the region is forced to move his headquarters to his superior's quarters at Rome. But evidently the latter does not have much time left, either.

VIII.7   *Milan, Vercelli each the news proclaims:*
             Peace in Pavia is declared to all.
             Floods in Siena, Florentine blood and flames.
             As May comes in how shall the Mighty fall!

Despite continued conflict further south, late springtime sees peace established in northern Italy.

IV.36   *Once more the games in France they shall refound*
             Once the campaign around Milan is won.
             On western mountains chiefs are gagged and bound:
             Romans and Spaniards quake with fear and run.

Almost as though in celebration, in France mass entertainments of a classical type are reintroduced – unless it should be the more modern form of Olympic Games that are now resumed. In the Pyrenees, however, the south-western conflict is not over yet. The

'Romans' and 'Spaniards' are presumably the still-fleeing remnants of the Asiatic invasion-force.

III.43   *Beware, you men of Tarn, Garonne and Lot!*
Trace not beyond the Apennines your ways.
Near Rome, Ancona to your graves you'll go.
Black Curly-Beard your cenotaph shall raise.

The fight will not be easy, however. The allies are likely to suffer heavy losses as they attempt to storm both coastal flanks of central Italy. As we shall see, 'Black Curly-Beard' is Nostradamus's way of describing Hercules' even more illustrious successor, to whom will fall the task of pursuing the war to its eventual close and raising whatever monuments are subsequently felt to be appropriate.

III.32   *Vast killing-fields for those from Aquitaine*
Not far from Tuscany await their dead
When war not far from Germany shall reign
And over all the Mantuan lands shall spread.

Nostradamus drives the point home. Even as the allies head south-eastwards across the Lombardy plain towards the Adriatic coast, stiff resistance is likely to be encountered and heavy losses sustained. The warning in III.43, above, therefore applies: those who do not wish to risk life and limb should make every effort to stay well clear.

III.38   *Both armies French and alien forces vast*
Beyond the mountains casualties record.
Six months from thence, ere harvest shall be past,
Their leaders shall strike up a grand accord.

As ever with Nostradamus, however, there is always a light at the end of the tunnel, unbearably dark though it may seem at the time. Only six months after the murderous spring offensive in northern and central Italy the allies will be negotiating the remaining Asiatic invaders' surrender.

V.50   *The year when brothers French shall be of age,*
One of them Italy shall hold as fief:
Hills quake: free road to Rome he shall engage,
Plotting to march against Armenia's chief.

Thus it is that 'Hercules' can advance into central Italy virtually unopposed. Meanwhile it would seem that he has a younger brother who has just come of age. Possibly we shall hear more of him later.

IX.2   *Hear now the voice proclaim from Roman hill:*
'Away! Forsake the land while it is riven!
The wrath shall pass: the reds their life-blood spill,
From Prato, Rimini, Colorno driven.'

As the beleagured inhabitants of Italy are warned in quasi-biblical terms to keep their heads down, the liberating armies press down towards Rome, eventually expelling the occupation-forces from the whole country. Unless the last line's *Columna* is an anachronistic reference to the Colonna family of sixteenth-century Rome, it would seem to refer to Colorno, just north of Parma.

II.16   *Naples, Palermo, Sicilian Syracuse*
       New powers shall rule, new lightnings scorch
         the sky;
       For now 'tis London, Ghent, Brussels and Suze
       Shall triumph keep, once the great slaughter's by.

So it is that the liberation-forces eventually clear the invaders out of the whole of Italy and Sicily, albeit only after further massive bombardments. Once again, in other words, Western Europe is free, with the possible exception of the Iberian peninsula. The enigmatic *Suses* could be Suze-sur-Sarthe, near Le Mans, Suze-la-Rousse near Avignon or Sus in Switzerland – to say nothing of Susa in north-western Italy itself. However, Nostradamus's determined spelling of the name with a final 's' (not necessitated by any consideration of rhyme, for he also adds one to *Syracuse*) actually suggests that he means 'Sussex'. This line refers, in other words, primarily to an alliance of British and Belgians.

IX.33   *From Rome to Denmark Hercules shall reign,*
       Surnamed the leader of tripartite Gaul.
       Venice and Italy shall quake amain:
       Renowned he'll be as high king over all.

The acquired stature of 'Hercules' is becoming ever more apparent. In this anticipatory stanza Nostradamus is starting to treat him not merely as a conquering hero, but almost as royalty itself. Certainly the area he controls is immense. The term 'tripartite Gaul' seems to be a reference to the celebrated first sentence of Julius Caesar's *Gallic War*, which referred to all of France and Belgium.

VIII.78   *A mercenary with a twisted tongue*
Of holy church arrives before the doors:
When out of them the heretics he's flung,
The church once militant he then restores.

Thus it is that an officer of the liberation-forces eventually reaches the Basilica of St Peter itself, and takes it upon himself to open it up once more.

X.80   *When o'er the realm the great King comes to reign,*
By force of arms the gates of bronze are seen
Opened to be by King and chief again.
Port ruined, shipping sunk, yet day serene.

This highly symbolic event is a source of great contentment to 'Hercules' and his leading aide, for all the chaos and destruction reigning around him.

X.27   *For him that's fifth and mighty Hercules,*
The church by act of war they'll open wide:
Never such strife 'twixt eagle, sword and keys:
Ascanus, Julius, Clement step aside.

This verse, similarly, seems to foresee a determined attempt to reopen St Peter's in Rome by force of arms on behalf of 'Hercules'. Evidently, though, this causes great controversy between the Church on the one hand (the 'keys' seem to be the papal ones of St Peter), and the military and state on the other. The last line seems to suggest that the papacy is offered to three different candidates (I have reversed their order for metrical reasons), all of whom decline. In the rather strange first line, meanwhile, Nostradamus almost seems to be referring not only to 'Hercules', but also to another (possibly the aide of the foregoing stanza) whom he seems to see as one of a line of French kings – specifically the fifth, possibly of a particular name. If so, no doubt we shall hear more of him later . . .

IX.84   *Revealed, the King completes the mighty slaughter*
             Once he has traced its source and its producer.
             The lead-and-marble tomb's revealed by water
             Of a great Roman, masked with dread Medusa.

Thus it is that 'Hercules' reveals his full power by tracking down his arch-opponent at the very same moment as natural events are unearthing other secrets from the past. Nostradamus, in fact, has a golden opportunity to indulge once again his passion for incorporating parallel ideas into both halves of his quatrains.

VI.66   *When they shall come to found the sect anew*
             The bones of the great Roman shall be found.
             Clad all in marble springs the tomb to view
             When earth in April quakes, half-underground.

The theme continues. The attempt to refound the Vatican regime in Rome is marked by the discovery of what many commentators assume to be the tomb of St Peter following a local earthquake. However, the Medusan symbolism of the foregoing stanza would tend to argue against this particular identification.

III.65   *One day the mighty Roman's tomb is found:*
           The next, elected Pope, he'll tread the palace.
           The Senate, though, the choice shall straight
               confound.
           Poisoned he'll be – and by the sacred chalice.

The attempt to re-establish the Vatican continues to arouse violent controversy. A new pope is elected the day after the momentous discovery, but is then promptly poisoned, apparently at the instigation of the new Italian parliament. Clearly there is enormous popular opposition to any attempt to return to the former ecclesiastical regime, almost as if it is being blamed for the catastrophe that has recently befallen Europe.

III.40   *The mighty theatre shall rise up again,*
           The dice be thrown, the nets be cast about.
           The first to toll the bell shall feel the strain,
           Worn out by bows so long ago cut out.

Possibly in order to placate public opinion, 'Hercules' now attempts to resurrect the ancient Roman regime of 'bread and circuses'. The ancient entertainments prove all too much for the first participants, however: as Nostradamus points out via a metaphor much more familiar to his own age than to ours, old bows are hard to stretch – the ancient practices, in other words,

221

will demand physical skills that have long since been lost and will need to be slowly redeveloped.

X.79 *Old roads with new embellishments they'll fit:*
With psalms to ancient Memphis they shall go,
As Gallic Hercules' mercurial writ
Earth, sea and all the lands shall trembling know.

In other ways, too, 'Hercules' is much drawn to resurrecting the classical past. Much effort is devoted to restoring the ancient Roman roads and streets to their former glory, while communication links generally are restored.

II.71 *Those long-exiled to Sicily shall sail*
To save from hunger alien victims thin.
At daybreak shall the French to show still fail.
Yet life goes on – for now the King joins in.

There now seems to be a sudden compassionate initiative by Italian anti-war groups to bring succour to the alien settlers in their homeland of Sicily, who have apparently been long neglected by their own Asiatic overlords. After their recent experiences the French are naturally reluctant to join in, despite apparent assurances of support. However, much to everybody's surprise, 'Hercules' evidently decides to commit himself to the action on his own responsibility.

IV.95   *Once placed in power, not long shall rule the pair.*
After three years seven months at war they'll be,
Till both the vestal lands revolt declare.
The junior wins the war in Brittany.

This quatrain is extremely vague. It seems to suggest that the two joint commanders of the allied forces will now fall out with each other in the most dramatic way. The squabble (possibly military) will spread all across liberated Europe, until what appear to be Italy and Greece refuse to play ball, and so put an end to the argument. The geographical extent of the quarrel seems to be confirmed by the fact that the junior partner comes out on top in north-western France, while (as we shall see) the fighting has dire effects in the east, too.

V.23   *Both continents shall happily unite*
Once most themselves to Martial war have given.
Afric's great lord shall tremble in his fright,
Till the duumvirate by sea is riven.

Nostradamus does not identify the two continents, but Europe and America could well be candidates. Possibly the sheer horror of what has been taking place in France and Italy has at some stage brought about transatlantic intervention. If so, then it is entirely understandable that the new oriental commander should quake in his boots. The 'duumvirate' seems to refer to the two commanders mentioned above, whose quarrel eventually extends as far as the Mediterranean itself. No wonder the pressure is taken off the oriental leader for a while.

VI.58   *Between the now far-distanced monarchs twain,*
When by the Sun the Moon's light dimmed shall be,
Great rivalry and indignation reign
Now that Siena and the Isles are free.

Thus it is that the discord whose rumblings have already been felt
across newly-liberated Europe finally breaks out into the open.
No sooner does it become possible for everybody to relax a little,
than the two commanders use the opportunity to pick a quarrel.
Possibly they are 'Hercules' himself and his aide and would-be
successor.

VI.95   *A slanderer the younger shall attack*
When warlike deeds and great o'er all shall reign.
Not much of it the elder one shall back,
But soon the kingdom shall be torn in twain.

Whether this quatrain applies to the quarrel in question is difficult to tell. If it does, though, the 'elder' could be 'Hercules', the
'younger' his prospective successor. At all events, the dispute
now seems likely to tear the whole regime apart.

II.34   *Th' insensate fury of an angry fight*
Sees mess-companions draw their flashing arms.
Injured and split, offended at some slight,
Their stiff-necked feud fair France severely harms.

The quarrel is clearly a deeply personal one, having no necessary
connection with matters military at all. Yet its ramifications are
destined to prove immensely far-reaching, as we shall see.

V.64   *To calm the greater number of their peers*
            They'll countermand advice by sea and land:
            Geneva, Nice shall loom as autumn nears
            O'er field and town: against their chief they'll band.

The details are extremely confused: indeed, such squabbles are
an area that Nostradamus frequently tends to get back to front.
But it does rather seem that the two main protagonists will at
some stage be pressurised by their colleagues to stop their more
aggressive actions, even if only temporarily. The urgency of some
kind of settlement is underlined as local garrisons start to take
sides.

VI.7   *Norway, Romania and the British Isles*
            Shall by the pair of brothers troubled be.
            Rome's mighty chief, of French blood, forced
                 the whiles
            To seek in wooded land security.

This stanza fills in the picture slightly more. To judge by the
countries listed in the first line, the two 'brothers' seem to have
dire effects on the European allies to the north and east. Once
again, though, the suggestion seems to be that their feud will
extend right down into the Mediterranean. Eventually the great
'Hercules' is forced to flee, and (as the original text reveals) his
armies with him.

V.45   *The mighty Empire shall be desolated,*
Power transferred to Ardennes' forests cool.
The bastards by their elder separated,
Hawk-nosed Ahenobarbus then shall rule.

For a while, at least, the effects are devastating. The new continental regime is disrupted, its leader ('Hercules', presumably) forced to seek refuge near the Franco-Belgian border. Eventually, however, a senior commander intervenes to put a stop to the quarrel. Possibly it is 'Ahenobarbus' himself. At all events, he now assumes full command. Unless Nostradamus is so disgusted with the two protagonists as to use the word 'bastards' to refer to *them*, the meaning of line three is unclear.

II.38   *Many are they who shall be damned outright*
When reconciled shall be the leaders twain,
But one of them shall soon be in such plight
That their alliance scarce stands up again.

Nevertheless, the quarrel will have had its severe effects on all those involved – and not least on the two feuding leaders themselves. One of them is evidently no longer in a fit state to permit any real resumption of their former friendly relationship – or possibly some further misfortune befalls him.

VIII.5   *By Borne and at Breteuil lamps, candles burn.*
He shall appear in church ornate and shining.
Then to Lucerne shall all the Canton turn
When in his coffin Cock is seen reclining.

226

We now see the reason why. Evidently 'Hercules' has either died or been killed, apparently still somewhere in the east. His coffin is borne into central Switzerland, lying in state at various places on the way (there are two towns called Breteuil, one of which lies south of Amiens in north-eastern France, not far from Arras and St Quentin: Borne – if it is not either the name of a village in the Netherlands or a misprint for Berne in Switzerland – probably refers to the River Borne in the area of Annecy, just south of Geneva).

V.21   *Upon the Roman monarch's death, to those*
Whom he throughout his reign has helped and aided
'Mid burning fires th' ill-gotten booty goes.
For death, though, shall the honest be paraded.

The deceased, it would seem, is indeed 'Hercules', but it now turns out that his regime has been a pretty corrupt one, so much so that on his death his cronies blatantly attempt to take everything for themselves. Possibly, indeed, it was this corruption that lay at the basis of the deadly quarrel in the first place.

IV.14   *The first king's sudden death at first appears*
All things to change. Another comes to power
Sooner or later, though of tender years,
Who o'er both land and sea shall fearful lour.

However, a successor eventually steps into his shoes. As X.26 (p. 229) possibly suggests, he seems not to be the late opponent of 'Hercules', but another leader entirely. Nostradamus suggests that, though young, he was bound to reach the top sooner or later. He promises to be just as doughty a military leader, too.

V.74   *From royal blood of France a heart shall grow*
That is Germanic, lofty power attaining.
Far from the land he'll chase the Arab foe,
The church's former eminence regaining.

Nostradamus goes further. His blood is to be *Troyen* – in other words he will be descended, as the French kings were alleged to be, from Priam of Troy. At the same time he will also be in some way German. The impression is considerable, then, that Nostradamus expects him to become nothing less than a virtual reincarnation of Charlemagne himself. His destiny, meanwhile, is finally to rid France of its invaders and to restore the Church to its former glory.

V.39   *Born from the true stock of the fleur-de-lys,*
His ancient blood the stuff of many hands,
Then set in place as heir to Italy,
His crest blooms with the flower of Florence' lands.

Quite apart from having French and German antecedents, indeed, he now goes on to inherit Italy from 'Hercules' as well.

V.41   *Shade-born where light is dim and sunbeams few,*
'Midst power and riches he'll the sceptre hold.
From th' ancient source he shall his line renew,
Replacing th' age of bronze with one of gold.

His prospects, in fact, seem to be little less than fabulous. From obscurity he is destined to rocket to something approaching world pre-eminence.

X.26   *Succeeding, he'll his brother-in-law requite:*
In vengeance' name to power he shall advance.
For all obstructions he'll his death indict.
Long shall Great Britain loyal stay to France.

Not only is the new leader actually related to 'Hercules', but he will use his strong feelings about his kinsman's death as a kind of motivation and excuse for imposing his own stamp on events.

IX.41   *Avignon Henry seizes for his own.*
From Rome come honeyed letters of complaint,
By envoys from Canino to him shown:
Carpentras seized by black of reddish taint.

At this point we are introduced by name to the new leader. Nostradamus repeatedly gives his name as 'Chyren' – generally assumed to be an anagram for Henryc, or Henricus ('Henry'). There is a hint that he may previously have been on the administrative staff at Avignon, and therefore well placed to take over control on the death of 'Hercules'. If the latter had set up his headquarters in Rome before his death in the far north-east (he is, after all, described in VI.7, p. 225, as the 'Roman chief'), this might account for the bitter complaints from that city, especially in the light of the endemic corruption referred to above. Meanwhile there seems to be a local revolt against the new regime at Carpentras, on the Rhône delta, led by a black, dissenting general with views allied to those prominent among the local regimes in the far south-west.

VIII.54   *Beneath the cover of a marriage pact*
        Muslims shall Henry for his largesse thank.
        Thereby Arras, St Quentin he'll exact.
        Spain shall become a power of second rank.

But Henry is not merely a soldier. Clearly, too, he is a master diplomat, as adept at using words and promises to gain his ends as military might. In this case his initial aim seems to be to eradicate a still-surviving pocket of Asiatic resistance near Breteuil, at whose hands his predecessor may possibly have met his demise. At the same time he also apparently takes steps to force the invaders' final withdrawal from a weakened Iberian peninsula.

IV.3   *From Bourges and Arras easterners shall flood.*
        Of Gascons more shall fight upon their feet.
        Those from the Rhône in Spain shall spill
            much blood
        Near to Sagunto's lofty mountain seat.

Thus it is that the last pocket of Asiatic resistance collapses. In due course Henry's forces, advancing along Spain's Mediterranean coastal pass, are destined to win a great victory in the shadow of the mountains near Sagunto. But first other matters are destined to demand his attention . . .

I.99   *The Mighty King shall love to spend his days*
        With two more kings in friendship's bond at one.
        What dark suspicions shall their ménage raise!
        Pity the children round about Narbonne!

Rebellion continues to brew in the far south-west of France —
apparently a kind of residue of the former occupation, possibly
encouraged by the still-surviving Asiatic regimes over the border
in Spain. Nostradamus hints that the future consequences may
well be unpleasant.

VII.12   *The younger brother ends the mighty war,*
         But leaves to fate those who will mend their ways.
         Moissac his grasp shall flee; so shall Cahors:
         Lectoure shall he repulse, Agen he'll raze.

Here Henry is apparently being described as if he were actually
the *younger brother* of 'Hercules': this is of course always possible, especially as we earlier saw him describe Henry and
Hercules as brothers-*in-law*. At all events, there is still much
unfinished military business to be concluded in the south-west.

IV.72   *Agen and Lectoure past, the northern power*
         At St Félix discussions shall assay.
         Those from Bazas shall come at the wrong hour
         Condom, Marsan to take without delay.

In an effort to avoid further bloodshed, Henry once again tries
his negotiating skills, taking advantage of the fact that one wing
of his forces is still held up at Condom and Mont-de-Marsan.

IX.92   *Wishing to enter Villeneuve shall the king*
Approach, the foe to conquer and subdue.
A captive freed says many a false thing.
The king remains outside, at distance due.

Once again we encounter Nostradamus's *cité neufue*, which we formerly identified as Villeneuve-sur-Lot. With enemies on every side, Henry still has to tread carefully.

IX.15   *Near Perpignan the reds shall be detained,*
Sapped from within, they shall be led away.
Three are dismembered, five have food restrained,
Upon Bourgogne's great lord and bishop's say.

Nevertheless, the local rebel leaders are duly captured and very roughly treated indeed. Apparently the vengeful local Church hierarchy is starting to show its teeth at the time, too.

X.11   *The last-born with his multitude shall press*
Beneath Jonchères and through its perilous gate,
Then o'er the Pyrenees, quite baggageless,
Perpignan's mighty general to await.

This further stage in the campaign is difficult to decode, but it seems as though Henry will lead troops from the Limoges area south-westwards, with a view to crossing one of the Pyrenean passes into Spain.

VI.1   *Around the Pyrenees a concourse great*
Of foreigners the king shall come to aid.
Near Garonne and Mas d'Agenais's temple gate
Shall fearful Roman chief in water wade.

At the same time there is a massive clean-up campaign in the
south-west which does not go all Henry's way. The 'foreigners'
may be English occupation-troops from Guyenne. At one stage
either he or one of his local commanders is evidently trapped in
marshes and fearful for his own survival. The weather seems to
be extremely wet at the time.

II.17   *The vestal virgin's precinct shall be sought*
Not far from Elne and lofty Pyrenees.
The Great One in a trunk is thither brought.
Northward the vines shall rot, the rivers freeze.

As the bad weather continues, a further development ensues
closer to the Mediterranean coast, near Perpignan. What seems
to be the body of a rebel leader is delivered to the site of some
ancient Roman ruins. Alternatively, perhaps it is one of Henry's
generals who thereby arrives in the area secretly.

II.48   *Over the mountains goes the host abroad*
Saturn in th' Archer, Mars the Fishes quitting.
Their leader hanging from a piece of cord,
Poison concealed in fish-shaped warheads sitting.

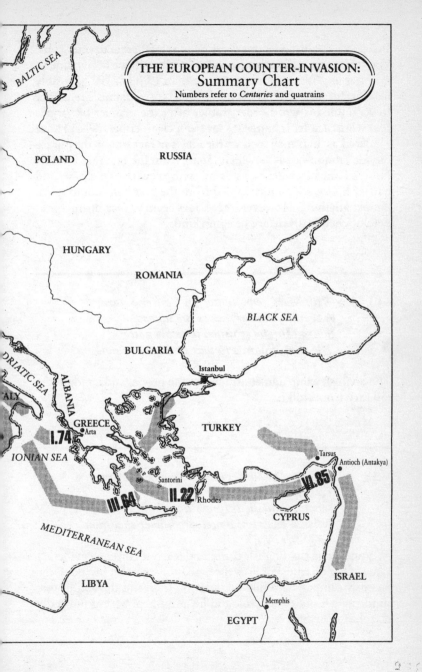

THE EUROPEAN COUNTER-INVASION:
Summary Chart
Numbers refer to *Centuries* and quatrains

Just as hard to decode, this verse does at least seem to offer some kind of dating – though such calculations as have been made so far offer us nothing more promising than 13 July 2193. (Possibly insufficient account has been taken of Nostradamus's tendency to scramble his word order, rather after the manner of Virgil.) Just whose leader is hanged is far from clear, either. What I have rendered as 'in fish-shaped warheads' is in fact simply the phrase 'under salmon-heads' – which (apart from the fact that it fulfils Nostradamus's evident obsession with repeating in the second half of his verses an idea culled from the first half) could mean almost anything. However, there does seem to be a distinct hint here of chemical warfare of some kind.

VIII.48 *With Mars near Jupiter, in Cancer Saturn,*
A seer in February saves the lands.
Sierra Morena stormed in triple pattern:
The war of words to war of arms expands.

The Spanish campaign continues on the propaganda and on the military fronts alike.

V.59 *Too long at Nîmes the English chief shall stay.*
To help, Ahenobarbus heads for Spain.
Several shall die through war that starts that day
When o'er Artois a meteor shower shall rain.

At some stage the English commander from Guyenne evidently visits 'Ahenobarbus' in Provence, possibly to enlist his aid in the Spanish campaign. While he is away, things in the south-west suddenly get out of control, and he and Ahenobarbus hurriedly travel to the front.

X.95   *Down into Spain the mighty King shall sweep:*
       Such ill he'll do the Crescent down to beat!
       He'll clip the wings of those who Friday keep.
       By land and sea the south he shall defeat.

Thus it is that Henry eventually succeeds in pushing the Muslim forces — 'those who Friday keep' — out of Spain and back into Africa.

II.69   *The King of France upon the Celtic right*
        Seeing how much discord at large shall be
        In all three parts of Gaul shall press his might
        Against the dead hand of the hierarchy.

At this point Henry (if Henry it is) finally decides that enough is enough. A stop has to be put to all the factionalism among local commanders for good and all. What is needed is some kind of firm overall command, if the Asiatics are ever to be finally eradicated from the world scene.

IV.50   *Autumn shall see the West's full power deployed,*
        Dominion wielding over land and sky:
        Yet none shall see the Asian power destroyed
        Till seven in turn have raised the sceptre high.

Nostradamus now gives us some kind of time-scale for the whole operation to expel the invaders from Europe. It will, he suggests, take six changes of regime before the entire continent is free. Bearing in mind that Nostradamus was a Frenchman, this presumably refers specifically to France. Indeed, it could conceivably indicate a period spanning seven presidential terms (however he would have understood the idea), or forty-nine years. If so, and if this is meant to be counted from the beginning of the great Western counter-attack, it could suggest that final victory will not be achieved until quite late in the twenty-first century. If, on the other hand, we are meant (as seems more likely) to count from the beginning of the whole European conflict in around 1999, it would tend to date final victory to 2048 or so. On the other hand, since the first French presidential elections after 1999 are theoretically due in 2002, six further terms would bring us to the earlier date of 2044, while deaths and/or resignations could quite easily bring the final victory celebrations forward into the late 2030s. Interestingly enough, 2037 is the date proposed by the modern prophetess Jeane Dixon[6] for precisely the same event.

VIII.4a   *Many shall be desirous to confer*
            And beg the warlords their attacks to cease.
            In no wise shall the lords to them defer.
            Alas for all, unless God sends us peace!

Relatively weak by the standards of the 'regular' *Centuries*, this is one of the late additions to *Century* VIII. It suggests that the world's peoples – or even people in some unspecified local context such as Western Europe – will, as ever, start to undermine their leaders' military initiatives as soon as the direct danger to themselves is removed, especially as the conflict drags on. Possibly what they are really opposed to is the imminent prospect of pursuing the invaders back to their own heartlands, with all the extra loss of life that that is likely to involve. But, not for the first time, they will have little success in persuading their leaders to stop making war on each other. The 'peace movement' phenomenon is not a new one, and thankfully we may confidently expect it to continue far into the future – as, no doubt, will the politicians' traditional response.

VIII.2a   *To speak of peace there shall come many a one,*
Be they great lords or puissant royalty;
But not so readily shall it be won
Till more than others they shall listeners be.

Another supplementary quatrain is once again characterised by even more vagueness and blandness than usual. Nevertheless, even if undated and unplaced, the prediction seems apt. World leaders, it seems, will continue to pay lip-service to peace, while grandly preserving all their old dreams of power and empire. Nostradamus correctly perceives that the process will always be self-defeating. The politicians have to learn to be responsive (*obeissans*) to their electors, the dictators to the needs of their peoples. Charity begins at home: peace begins in the heart.

X.86   *Like griffon shall the king from Europe speed,*
Accompanied by all those from the North.
Of reds and whites great numbers he shall lead
'Gainst Babylon's great ruler boldly forth.

In the light of the suggestive reference to the King of Babylon in the last line, it has been all too easy for past commentators to place this prediction in some kind of gloomy apocalyptic context. As ever, though, the reference seems to be to something much more down-to-earth – namely the final onslaught on the Asiatic coalition by the countries of northern Europe, who will have decided not only to chase the orientals out of Europe, but to pursue them all the way to the Middle East, there to destroy their power utterly. The curious, composite image of the 'griffon' could conceivably refer to the traditional lion-body of Britain, allied to the equally traditional eagle of Italy, of Germany, of Poland, of former Imperial France – even, perhaps, of the United States of America. The 'reds' and 'whites' are more difficult to identify: the reference could be either political or racial, or even of some other kind entirely: it seems unlikely that the 'reds' are to be identified with the already-mentioned post-invasion regimes in the south-west of France, unless they have been persuaded to switch sides in the interim as a result of the recent military campaign against them.

III.64   *The chief the Persian cargo-ships shall pack*
And send a war-fleet 'gainst the Muslim foes
From Persia. Then the Cyclades he'll sack
And in Ionian port take long repose.

In his efforts to perform his customary literary trick of repeating in the second half of the verse an idea first mooted in the first half, Nostradamus comes perilously near having his Persians attacked by Persians. In fact, however, what seems to have happened is that Henry has captured a large number of the oriental invaders' merchantmen, which he himself is now putting to good use as troopships and supply-vessels. As for the war-fleet itself, the *triremes* mentioned in line two of the French text would, to Nostradamus's contemporaries, simply have called up a picture of large, powerful, self-propelled warships. We should therefore interpret them in precisely the same terms. After routing the invaders – here picturesquely described as 'Medes and Parthians' – in the Greek islands, no doubt partly to sap their morale and partly to give himself some suitable jumping-off points for further expeditions, Henry retires to one of the safe ports on the Ionian sea, quite possibly Taranto in Italy, for recuperation and resupply.

VI.27
*Within the Isles where five streams join in one
'Gainst lunar crescent is great Henry ridden.
Through drizzle shall his single fury run.
Six shall escape, in flaxen bundles hidden.*

I have not so far been able to identify the island where five rivers
join, but the mention of 'drizzle' suggests once again that Henry
will have to face chemical weapons as he attacks one particular
Muslim fortress.

I.74
*Rested, on Western Greece they'll set their sights.
Deliverance next to Antioch they'll bring.
The king with black, curled beard for th' Empire
   fights.
Roasted shall be the copper-bearded king.*

At this point Nostradamus actually offers a physical description
of Henry, as well as of his doomed leading opponent. After a
pause for recuperation and resupply, a massive European
counter-attack is directed through the former Epirus – i.e.
Albania and western Greece – towards the Middle East. The site
of ancient Antioch is nowadays occupied by the Turkish town of
Antakya, some fifty miles west of Aleppo in Syria.

IX.75
*Far overseas in Arta and in Thrace
The French shall to a sick race aid assign
Who in Provence have long since left their trace
And of their laws and customs many a sign.*

In what Nostradamus sees as a kind of cultural reciprocation, France now brings aid and succour to Greece, the very nation that at one time settled and civilised ancient Provence itself, and which is still suffering the after-effects of the earlier earthquakes and catastrophic floods (see V.31, p. 127).

II.22   *Seaward from Europe sails th' amazing force:*
         The Northern fleet its battle-line deploys.
         Near isle submerged it sets a common course.
         The great world's centre yields to stronger voice.

Evidently the land campaign is to be accompanied by a huge sea-borne expedition as well, and the eventual result is destined to be a change of regime in the Middle East, and specifically in Jerusalem, traditionally the centre of the world. (This means that III.97, p. 45, could conceivably apply at this point, rather than referring to the re-establishment of Israel in 1948). The 'submerged island' is not identified, but in the light of III.64 (p. 240) the collapsed volcano of Santorini seems a good candidate.

VI.85   *By forces French shall mighty Tarsus be*
         Destroyed, all Muslims captured, led away –
         Helped by the mighty Portuguese at sea –
         When summer starts, on blessed Urban's day.

The invasion of Turkey continues, with further landings at Tarsus, only a few miles to the north-west of ancient Antioch.

IV.39   *For urgent help shall plead the Rhodian race,*
               By Muslim overlords long left to waste.
               The Arab forces shall their steps retrace.
               The Westerners shall put things right in haste.

The island of Rhodes is in need of special attention, its inhabitants having been badly neglected by the occupiers, rather like their counterparts in Sicily (see II.71, p. 222). Urgent humanitarian aid is provided by the incoming Europeans.

VI.21   *Once the north hemisphere as one assembles*
               The East shall be affrighted and dismayed.
               Its new-elected chief, supported, trembles.
               Byzantium, Rhodes with Arab blood are sprayed.

The Western counter-attack has a salutary effect on ruling circles in the East. The original overlord, as we saw, has either died or been killed. For all his successor's confidence as a result of being elected to office and perhaps spurred on by his allies, he is too shaken effectively to resist the furious Western onslaught, which has already advanced via the Greek islands as far as his own Middle Eastern doorstep.

II.70   *Through heaven the mighty missile forth shall go.*
               Death in mid-sentence everywhere is sown.
               Blasted the tree, a haughty race laid low,
               Alarums, omens, efforts to atone.

This verse seems to show how. Apparently some kind of missile is launched against the invaders' heartlands. Its effects are devastating, totally shaking the orientals' confidence. (It has to be said, though, that this verse is not specific as to the target: the sole clue is the phrase 'haughty race'.)

IX.43   *Ready to land, the Christian ships approach,*
While Arabs watch with dark, suspicious eyes.
On every side marauding ships encroach,
Ten chosen ones attacking by surprise.

More European ships now come ashore. Quite what Nostradamus means by his emphasis on their Christian nature, though, we shall possibly see in the next stanza.

VII.36   *God's Word at Istanbul shall come ashore*
With seven red shaven-heads, each one a chief.
Against their Graces Trabzon's fifteen score
Shall make two laws: first horror, then belief.

Incredibly, what now apparently follows is the arrival in the former Byzantium of a delegation of missionary cardinals, intent on converting the defeated Muslims to Christianity as it were by the sword – unless, of course, line three really means that they are themselves converted Asiatics. Understandably, the local inhabitants' first reaction is one of sheer horror. The missionaries are anathematised by the parliament currently meeting further east in Trabzon, whither it has fled from the European invaders. Yet, possibly in the light of the latter's newly acquired status as victors, the delegation actually starts to make converts.

II.79 *By skill he of the curly beard and black*
   The race both cruel and proud soon subjugates.
   Henry the Great from far away brings back
   All those still penned by Muslim prison-gates.

Henry, having pursued the invaders abroad, now subdues them in their heartlands, or at very least (it would seem) in the Middle East.

II.60 *Conspiracy collapses in the East.*
   Jordan, Rhône, Loire and Tagus changed shall be.
   When lust for riches shall at last have ceased,
   Fleet scattered, bodies float on bloody sea.

Thus it is that the Eastern alliance collapses, almost of its own accord, under continued pressure from the West. From the Middle East to Portugal (Nostradamus is particularly prone to refer to peoples by the names of their rivers) things are transformed. The invaders, having at last slaked their understandable thirst for the West's riches, either settle down or return home, leaving their military machine in ruins, and especially their naval wing. Here, in other words, Nostradamus seems to be describing the final petering out of the great Asiatic invasion-cum-migration: certainly little more is heard of it from now on. Other seers[14, 20] refer at this point to a great mingling of the races, just as Nostradamus himself, in his *Letter to Henri King of France the Second*, refers to a mingling of tongues (see the quotation at the beginning of this chapter).

As suggested previously, III.97 (p. 45), may likewise find its intended application at this point.

V.52   *A king there'll be who'll turn things upside down,*
          Placing the exiles high in men's esteem.
          The pure and chaste, once used in blood to drown,
          Long time shall flourish under such regime.

Unless it refers to a much later, millennial age, the original French suggests that Henry will place the exiles and returning refugees in positions of power, always tending to favour the underdog. Indeed, so often does Nostradamus use the term *exilés* throughout his writings as to suggest that refugees are likely to be a major feature of the world of the twenty-first century.

VI.70   *Lord over all great Henry is acclaimed,*
           Like Charles the Fifth himself feared and adored,
           Well pleased the only victor to be named.
           Heaven-high his fame and praise shall soon
              have soared.

Henry is now triumphant. Nostradamus likens him to the former Holy Roman Emperor Charles V.

Présage 41   *Bandits at large, much heat and searing drought:*
               In that there will be nothing new, at least.
               Abroad, the friendly hand too much held out:
               The land's new leader dazzles all the East.

At last, then, there is cause for hope. The new leader starts to conduct a brilliant *Ostpolitik* in which forgiveness figures prominently – rather more, in fact, than Nostradamus can stomach. The bandits, heat and drought of the first line may *sound* somewhat apocalyptic, but as Nostradamus points out, they do not need to be anything of the kind. Lawlessness and bad weather, as he nearly says, are always with us. Nevertheless, as later quatrains will suggest, there do seem to be some worrying meteorological phenomena about in southern Europe at this juncture – though whether they are connected with the earlier 'fire from the sky' episodes is not clear.

IV.86   *When in Aquarius sun with Saturn makes*
       Conjunction, shall the mighty king and great
       Received, anointed be at Reims and Aix:
       War won, he'll many wrongly immolate.

Henry now seals his triumph by resurrecting the ancient French monarchy and having himself crowned and anointed at Reims (where no less than six French kings were crowned during the Middle Ages) and – even more significantly – at Aix-la-Chapelle, where the former emperor Charlemagne was both crowned and buried. However, there are signs that he will start to over-estimate himself and take violent recriminations against many who were innocent of all crimes during the conflict. If, that is, I have not mis-sequenced this verse.

V.6   *On the king's head the Prophet lays his hand*
      Praying the while for peace in Italy.
      The sceptre changing then to his left hand,
      The King an Emperor of peace shall be.

Clearly we are still at Henry's coronation. The mention of Italy suggests that the 'Prophet' is a high cleric from Rome. At last, it would seem, war has all but come to an end.

X.73   *The present time and all that once transpired*
        The mighty man of God shall judge that day.
        But in the end they'll all of him grow tired,
        And legal-minded priests shall him betray.

The cleric in question is evidently a charismatic character. One
has the feeling that he will endeavour to refound the Church on
new bases that go much nearer to the heart of true religion than
much that has passed for it previously. In this, however, his
efforts will be subverted by the surviving priesthood, who (predictably perhaps) would much rather return to the old theocratic
bureaucracy and its worn-out doctrines in which their power
formerly resided.

IV.34   *The mighty captive's summoned from abroad*
        Before King Henry chained with gold embossed;
        His host entire put to the flames and sword,
        Italy's war, Milan's great battle lost.

As a final act of victory, the supreme leader of the whole Asiatic
campaign – or, at very least, of that in Italy – is brought captive
before the new king in his ceremonial regalia to eat humble pie.
The last two lines evidently refer not to current events, but to the
history of his defeat.

IV.77   *Araby conquered, Italy at peace,*
        A Christian king a world at one shall rule.
        Near Blois he'll wish to rest at his decease,
        Once he has freed the seas of brigands cruel.

With only a few mopping-up operations still to complete, Henry has evidently become the pre-eminent world leader. Indeed, Nostradamus makes him sound distinctly Messiah-like (thus possibly giving rise to the persistent French royalist tradition to that very effect). Now he can contemplate his own old age and death. He would, he decides, like to be buried in or near his ancestral city of Blois, former haunt and alternative capital of the French kings. The decision seems apt.

V.79   *All sacred pomp its wings shall soon abase*
        Once the great legislator starts his reign.
        He'll raise the lowly, far the rebels chase.
        None like him shall be born on earth again.

Once again Nostradamus makes Henry sound distinctly Messianic – unless of course this verse really refers to the later Millennium itself, some eight hundred years in the future.

IX.66   *Peace there shall be, unity, many a change;*
        Those that were high brought low and low
        *   raised high;*
        The first fruit's torment travel to arrange,
        To stop all war, cases at law to try.

But re-laying the foundations of a new civilisation is never easy. There is much administrative work to be done.

II.95   *Where once lived crowds, now nobody can live.*
          The fields must be re-marked and redefined.
          Kingdoms to wise incompetents they'll give.
          Great brothers dead, can feuds be far behind?

Conditions, indeed, are decidedly difficult. The war has evidently
had dreadful environmental effects. While some areas are un-
cultivable, others are merely deserted. Even leaders of the stature
of 'Hercules' and Henry will find such conditions hard enough to
cope with. How much harder, then, will they seem to their less
charismatic successors!

IV.20   *Long time the place shall reap abundant peace:*
          Through all its desert realm lilies shall blow.
          Thither they'll bring the dead o'er land and seas
          Who hoped 'gainst hope there to their graves to go.

At the same time there will be a rather touching episode, as the
bodies of former refugees are brought back to be buried in their
still-deserted homelands.

II.19   *The newcomers shall find towns undefended*
          And people lands that none till now could fill.
          Famine, plague, war; then acres to be tended.
          Meadows, fields, houses, towns they'll take at will.

Inevitably there will be further squabbles over land rights in these
areas, but only between the settlers themselves. In all other
respects they will be taking over virtually virgin country.

III.26   *Of kings and princes icons they'll adorn*
         And empty auguries hold up to view.
         Gilded and azure-tipped the victim's horn.
         The oracles shall be explained anew.

In this verse, meanwhile, Nostradamus seems to predict a rise in
public credulity and idolatry – idolatry of their leaders in the
form of the so-called 'personality cult', credulity in the form of a
return to a form of ritualistic paganism with a pronounced
emphasis on 'reading the entrails'. Of recent years we have seen
both, and the latter especially seems set to continue for a good
while yet, if not actually to increase, mainly via the medium of
what is loosely described as the New Age movement. In the last
line Nostradamus even seems to be predicting the appearance of
books such as this. Possibly, though, he is really referring to the
final decoding of his prophecies, which he himself elsewhere
(III.94, p. 271) dates to five hundred years after the publication of
his first edition – i.e. around the year 2055. At least, though, he is
describing what are essentially peaceful, rather than warlike
pursuits. This in itself has to be a sign of hope for the future.

V.77   *All the degrees of honour in the church*
       For Jovial Quirinus they'll revise.
       To Mars Quirinal priests berobed shall lurch,
       Till France's monarch shall them Vulcanise.

The new lurch towards paganism is not popular with the reigning
establishment, and it eventually takes vigorous steps to stamp it
out.

III.76   *In Germany strange sects shall come to be*
That almost shall the happy pagan play.
Captive their hearts, but little gain they'll see.
They shall return their proper tithes to pay.

The delights of the flirtation with paganism, however – especially in Germany – will eventually start to pall in any case, and there will be a widespread return to mainstream religion.

II.8   *Of churches hallowed in old Roman manner*
They shall reject the very fundaments,
Making base-principles their human banner
At many a former saintly cult's expense.

Nevertheless, the return to mainstream religion is destined to be based not on received practice, but on a return to Christian first principles – i.e. the simple, homespun practices of the early Church. The whole, complex edifice of traditional Roman Catholicism is likely to be severely shaken, even though some of its major saintly cults are likely to survive, reflecting as they do some very deep, even pre-Christian instincts within the human psyche.

X.6   *At Nîmes shall Gardon's river flood so high*
That they shall think Deucalion returns.
Into the colosseum most shall fly.
In vestal tomb fire once-extinguished burns.

Nothing is ever perfect, however, and at some stage severe weather hits the south of France. Serious flooding results:

Deucalion, after all, was the ancient Greek equivalent of the biblical Noah. The local populace take refuge in the famous amphitheatre. On the other hand, even disasters such as this can have their bright side, as line four and the succeeding stanzas go on to reveal.

V.66   *Beneath the ancient vestal buildings deep*
        Not far from ruined aqueduct so old
        Like sun and moon still-shiny metals sleep
        And burning Trojan lamp engraved in gold.

Possibly as a result of the flooding (not for the first time) some remarkable discoveries are unearthed – in this case an ancient vault containing what (despite line four of the foregoing verse) seems to be an ever-burning lamp. The details confirm that the discovery will indeed take place at Nîmes, where the convent of St Sauveur-de-la-Fontaine is built on the site of an ancient temple to Diana. Rather than being 'Trojan' (the conventional interpretation), the lamp may in fact date from the reign of Trajan – which is the word that Nostradamus actually writes.

IX.9   *When shall be found the lamp that's ever-living,*
        Hidden beneath the vestal temple's walls
        (The flame found by a child through water sieving),
        Flood destroy Nîmes; down fall Toulouse's halls.

Whether the floods really lead to the discovery, or the discovery merely presages the floods, is not entirely clear from this verse. But then not much of Nostradamus ever is. Probably, though, the former is the correct explanation.

IX.37   *Bridges and mills December shall throw down:*
        So high the torrent of Garonne shall race,
        Buildings and halls throughout Toulouse's town
        Destroyed: scarce should an old girl know the place.

What *is* clear, however, is that the flooding will be extra-ordinarily severe at the time, not merely at Nîmes, but in south-western France too.

VIII.30   *Not far from digger's scoop within Toulouse,*
          Excavating a palais de spectacles,
          A treasure's found that all shall sore bemuse
          In caches twain quite near to the Basacle.

Perhaps it is during the course of reconstruction work that yet further valuable archaeological discoveries are made. Certainly the *Basacle* is the name of the former mill area of the city, as well of the castle that protects it – and Nostradamus specifically mentions damage to mills in IX.37, immediately above.

VIII.29   *By Saint-Sernin's fourth pillar shall be found*
          (Split by a 'quake when floods are at the door)
          The pot beneath the building underground
          Of Caepio's stolen gold; then handed o'er.

Indeed, Toulouse is destined to yield up even more treasures, this time under the celebrated basilica of Saint-Sernin. Caepio, the Roman consul who sacked Toulouse in 106 BC, somehow man-aged to mislay the treasures he 'liberated' there, carefully ensuring that they never reached Rome. In consequence, he was impeached and sacked from the Senate. If Nostradamus is right, the floods will at last find him out and reveal just where he hid them.

IX.12   *So many silver images are found*
            Of Hermes and Diana in the lake
            By potter seeking new clay underground
            As him and his rich beyond dreams to make.

Meanwhile, back at the convent ... As ever, Nostradamus invokes a double image: in the original, immersion in water has its golden counterpart. Could it be his way of suggesting that every cloud has its silver lining? And can the discovery of new riches underground itself be symbolic of what humanity is now destined to discover deep within its own psyche?

X.89   *Brick walls they shall in marble reconstruct:*
           Of peace seven years and fifty shall there be.
           For humans, joy; rebuilt each aquaduct;
           Health, honeyed times and rich fecundity.

As the crumbling post-war ruins are replaced with white, wooden buildings, possibly in concrete, at last the picture is definitely one of full recovery and prosperity which will last for over half a century. True, this very fact means that the world – or Europe, at least – is eventually likely to be overtaken by war once again. But then it is relatively rare for peace to last even that long, so presumably humanity will have to be thankful for small mercies. Certainly a long era of unprecedented conflict for the Mediterranean area and Western Europe will at last have come to an end, and humanity can look forward to a period of some centuries during which the world may not always be nice, but whose major problems and triumphs are at least likely to be of a very different order from anything than has ever been experienced before.

6

INTO THE FAR FUTURE

Both soon and late you shall see changes great.
Vast horrors, vengeance cruel the signs portend,
While moon, on whom her angel-guide shall wait,
In highest heaven her angles shall subtend.

Centuries: I.56

As was ever the case, the exact sequence of Nostradamus's predictions cannot easily be established very far in advance. The nearer the events referred to, the more it becomes possible to refine the sequence. Nevertheless, 100 per cent reliability can never be claimed until afterwards – and sometimes not even then. The order of the predictions listed in the foregoing chapters may thus still be susceptible of improvement. As far as those applying to the far future are concerned, however, the exact sequence can as yet be projected only very approximately indeed.

Even so, there are certain characteristics which do permit a rough ordering of the remaining material, and it is that fact that has informed the sequence presented in this chapter, which consequently represents my own best estimate of Nostradamus's picture of the lead-up to the distant Millennium.

What is perhaps most noteworthy about these last predictions is possibly their broad generality and lack of specific detail, almost as though after the traumas and triumphs of the twenty-first century the world will be so changed as to be virtually unrecognisable, even to Nostradamus . . .

I.63   *The woes once past, the world shall smaller grow:*
With lands unpeopled, peace shall long survive.
Through sky, o'er land and sea they'll safely go.
Then once again shall ghastly war revive.

After the various disasters of the foregoing forty years or so there will, it seems be a long period of peace and progress. Not that the first line should necessarily be seen (as some commentators would have us believe) as a direct prediction of improved communications links, even though Nostradamus certainly foresees routine air travel: it is just that the population of parts of Europe especially will have been so reduced by war, famine and disease — possibly in that order — that there will be little incentive to fight, and even fewer people left to do it. Whole areas, in fact will be deserted or — as Nostradamus puts it — *inhabitées* (far from meaning 'inhabited', as might appear at first sight, the French word in fact means '*un*inhabited'). Italy and France in particular may suffer in this way. Only after this prolonged peaceful era will the final woes eventually return that are to lead up to the final change of cycle.

V.32   *Where all is well 'neath sun and moon and star*
'Midst great abundance comes your ruin near.
E'en while you boast how fortunate you are
Like John's seventh stone from heaven it
*   shall appear.*

If Nostradamus is to be believed, the first sign that the era of peace and abundance is about to end will be the appearance from the heavens of some kind of cometary body that will burn like the seventh stone of St John's Revelation in the Bible, which is described in terms of chrysolite, golden topaz or yellow olivine. Possibly, then, we are here brought face to face with the return of comet Swift-Tuttle in the year 2126. If not, then some other heavenly body is apparently destined to collide with the earth, bringing ruin to the more prosperous parts of the world particularly.

II.45   *Too much high heaven the Androgyne bewails.*
New-born aloft the sky where blood is sprayed.
Too late that death a mighty race avails.
Sooner or later comes the hoped-for aid.

This mysterious stanza could mean almost anything. Who is the newly-born sexless being so mourned by the celestial powers – and who, for that matter, are they? Why is human blood shed either in the upper air or even in space itself? If the Androgyne's death is designed somehow to revivify the race, why is it too late? And is the hoped-for aid an extraterrestrial saviour or merely some kind of earthly succour? Certainly the extraterrestrial explanation seems particularly seductive. It is as though a would-be helper from space has been bloodily repulsed and so prevented from carrying out some kind of redemptive mission to Planet Earth. One is reminded of Marlowe's extraordinary line in *Doctor Faustus*:

See, see where Christ's blood streams in the firmament!

Nevertheless, yet further redemptive initiatives of similar type will apparently be attempted.

X.99   *No more lies wolf with ox or lion with ass:*
The timid deer is cast among the pack.
No more shall gentle manna fall, alas!
For vigilance and care the mastiffs lack.

In vague, misty terms Nostradamus now foreshadows a future time when the former order and prosperity will once again start to break down. His use of semi-biblical metaphor suggests that he associates this development with the far future, while in his last line he actually hints that more vigilance on humanity's part could still keep the decline in check.

I.44   *Soon shall the slaughter once again return.*
Those who resist are laid upon the racks.
No abbots, monks, no novices to learn:
Honey shall cost far more than candle-wax.

In particular, Nostradamus foresees an era of renewed brutality, with religion once again repressed. In association with this he also seems to foreshadow increasing inflation, particularly where the price of food is concerned. This in turn could suggest that food shortages will be starting to be experienced.

IV.67   *When Mars and Saturn equally shall burn*
The dried-up winds shall blow those countries o'er.
To ashes hidden fires great swathes shall turn.
Scarce rain, hot winds there'll be, then raids
*   and war.*

Possibly we have here the reason why. A period of severe drought commences. The 'secret fires' with which it is associated could refer either to fires that nobody notices, or to some kind of underground combustion or radiation. In the latter case one wonders whether there could be any connection with the former fire-weapon wielded by the former Asiatic invaders in south-western France particularly. Nostradamus, after all, does not suggest that the drought will be a world-wide phenomenon. The consequent food shortages meanwhile lead, as ever, to skirmishes and conflict.

I.67   *The mighty famine whose approach I feel*
First comes and goes, then reigns from east to west.
So great, so long it is that they shall steal
From trees their roots, babes from their mother's
    breast.

Once again the theme of food shortages surfaces, with the last line indicating the dire extent of the anticipated problem – though just how literally we should take the suggested cannibalistic element, or how broad a spectrum of people or nationalities the word 'they' (*on*) is meant to cover is uncertain. Although neither in this stanza nor in the one above are time or place specified, it is clear that Nostradamus sees food shortages – already starkly apparent even in our own day – eventually becoming world-wide, very much in line with the famines predicted by the biblical 'little apocalypse' of Matthew 24. Nor does this seem at all unlikely on present estimates, bearing in mind the world's rapidly rising population, spreading desertification and the possible effects of atmospheric pollution. The answers, in other words, lie (as ever) largely in our own hands. One way or the other, then, Nostradamus's quatrain deserves to be taken as a dire warning to us. Such was ever the role of the true prophet.

II.75 *The voice of an unwonted bird is heard*
On cruel cannon and on winding stair:
So high the price of wheat, that man is stirred
His fellow man to eat in his despair.

In this somewhat obscure verse Nostradamus once again fore-tells eventual food shortages, rampant inflation and their almost inevitable effects. The 'unwonted bird' image (not 'un*want*ed bird' as some versions have it)[4] is also to be found in the *Letter to Henri II*. Whether the 'man eats man' description is meant to be taken literally or merely figuratively is not clear: it is, after all, highly unusual for starving people to experience the urge to eat each other, still less to give way to it. No date is suggested, but this quatrain, like the one above, has the feel of events that still lie far in the future.

III.5 *When heaven its two lights' long default prepares*
('Twixt March and April shall that time befall),
How costly! Yet two mighty debonairs
By land and sea shall succour bring to all.

By the 'two great luminaries' mentioned in the original text, Nostradamus is apparently referring to the 'two great lights' of the Genesis creation-account which are set in the firmament to rule the day and night – i.e. the sun and moon. Their 'default' would appear to refer to their expected disappearance just prior to the advent of the Kingdom of Heaven on earth, as predicted by Jesus himself at Matthew 24: 29 (albeit on the basis of the earlier, Old Testament prophecies):

As soon as the woes of those days are past, the sun shall be darkened, the moon shall not give her light, the stars shall fall from heaven and the powers of heaven shall be shaken.

We may speculate on the true reasons for the extraordinary phenomenon: the most obvious explanation would be severe atmospheric pollution, however caused (in probable order of likelihood, volcanic eruptions and industrial smog: it is quite unnecessary for us to think in terms of nuclear winter). However, Nostradamus brings two new variables into the equation. First, he actually attempts to date the early signs of this event – even though not to any particular year. And second, he foresees some measure of hope, in that what are probably two benevolent world powers (unless they are another reference to the presumed celestial powers or extraterrestrials of II.45, p. 259) will do their utmost to bring emergency relief to those most affected by the ensuing food shortages and consequent explosive inflation as the crisis closes in.

III.4   *Ere sun and moon cease their appointed work*
When distant but in minuscule degree
Cold, drought and peril near the borders lurk,
E'en where the oracle first came to be.

Despite attempts by commentators to make Nostradamus's word *lunaires* refer to present-day Muslim countries by virtue of the crescent moon on their flag, the similarity of wording makes it overwhelmingly probable that this quatrain is linked (unusually) to its direct successor, and that the word is actually a Nostradamian compression of the word *luminaires*. The prediction, in other words, refers to the same phenomenon as in III.5, above. The inevitable consequence of the masking of sun and moon by cloud and/or smoke in the upper atmosphere would indeed be cold – and possibly drought, too, as a result of a severe reduction in solar heating and a consequent weakening of the earth's weather systems. There seems, however, to be the probability of special danger 'near the borders', which might perhaps suggest (not unreasonably) that armed forays into neighbouring countries in search of food are likely to follow. The last line looks like an attempt by the seer to pinpoint the area where the problem is likely to be felt most acutely. Unfortunately, though, he does not state which 'oracle' he means. The natural interpretation would suggest Delphi in Greece, but he could as easily be referring to his own birthplace in southern France.

III.34   *When heavenly sun no further beams shall shed,*
In daylight broad the monster shall appear.
In many different ways interpreted,
None shall support it, lest it cost them dear.

Nostradamus makes no attempt to explain this mysterious omen or apparition, be it extraterrestrial or otherwise: I should be foolish to attempt to do so either.

I.91   *The gods to men shall make it fully clear*
How of the mighty war they'll be the source.
Before the sky shall clear shall sword and spear
To leftward turn with even greater force.

Line three suggests that this quatrain belongs not long after III.4 and III.5 (pp. 262, 263), when the skies are at long last showing signs of clearing again, and the earth's people have consequently started to resume their old, unregenerate ways. However, the syntax is more than a little woolly. It may suggest that everything is literally in the lap of the gods, in which case there is nothing to be done. Equally, though, it may be suggesting that humanity is the ultimate source of its own woes. In the words of Shakespeare's Cassius in *Julius Caesar*,

> *The fault, dear Brutus, is not in our stars,*
> *But in ourselves.*

The message – if message it consequently is – may seem gloomy, but it is in fact potentially a highly positive one. If we are the source of our own woes, then clearly we have it within us to be the source of our own salvation, too. Whether this prediction, like those before and after it, is ever fulfilled thus depends very largely on what we choose to do about it. Nothing, it seems, is irrevocable. Everything, though, hinges in this case on just who the 'gods' in the first line are meant to be. Ufologists and Erich von Däniken, for example, will naturally assume that they are once again extraterrestrials. Who knows, they may even be right.

I.17   *Full forty years no rainbow they shall know,*
   Then forty years shall it be seen each day.
   First arid land shall yet more arid grow:
   Then mighty floods there'll be, shine though it may.

Evidently the weather will be no less contrary in the future than ever it was. Forty years of sunless and consequently rainbowless drought will be followed by forty years of rain and floods.

VI.5   *A wave of plague shall bring so great a dearth*
   While ceaseless rains the Arctic Pole shall sweep:
   Samarobryn, a hundred leagues from earth,
   Law-free themselves from politics shall keep.

The last two lines of this extraordinary prediction appear to describe some kind of space-station a hundred French leagues (i.e. 276.4 miles) above the earth's surface – at almost exactly the orbital altitude, in fact, of the former American Skylab, and only slightly above that of the Soviet Mir. Yet the name proposed is neither Skylab nor Mir, but 'Samarobryn'. This ominous-sounding term (which Nostradamus treats as a *plural*, incidentally) has long puzzled commentators, yet astonishingly enough it seems to be directly related to the Russian words *samo* ('self') and *robotnik* ('worker') – almost as if to indicate that the orbiting space-stations are not only Russian, but in some way autonomous. The space-crew seem to be supranational – though the law from whose effects they are immune (whether or not Nostradamus realised the fact) could well be no more than the law of gravity. This would tend to place them a good many years – perhaps even decades or centuries – in the future. The first two lines, meanwhile, suggest that some kind of major epidemic will be sweeping the northern hemisphere at the time, accompanied by the 'long rains' which in Nostradamus's own day certainly tended to produce outbreaks of the familiar plague by flushing the rats from their dens, and which seem also to have been predicted in the preceding quatrain.

II.46   *The wheel's great Mover turns the wheel again:*
One cycle done, a greater is at hand.
Famine, war, plague and bloody, milky rain.
Fire across heaven shall trail its blazing brand.

Here at last Nostradamus approaches the advent of the Millennium itself. True, by wildly misrepresenting the word *troche* (see 'Academic Notes'), commentators commonly interpret line one (transposed with line two in my version) to indicate nuclear Armageddon and all manner of other monstrosities. Fortunately, though, this line of the text at least is totally innocent of all such suggestions. As for the last two lines, care needs to be taken in reading them at face value: clearly they are so closely based on the biblical Apocalypse as to raise serious doubts about their validity under the terms of prophetic Law 3 (p. 20). The 'bloody, milky rain' is perhaps something of an oddity, though Nostradamus does use such images elsewhere (II.32, III.18, III.19 and possibly VIII.77 – see pp. 84, 178, 103, 58). Certainly reddened or milky raindrops are not unknown under certain weather conditions. On the other hand, *pluye, sang, laict* could, in context, simply be Nostradamian code for *pluie sans (re)lâche*, 'never-ending rain' – possibly a further reference to the 'long rains' mentioned in the two predictions just quoted. This time, however, the heavenly fire does seem to represent the long-predicted great star of the Apocalypse (Rev. 8: 10–11): indeed, the fact could conceivably help 'date' the quatrain, since Halley's comet (if such it turns out to be) is due to return in around the year 2822, only six years or so before Nostradamus's date for the inception of the Millennium.

IX.83   *Twenty degrees of Taurus – thus the sun –*
The crowded theatre shall an earthquake strike.
Air, sky and sea it shall disturb, turn dun.
Faithless, they'll call on God and saints alike!

In the month of May, seismic events are, it seems, destined to strike some at least of humanity at the very moment when ultimate events are furthest from their minds. Even those who have long forgotten their religion are suddenly inspired to return to it.

X.74   *When turns at last the mighty number seven,*
At time of Ritual Games it shall be found
Not long before earth cedes its sway to heaven
That those long dead are rising from the ground.

Possibly this verse refers to the same occasion. But there is more to it than a mere earthquake. Once again leaning heavily on familiar biblical eschatology, Nostradamus is here clearly referring to the expected general resurrection of the dead prior to the inception of the Millennium – however bizarre the whole notion may nowadays seem to us, and however we may choose to understand it in rational terms (readers are gently reminded at this point of the operation of prophetic Law 8 on page 20). What is particularly interesting, however, is that he chooses to link it with two predictive features of his own. First, he ties it in chronologically with what, in the original French, he calls the 'Hecatombic (i.e. sacrificial) Games' – possibly some future form of the Olympics. At the same time he actually puts a date on it. This culminating event for the current world order will, it seems, take place at the end of the seventh millennium – i.e. according to Nostradamus's version of biblical chronology, in or around the year AD 2827/8 (see I.48, p. 270). Interestingly enough, Mario de Sabato, too, predicts the beginning of an entirely new world order in around 2800,[20] while the Great Pyramid of Giza itself seems to date the beginning of the Millennium to July of AD 2989.[14] Nostradamus's whole prediction, in fact, is an odd and – it has to be said in the light of prophetic Law 3 – rather unpromising mixture of the expected and the foreseen, and only time will tell just how successful it turns out to be.

II.13   *The soulless corpse shall never suffer more:*
The day of death leads on to birth anew.
The Holy Ghost its rapture shall restore
As soul th' eternal Word shall plainly view.

Indeed, the Millennium he foresees looks to be very much a spiritual, rather than blood-and-guts affair – more earth-in-heaven, it could be said, than heaven-on-earth. Possibly this is a reflection of St Paul's anticipated spiritual universe, which in turn mirrors the ancient Essenes' view of the matter. Certainly it reflects standard Christian dogma – for all the latter's evident contradiction of Old Testament and gospel teaching, and not least of the Lord's Prayer itself, with its clear injunction:

> *Thy Kingdom come . . .*
> *On earth as it is in heaven.*

Once again, therefore, we should do well to be suspicious of taking on board too uncritically what appear to be more in the nature of conditioned Nostradamian expectations than actual Nostradamian visions. Better by far, it might be thought, for Nostradamus to stick to his last: he may have been a prophet, but that is not at all the same thing as being a theologian, let alone a reliable one.

III.2 *The Word Divine shall grant to substance crude*
All heaven and earth, all mystic gold occult.
To body, spirit, soul all power accrued
O'er earth and heaven – such is the great result.

Thus it is that Nostradamus now sees as his ultimate vision a universe in which heaven and earth are one, man has achieved ultimate union with the divine and all humanity's great ideals – religious, alchemical and, it has to be said, political too – are finally attained.

V.53 *The laws of Sun and Venus disagree*
Touching which shall true prophecy inspire.
Never the twain shall in agreement be.
The solar law follows the great Messiah.

Finally, Nostradamus turns his attention to prophecy itself and its fulfilment. There are, it seems, two prophetic paths – possibly the male and the female – of which the Messiah himself is destined to pursue the solar one. This might imply that Nostradamus himself claims to adhere to it, too.

I.48 *These twenty years the moon pursues her reign.*
    Till year seven thousand then another's crowned.
    Ere next the sun takes up his course again
    My words their last fulfilment shall have found.

This is perhaps Nostradamus's culminating prediction: all his prophecies, he claims, will have come true by the year seven thousand – seven thousand years, that is, after the biblical Creation. Since, in his *Letter to Henri King of France the Second*, he dates this event at 4173 years before the birth of Christ, it follows that his 'seventh millennium' will end in AD 2827/8. (Mathematicians please note: there was never a 'Year 0', since under the present system, devised by Dionysus Exiguus in the sixth century of our own era, 1 BC – the 'first year before Christ' – is followed immediately by AD 1 – the first 'year of our Lord'. On the other hand, in terms of the rest of the datings since established by the same system, it turns out that Jesus of Nazareth was probably born in the autumn of what we now call 2 BC.[14] The overall effect, then, is to leave the mathematical calculation more or less as it was, give or take four months or so.) The first line, meanwhile, apparently dates the quatrain itself to 1555, the year of its first publication, since according to Roussat and others[3, 11] the last great astrological lunar cycle lasted from 1535 to 1889.

7

FOREWARNED IS FOREARMED

Five hundred years, then more heed they shall take
Of him who was the jewel of his age.
Suddenly then shall light resplendent break
Such as that time's approval to engage.

Centuries: III.94 ·

NEVER A MAN FOR FALSE MODESTY, it was with these glowing words — apparently about himself — that Nostradamus seems to have predicted the final triumph of his predictions and their recognition by society at large by about the year 2055. This would suggest that most of the major ones will have come true by then, so making their acceptance virtually inevitable, even by the sceptics.

Perhaps, indeed, that is what it will take to bring about such an unlikely volte-face. Until they are actually borne out, certainly, most of Nostradamus's predictions seem improbable, to say the least — and all the more so for his own apparent suggestion, oft repeated, that a good many of them are not in fact inevitable at all. Much, it seems, will hinge on our reactions to events, as well as on our responses to the predictions themselves.

History repeats itself

Thus, we need to be constantly alive to the fact that some of the supposed 'future' prophecies may already have been fulfilled, whether in whole or in part. Europe and North Africa, after all, have already long since been invaded from the East by Muslim forces via Constantinople. To a greater or lesser extent, the Ottoman occupation lasted over four hundred years from around 1453, and its dire consequences in terms of religious and ethnic conflict still persist even today, especially in the Balkans. Nostradamus himself referred to it repeatedly, naming not only his own contemporary, the Ottoman Sultan Selim I, but also his successor on the Peacock Throne, Suleiman the Magnificent – both directly as *Soliman* and via the anagram *(L')Ogmios* (presumably intended to be read as 'Solimog'), which was itself the name of the eloquent Gallic god corresponding to the classical Hercules . . .

Again, the popes have long since fulfilled Nostradamus's predictions by fleeing Rome for the valley of the Rhône. During the fourteenth century the French popes remained there for nearly seventy years. Their palace at Avignon still survives. Even when they returned to the Vatican, the French papacy continued, leading to an extraordinary situation in which there were two popes at once. These were (and still are) referred to as the pope and the anti-pope, so ringing suggestive bells in the minds of those who can think of nothing but apocalypses and Antichrists. A later pope, too, was held captive by Napoleon at Valence, where he subsequently died, though apparently of natural causes.

Meanwhile, in Napoleon himself, together with Hitler and Stalin, we have already had three anti-Christian dictators who, in some people's minds at least, have amply merited Nostradamus's title of 'Antichrist' without even having had the decency to wait for the end of the age.

Thus, oriental invasions, papal shenanigans and even Antichrists are nothing new. Neither are bloody times generally. There have been plenty of them in the past, and no doubt there will be plenty more in the future, too. Human nature – for-

272

tunately or unfortunately – does not change. It is not entirely unlikely, consequently, that the darker themes of history will tend to resurface repeatedly in the future, much in the way that Nostradamus's predictions seem to suggest, right up until the dawning of whatever Millennium eventually arrives. Nostradamus, apparently like King Solomon – to say nothing of the Hindus and Buddhists – believed as much both implicitly and explicitly.

Blaming the messenger

In reporting the fact, however, we may be accused of spreading only bad news, of actually creating the future that we most dread under the terms of prophetic Law 4 (p. 20). But then when was news ever other than predominantly bad? The retrospective equivalent of Nostradamus's predictions, after all, would be thirteen hundred years of newspapers. Can anyone imagine how much bad news *they* would contain? As for the accusation of creating the dark times by the very act of anticipating them, it needs to be said that the deed has been done long since. Blame the Bible, even blame Nostradamus if you must – notwithstanding the fact that it sounds suspiciously like blaming the messenger for the message. (Ask yourself, too, how Nostradamus can possibly be blamed for the effects of a prophetic message that until now nobody has fully understood.) But it is too late now to blame me, or indeed any other translator or commentator, for the coming Asiatic invasion, if come indeed it does. The prophetic wheels, if such they were, were set spinning long centuries ago, and whether in Central Asia, the Middle East or the former Yugoslavia their political and social counterparts are already stirring into motion quite independently of anything that I or anybody else can now do about it – as even the most casual glance at *today's* newspapers will soon confirm.

Prophecy's fourth law demands time to take effect. Without it, it is impotent. For years the would-be commentators, after all, have been using Nostradamus to predict nuclear Armageddon and a third world war involving the Soviet Union, the Warsaw Pact and West Germany, yet nothing of the kind has ever happened. Moreover, there is virtually no chance now that it will. Not only has there been insufficient time for the predictions to exert their spell: the proposed participants no longer exist to fulfil the predictions in the first place. Where circumstances do not allow, in other words, the law of self-fulfilment simply cannot operate. Even the fourth law demands *some* semblance of reality to work on.

But if it is too late now to blame interpreters such as myself for the bad times to come, there is plenty of time yet for the laws of prophecy to bring about the good times that I also anticipate for the distant future on the basis of Nostradamus's prophecies, once the great invasion and war is over at long last. Blame me for that, then, if you like.

Changing human consciousness

Questions of blame aside, though, it actually seems quite likely that past events will indeed have their future counterparts, quite independently of whether they are predicted or not – and that these, as is the way of things, will be even bigger and better (or worse) than before. Possibly this is because the human consciousness that produces them will be the same old human consciousness as before. If so, then the only reliable way to prevent them will be to change human consciousness, not to attempt to muzzle either the prophets or their interpreters.

And would-be missionaries should bear in mind that this means changing *their* consciousness, not somebody else's.

The case for Nostradamus

Whether Nostradamus's predictions will turn out accurately to have reflected those forthcoming events is a moot point. But it is difficult to deny that, while his verses often do have a distinct air of *déjà vu* about them, they also contain a large element that has no relevance to past events at all. They speak of air travel. They have the Asiatic invaders of Europe also moving into Persia, as well as overrunning Italy and France. They hint at the use of particularly nasty aerial weapons. They all but name Polaris and

Trident. They spell out in enormous detail the various stages of a campaign in Western Europe that has no historical counterpart. They even set out some sort of time-scale for the conflict which seems to have no relevance to history.

In all these respects, then, those of Nostradamus's prophecies that clearly do not refer to the past still remain unfulfilled. At the same time they are remarkably detailed and consistent, constantly tying in one with the other. As a result they must for the most part either stand or fall together. All in all, then, these facts have to mean one of two things. Either the still-outstanding prophecies of Nostradamus are likely to be fulfilled in the future, more or less *en bloc*, or they are just plain wrong for page after page after page. This last point cannot just be glossed over. We have already seen that he can indeed get his detailed facts wrong – even back to front. We know that he tends to confuse human motivations and exaggerate apocalyptic events. We are fully cognisant of his tendency to write in riddles capable of more than one interpretation.

But that Nostradamus could be so utterly and comprehensively wrong as to make a major part of his opus totally inapplicable to the future it purports to describe does seem – in the light of such past accuracy as is grudgingly allowed him even by his critics – distinctly unlikely. Had he predicted an Asiatic invasion in only one or two verses here and there, it might conceivably be possible for us to accuse him of a momentary aberration, or to explain any isolated successes in this area as mere flashes in the pan. But he did not. He went on and on about it, repeatedly and in the most sickening detail. Either, consequently, he was a deluded obsessive who was wrong more often than he was right – or we have at least to consider seriously the possibility that there may be something in his predictions.

What can we do about it?

Perhaps, indeed, that was all that he intended. If, after all, those predictions are not by any means all inevitable, then our own reactions are actually important. We still have some choice in the

275

matter. We can ensure that our own thoughts and actions are not such as to bring about the events that we most wish to avoid. We can encourage our religious activists – whether Muslim or Christian in this case – to exercise mutual respect and tolerance. We can look out for advance warning signs of the events predicted. We can choose where to live, carefully avoiding the areas likely to be worst affected (a good many of Nostradamus's predictions, it is worth remembering, are clearly designed to warn local inhabitants). We can lean on our politicians to adopt suitably prophylactic policies, draw up tentative contingency plans, and respond appropriately if and when events do swing into motion. We can urge our military authorities to take suitable precautions of a fairly generalised kind. In our own homes (if we are lucky enough to have them), we can make ourselves less vulnerable to social disruption by assuring our own fuel supplies, reducing our energy requirements, adopting alternative energy sources, preserving our more primitive forms of heating and lighting, growing more of our own food, retaining our old hand- and foot-operated machines, and learning once again how to make do and mend and practise recycling in every area of our lives. Forewarned, as they say, is forearmed. And if, in the event, Nostradamus were to prove to be as wrong as he would have to be to render such precautions unnecessary, perhaps the resulting benefits for our planetary environment would not be such a high price to pay after all.

Dead prophet, then, or dead loss? Only time will tell. But if the critics really want to prove Nostradamus as wrong as they would have him be, then the best way for them to do it is not merely to *say* as much, citing in evidence the distinctly unpersuasive fact that he offends their theoretical presuppositions. Instead, they need to *prove* as much in terms of actual practice – to take a variety of steps, in other words, designed either to make the fulfilment of his predictions impossible or to mitigate their effects should they ever dare to occur. Then they could quite reasonably say 'I told you so'.

And I have no doubt that Nostradamus, for his part, would be the last to object.

ACADEMIC NOTES

Centuries

(References are to the 1568 edition)

I 1 *l.2* *seul* = s[on] oeil
    l.4 *psperer* = prospérer
I 9 *l.2* *Hadrie*, 'the Adriatic'
    les hoirs (O.Fr., 'heirs')
    Romulides, 'the heirs of
    Romulus': thus, 'the
    Italians'
    l.3 *classe* ⟨ Lat. *classis*, 'fleet'
    l.4 *Mellites* ⟨ Grk. *Melite*, 'Malta'
I 11 *l.3* *glaives* ⟨ Lat. *gladius*, 'sword':
standard Nostradamian term for 'war'
I 15 *l.3* *auge* ⟨ Lat. *augere*, 'to
increase, augment'
I 16 *l.4* *siecle* (⟨ Lat. *saeculum*,
'generation') = cycle
I 17 *l.1* *l'Iris* (⟨ Grk.), 'the rainbow'
I 18 *l.3* *Senoise* = Siennoise, 'of Siena'
    l.4 *Phocen* (⟨ Lat. *Phocaea*), 'of
Marseille'
I 20 *l.1* *Nātes* = Nantes
    l.4 *fleues* = fléaux
I 25 *l.3* *siecle* (⟨ Lat. *saeculum*,
'generation') = cycle
I 28 *l.1* *fuste*, originally a shallow-
draught galley, thus, 'landing craft' (?)
    l.3 *gês* = gens
    tare (O.Fr.), 'loss'
    l.4 *morelle pique?* = mortelle
pique! (*?* is often printed for *!* in the
original text)
I 32 *l.1* *translaté* ⟨ Lat. *transferre*,
-latum, 'to transfer'

I 35 *l.4* *classes* ⟨ Lat. *summonses*
I 37 *l.4* *pont* ⟨ Grk. *pontos*, 'sea'
I 41 *l.1* Later editions have: *Siege a
cité & de nuit assaillie*
    l.4 Later editions have *Poison &
lettres caches dans le plic* (= pli)
I 43 *l.4* *translaté* ⟨ Lat. *transferre*,
-latum, 'to carry across, transfer'
I 48 *l.4* *& mine* = termine
I 51 *l.3* *siecle* (⟨ Lat. *saeculum*,
'generation') = cycle
I 52 *l.1* *les deux malins*: astrologically,
Mars and Saturn (?)
    l.4 *Septentrionale*, 'of the
Septentrion, or Great Bear': thus,
'northern'
I 63 *l.1* *fleurs* (f.) = fléaux (m.) note
the masculine *passés*
    l.3 *seur* = sûr
I 64 *l.4* *lon orra* = l'on ouïra ⟨ *ouïr*,
'to hear' (comp. Eng. 'Oyez! Oyez!')
I 69 *l.3* *contrades* ⟨ O.Prov. *contrada*,
'country'
I 70 *l.4* Meaning obscure
I 71 *l.2* *Ligurins*, 'Ligurians' (former
tribe of northern Italy)
    l.4 *vast* ⟨ Lat. *vastus*, 'devastated'
I 72 *l.1* *changee* = chargee (?): read as
Marseille déchargé de tout habitant
    l.3 *Tholoze* = Toulouse
    Bourdeaux = bord d'eaux (?)
I 73 *l.2* *Argel*, 'Algiers'

277

l.4   *classe* ⟨ Lat. *classis*, 'fleet'
Veniticns, 'Venetians': thus,
'Italians'

I 79   *l.3*   *Car Bourd.* = Carcassonne,
Bordeaux
Bay. = Bayonne
l.4   *tauropole* ⟨ Grk. *taurobolos*,
'bull sacrifice, slaughter'

I 83   *l.4*   *curieux* ⟨ Lat. *curiosus*,
'having care or charge of'

I 87   *l.1*   *ennosigee* ⟨ Grk. *ennosigaios*,
'earth-shaker' (normally applied to
Poseidon)

I 90   *l.1*   *campane* ⟨ Lat. *campana*, 'bell'
l.2   *classe* ⟨ Lat. *classis*, 'body of
men, fleet, army'
l.3   *tramontane* ⟨ It. *tramontana*,
'north wind', originally from over the
Alps

I 91   *l.3*   *veu* = vu

I 99   *l.3*   *souspir* ⟨ Lat. *suspicere*, 'to
look askance'
mesgnie ⟨ Lat. *mansionem*,
'house(hold)'

II 1   *l.1*   *insuls* ⟨ Lat. *insulae*, 'islands'

II 2   *l.3*   *anthene* = antenne, 'yard-
arm'

II 3   *l.2*   *Negrepont* ⟨ Lat. *niger*,
'black' + Grk. *pontos*, 'sea'

II 5   *l.3*   *classe* ⟨ Lat. *classis*, 'fleet'

II 8   *l.2*   *goffre* ⟨ Romance, 'deep'
(Cheetham)

II 15   *l.1*   *trucidé* ⟨ Lat. *trucidare*, 'to
slaughter'
l.2   *nef* ⟨ Lat. *navis*, 'ship'
astre crinite, 'bearded star':
thus, 'comet'
l.3   *erain* ⟨ Lat. *aerarium*,
'treasury'

II 16   *l.3*   *Gand* = Ghent
l.4   *hecatombe*, 'ritual sacrifice':
hence 'slaughter'

II 17   *l.2*   *Ethne*: presumably not 'Etna'
but 'Elne'
l.4   *north* ⟨ Eng. (unusually)
getez, misprint for *gelez*,
'frozen'
mastinées ⟨ O.Fr. 'damaged,
destroyed'

II 22   *l.1*   *camp* = champ, '(battle)field':
hence, 'army'
Ascop ⟨ Grk. *askopos*,
'unseen, inconceivable, incredible'
l.3   *Arton* ⟨ Grk. *arktos*, '(Great)
Bear', hence 'northern': alternatively
possible anagr. for *OTAN*, 'NATO'
l.4   *subrogée* ⟨ Lat. *subrogatus*,
'surrogate, substituted'

II 26   *l.3*   Another 'Virgilian' scrambled

line: read as *Fuyant Thesin vers Po se
versera: Thesin* = Ticino: *versera* ⟨ Lat.
vertere, 'to turn'

II 30   *l.3*   *oncq'* = jamais
l.4   *avint* = advint: read *Qu'avint
aux Romains viendra par Babel*

II 32   *l.1*   *escoudre* ⟨ Lat. *excudere*, 'to
make, forge'

II 34   *l.3*   *les* = lésé
curieux ⟨ Lat. *curiosus*, 'full
of care'

II 37   *l.4*   *profligez* ⟨ Lat. *profligati*,
'destroyed'

II 38   *l.3*   *malencombre* = O.Fr.
malencontre, 'misfortune'

II 40   *l.3*   *pugne* ⟨ Lat. *pugna*, 'battle'
l.4   *insulte* ⟨ Lat. *insultare*, 'to
leap at'

II 43   *l.4*   *Pau* = Po
Timbre = Tiber
umdans ⟨ Lat. *undo*, 'to wave,
be agitated'

II 46   *l.2*   originally line 1: *troche* ⟨ Grk.
trochos, 'wheel'
l.4   *veu* = vu

II 47   *l.4*   *par mort articles* = à l'article
de la mort, 'on the point of death'

II 48   *l.1*   *copie* ⟨ Lat. *copia*, 'army'
l.4   *polemars* = O. Prov. 'twine,
cord' or ⟨ Grk., *polemarchos*,
'commander'

II 51   *l.4*   *secte*, 'sect', but also possibly
'cut off': in Nostradamus's eyes, *any*
sect other than the Roman Catholic
mainstream was by definition heretical

II 52   *l.4*   *luite* = lutte

II 59   *l.1*   *classe* ⟨ Lat. *classis*, 'fleet'
l.2   *souldars* = soldats

II 60   *l.1*   *La foy Punicque* (⟨ Lat.), 'bad
faith'
l.2   *Iud* ⟨ Lat. *Judaei*, 'the Jews,
Palestine'
Tag. = Tagus
l.3   *mulet*: probable ref. to Philip
of Macedon's proverbial 'mule laden
with gold'
l.4   *classe* ⟨ Lat. *classis*, 'fleet'
espargie ⟨ O.Fr. *espargier*, 'to
sprinkle, scatter'

II 61   *l.1*   *Euge* (⟨(Lat.), 'Bravo!'
Tamins = Thamise,
'Thames': thus, 'England'

II 62   *l.4*   *cent, main* = sang humain

II 64   *l.3*   *Gebenoise*, 'of Cevennes
(south of France)'
l.4   *classe* ⟨ Lat. *classis*, 'army, fleet'

II 65   *l.1*   *parc* ⟨ Lat. *parcus*,
'economical, frugal'
enclin ⟨ Lat. *inclinare*, 'to
decline, lower, draw towards setting'

l.2 *l'Hesperie* (⟨ Grk. *Hesperides*), 'the west'
Insubre, the Milan region of Italy
l.3 *nef* ⟨ Lat. *navis*, 'ship'
II 68 *l*.1 *l'aquilon* ⟨ Lat. *aquilo*, 'the north'
II 69 *l*.4 *cappe*, ⟨ L.Lat. *cappa*, 'cape, priest's cope'
II 70 *l*.3 *pierre*, 'stone': here possibly 'thunderstone'
l.4 *monstre* ⟨ Lat. *monstrum*, 'omen'
II 72 *l*.4 *Thesin* = Ticino
pugne ⟨ Lat. *pugna*, 'battle'
II 75 *l*.2 *Sur le canon du respiral estage* = Sur le canon dur et spiral étage, 'Both on the battlefield and in academic circles' (?). The seer's own house had a particularly fine spiral staircase.
l.3 *viendra* = se vendra (?)
l.4 *Antropophage* ⟨ Grk. *anthropophagos*, 'man-eater, cannibal'
II 78 *l*.2 *Punique* = 'Carthaginian': thus, African
l.3 *à sang . . . ramer*, 'to swim in blood'
II 79 *l*.3 *longin* ⟨ O.Prov. *longinc*, 'afar'
l.4 *Seline* ⟨ Grk. *Selene*, goddess of the moon: thus, 'lunar'
II 81 *l*.1 *aduste* ⟨ Lat. *adustus*, 'burnt to ashes'
l.2 *urne*, 'water-jar', the celestial one of Aquarius(?): hence, January or February
Ceucalion: 'Deucalion' in later editions
Punique fuste, 'African shallow-draft galley'
l.4 *lairra* = laissera
II 84 *l*.1 *Tustie*, 'Tuscany'
l.4 *vastant* ⟨ Lat. *vastare*, 'to lay waste'
II 85 *l*.4 *Lygustique*, 'Ligurian': thus, 'Italian'
II 89 *l*.1 *seront demis* = seront amis
l.3 *estres* = astres
II 91 *l*.2 *Aquilon* (⟨ Lat. *aquilo*), 'the north'
l.3 *orra* ⟨ ouïr, 'to hear'
l.4 *glaive*, 'blade, sword': thus, 'war'
II 93 *l*.1 *Tymbre* = Tiber
la Lybitine = Libitina, Roman goddess of death
l.3 *nef*, 'vessel, nave (of church)', hence, 'church'
prins (⟨ Lat. *prehensus*) = pris

sentine, 'bilges'
II 100 *l*.3 *insulte* ⟨ Lat. *insultare*, 'to leap at'

III 2 *l*.2 *cāprins* = compris
laict, 'milk': later editions give *faict*, 'fact, deed'
l.4 *celique* = céleste
III 4 *l*.1 *lunaires* = luminaires (see III.5)
l.4 *prins* (⟨ Lat. *prehensus*) = pris
III 7 *l*.3 *celiques* = célestes
III 10 *l*.3 *Monech* ⟨ Lat. *Moneceus*, 'Monaco'
l.4 *croc* = croqué, 'hooked'
III 12 *l*.1 *Heb* = Ebro
Rome = (unusually) Rhône
l.2 *Aretin* ⟨ Lat. *Arentius*, 'Arezzo'
l.4 *prins* ⟨ Lat. *prehensus* = pris
III 13 *l*.1 *arche* ⟨ Lat. *arca*, 'ark': thus, 'ship'
l.4 *classe* ⟨ Lat. *classis*, 'fleet'
III 19 *l*.2 *preteur* ⟨ Lat. *praetor*, 'governor, ruler'
l.4 *recteur* ⟨ Lat. *rector*, 'ruler'; or Lat. *rectus*, 'right'(?)
III 20 *l*.1 *Bethique* ⟨ Lat. *Baetis*, the river Guadalquivir
III 26 *l*.2 *aruspices* ⟨ Lat. *haruspex*, 'seer, prophet'
l.2 *Ibere* (⟨ Grk.), the Iberian peninsula, especially around the River Ebro (Cheetham)
l.4 *contrade* ⟨ Prov. *contrada* (⟨ late Lat.), 'country'
l.3 *acre* ⟨ Grk. *akros*, 'tip'
l.4 *extipices* ⟨ Lat. *extispex*, 'soothsayer'
III 27 *l*.3 *fera* = ſera (sera) (?)
III 33 *l*.3 *copia* ⟨ Lat. *copia*, 'army'
l.3 *gastera* = gâtera
III 38 *l*.2 *prins* = pris
III 40 *l*.2/4 *ia* = déjà
III 44 *l*.3 *de fouldre à vierge* = à verge de foudre: the words have been re-ordered *à la* Virgil
l.4 *prinse* = prise: note careful noun/adjective agreement throughout
III 46 *l*.1 *Plancus*: Lucius Munatius Plancus, founder of Lyon in 43 BC.
III 49 *l*.4 *Roan* = Rouen
III 53 *l*.3 *Agrippine* ⟨ Lat. *Colonia Agrippina* = Cologne
III 62 *l*.1 *Cyrrene* ('Cyrenian') = Mediterranean
l.3 *percee*, 'way in'
gloze (⟨ Grk. *glossa*, 'word requiring explanation'), 'glossed, noted'

III 64 *l.2 olchade* ⟨ Grk. *holkas,
-ados,* 'cargo-ship': error for
olchades (as printed in later
editions), to rhyme with *Cyclades* in
line 3
III 68 *l.2 profligez* ⟨ Lat. *profligati,*
'dashed forward, overthrown,
defeated'
    cherroneſſe ⟨ Grk.
chersonesos, 'peninsula'
    l.3 dict ⟨ Lat. *edictum,* 'edict'
III 70 *l.3 Ausonne* ⟨ Lat. *Ausonia,*
'(lower) Italy'
III 70 *l.3 profligez* ⟨ Lat. *profligati,*
'laid forward, destroyed, ruined'
III 78 *l.3 Calpre* (⟨ Lat. *Calpe*),
'Gibraltar'
III 79 *l.3 Phocen* (⟨ Lat. *Phocaea*),
'of Marseille'
    l.4 quant et quant ⟨ Lat.
quantum, 'how many'
III 81 *l.4 pont* = tête de pont,
'bridgehead'
III 82 *l.1 Freins:* error for *Freius,*
'Fréjus'
    l.3 saturelles = sauterelles
    l.4 prins (⟨ Lat. *prehensi*) =
pris
III 83 *l.4 internitions* = intentions,
as per later editions
III·85 *l.1 prinse* (⟨ Lat. *prehensa*) =
prise
    l.3 Raubine = (river) Robine,
tributary of Aude
    LAUDE = l'Aude
(capitals often signal special
meanings or anagrams)
III 90 *l.2 presenté:* equivalent of
Latin ablative absolute
    l.3 istra ⟨ O.Fr. *issir* ⟨ Lat.
exire, 'to go out'
    l.4 Tyrren = tyrant, 'dictator,
ruler' (in early Greek the sense was
not necessarily pejorative)
    Phocean (⟨ Lat. *Phocaea*),
'of Marseille'
III 92 *l.3 Brodde:* see IV.3 below.
III 93 *l.3 Annibalique,* 'of
Hannibal', thus 'of the invaders
from Africa'
III 97 *l.3 barbare,* 'of Barbary,
Berber', hence (inaccurately) 'Arab'
III 99 *l.1 Alein* = Alleins:
Varneigne = Vernègues
    l.2 Lebron = Lubéron

IV 3 *l.1 Brodes* = Prov. term for
inhabitants of Alpine country around
River Isère (⟨ Lat. *Allobroges*); *also* =
O.Fr. *brode,*

'unworthy, dark, swarthy'. See
III.92, VIII.34.
IV 12 *l.1 de route* = déroute
IV 19 *l.1 Insubres* ⟨ Lat. *Insubria,*
Milan region of Italy.
    l.4 Par dons laenées (possibly
Pardons laenaés): meaning unclear:
laenées (⟨ Lat. *laena*), 'cloak, mantle'
IV 20 *l.1 uberté* ⟨ Lat. *ubertas,*
'abundance, plenty'
    l.4 sperants ⟨ Lat. *sperantes*
= espérants
IV 21 *l.3 coeur haut, prudent mis:*
read as *coeur prudent, haut mis*
IV 23 *l.1 classe* ⟨ Lat. *classis,* 'fleet'
IV 34 *l.3 Austone* ⟨ Lat. *Ausonia,*
'(lower) Italy'
    l.4 ost ⟨ O.Fr. *host,* 'army'
IV 36 *l.2 Insubre* ⟨ Lat. *Insubria,*
Milan region of Italy
IV 37 *l.2 Insubre:* see IV 36 *l.2*
    l.4 classe ⟨ Lat. *classis,* 'fleet'
    rubre ⟨ Lat. *ruber,* 'red'
IV 43 *l.3 debatre* ⟨ Lat. *debatuere,*
'to beat down'
IV 44 *l.2 malo sepmano* (Prov.) =
mauvaise semaine
    l.3 de nuech l'intrado (Prov.)
= de nuit l'entrée
    cailhau (Prov.) = caillou
IV 46 *l.3 Reims* = Rennes: compare
IX.20 below
    l.4 au toc de la campano =
au son du tocsin
IV 48 *l.1 Ausonne* ⟨ Lat. *Ausonia,*
'(lower) Italy'
IV 50 *l.1 Hesperies* ⟨ Grk.
hesperios, 'western'
IV 56 *l.3 aveugle* = aveuglement
    darbon = de Narbonne
IV 66 *l.1 rabieuse* = rabique,
'rabid'
IV 67 *l.3 adust* ⟨ Lat. *adustus,*
'burnt to ashes'
IV 72 *l.1 Artomiques* ⟨ Grk. *arktos,*
'(Great) bear': hence, 'northerners'
IV 74 *l.1 Brannonices* ⟨ Lat., tribe
from the Eure and Sarthe region
    l.4 d'Humaine = de Maine
IV 76 *l.1 Nictobriges,* inhabitants of
the Agen area
    l.3 Begorne = either Bigone or
Bigorre
IV 77 *l.1 SELIN* ⟨ Grk. *Selene,*
'moon': thus, '(over the) Crescent'
    l.3 blesique = blésoise, 'of Blois'
IV 79 *l.4 vorer* = dévorer
IV 82 *l.2 Olestant* ⟨ Grk. *olesthos,*
'destruction', oleter, 'destroyer,
murderer'

l.3 *Romanie*, 'area controlled by Rome'
IV 86 *l.1* *eau*, 'water': Nostradamian code for Aquarius
IV 89 *l.2* *pont* 〈 Grk. *pontos*, 'sea'
IV 90 *l.1* *copies* 〈 Lat. *copia*, 'army'
l.2 *Ticin* = Ticino: thus, 'Pavia'
l.4 *boucin*, Prov. 'scrap' (i.e. meat of old he-goat, hare or rabbit)
IV 94 *l.3* *lemam* = Leman (Geneva)
l.4 *Blyterre* 〈 Lat. *Julia Biterra*, 'Béziers'
Agath (〈 Lat.), 'Agde'
IV 95 *l.3* *vestales*, 'Vestales', virgins sacred to the state goddess Vesta, Roman equivalent of the Greek Hestia
l.4 *pui nay* = puîné, 'younger' (of two brothers)
Armonique: misprint for *Armorique*, 'of Armorica (Brittany and western Normandy)'
IV 98 *l.2* *demipler* 〈 Grk. *demiopleres*. 'abounding in public'
l.4 *morbilles* 〈 O.Fr. 'smallpox' *bleds* = blés
IV 99 *l.4* *Hesperiques* 〈 Grk. *hesperios*, 'western'

V 6 *l.1* *chef* 〈 Lat. *caput*, 'head'
V 11 *l.2* *Venus* = Venise: the city of Venice was known as the 'star of the sea' (i.e. Venus again)
V 13 *l.4* *Pannons* 〈 Lat. *Pannonia*, the region centred on Hungary
l.4 *Hercules*, 'Gibraltar'
la: pron., referring back to *gent*
hare 〈 O.Fr. *harer*, to harry, set a dog on s.o.
V 14 *l.3* *Heredde* 〈 Lat. *heres, -edis*, 'heir'
prinse = prise (the feminine could suggest a *female* prisoner)
V 15 *l.1* *prins* (〈 Lat. *prehensus*) = pris
l.3 *debise* (printed *debiſe*), error for *debiſe* 〈 débiſer, 'to weaken', to rhyme with *pontife* in line 1
V 17 *l.1* *andronne*, 'narrow lane or path'
l.3 *main* 〈 Lat. *manus*, 'force'
V 21 *l.4* *incoruz* 〈 Lat. *incorruptos*, 'uncorrupted'
V 23 *l.1* *contens*, contraction of *continents*
l.4 *classe* 〈 Lat. *classis*, 'fleet'
V 25 *l.4* *ver. serp* 〈 Lat. *versus serpens*, 'snake coiled back on itself'

V 26 *l.1* *esclaue*, O.Fr. 'slave' = medieval Lat. *sclavus*, 'Slav' 〈 late Grk. *sklabos* 〈 Slavonic *slovo*, 'word'; *sloviti*, 'speak'
l.4 *copie* 〈 Lat. *copia*, 'troops'
V 27 *l.1* *marnegro* 〈 Lat. *mare nigrum*, 'Black Sea'
l.3 *Phatos*: misprint for *Pharos* *Methelin* = Mitilini (Lesbos)
l.3 *Sol alegro*, 'in bright sunlight'
l.4 *Adrie*, 'Adriatic'
V 31 *l.4* *subdite* 〈 Lat. *subducta*, 'dragged under'
V 32 *l.4* *roche*: rhyme-imposed substitution. Read 'pierre': the Book of Revelation contains no 'seventh rock'
V 34 *l.3* *classe* 〈 Lat. *classis*, 'fleet'
l.4 *vin et sel*: literally 'wine and wit'
V 35 *l.1* *Seline*, 'of Selene the moon-goddess': thus, 'crescent'
l.3 *classe* 〈 Lat. *classis*, 'fleet'
V 39 *l.2* *Hetrurie*, 'Etruria': thus 'Italy'
V 43 *l.2* *Seez & Ponce* = Sées et Pons
l.4 *Magonce* 〈 Lat. *Magontiacum*, 'Mainz'
V 45 *l.2* *silve* 〈 Lat. *silva*, 'wood, forest'
l.4 *milve* 〈 Lat. *miluus*, 'kite'
V 47 *l.4* *austre* 〈 Lat. *austerus*, 'austere'
V 48 *l.3* *classe* 〈 Lat. *classis*, 'fleet'
V 49 *l.4* *fiance* 〈 O.Fr. 'engagement, promise'
V 50 *l.1* *lys* = fleur de lys: thus, 'France'
l.2 *Romanie*: the Roman kingdom
l.3 *Latin* 〈 Lat. *Latium*, Central Italy
V 51 *l.1* *Dace*: region of Romania
l.2 *Boesme*: Czechoslavakia
l.4 *Barcins* 〈 Lat. *Barcino*, 'Barcelona'
Tyrrens = tyrants
crue le brique = cruelle brigue
V 52 *l.3* *caste* 〈 Lat. *castus*, 'chaste, pure'
hyppolite (〈 Grk.), 'of (Saint) Hippolytus': thus, 'chaste, austere, religious'
V 54 *l.4* *lairra* = laissera
V 55 *l.1* *contrade* 〈 O.Prov. *contrada*, 'country'
l.4 *Lygustique*, 'Ligurian': thus, 'Italian'.
V 57 *l.1* *istra* 〈 O.Fr. *issir* 〈 Lat. *exire*, 'to leave'

mont Gaulsier (printed mont
Gaulſier – not, note, mont Gaulfier,
despite much hot air to the contrary) =
Gaule Cimonts, 'Cisalpine Gaul', or
Mont Gaulsier, near St. Rémy
    Aventine, one of Rome's
seven hills
    l.2   advertira ⟨ Lat. advertere, 'to
turn towards'
    l.4   SEXT ⟨ Lat. (per)secutus:
capitals nearly always signal some kind
of 'special' treatment in Nostradamus
    mansol ⟨ Lat. manus solis (see
VIII.46)
V 59 l.4 estoile en barbe, 'bearded
star', thus 'comet, meteor'
V 61 l.4 Senis = Cenis
V 62 l.4 nefs ⟨ Lat. naves, 'ships'
    prins (⟨ Lat. prehensus) =
pris
V 70 l.3 tout sexe deu = de tout sexe
V 71 l.2 exercite ⟨ Lat. exercitus,
'army'
V 75 l.2 sur ⟨ Lat. super, 'above'
    quarree = (place) carrée:
unless intended to mean 'apartment'
V 76 l.1 libere ⟨ Lat. liber, 'free, open'
    l.3   Carpen, 'Carpentras'
    l'isle volce: L'Isle-sur-Sorgue,
main town of Vaucluse
V 77 l.2 dial ⟨ Lat. Dialis, 'of Dis, or
Jupiter'
    quirinal, 'of Quirinus'
(Romulan version of Mars)
V 78 l.4 cappe ⟨ L.Lat. cappa, 'cloak,
(priest's) cope'
 85 l.1 Sueves ⟨ Lat. Suevi =
Swabians (inhabitants of the area
comprising south-east Germany and
Switzerland)
    l.3   gamp = camp (?)
V 92 l.2 Cinq changeront en tel reuolu
terme: read Tel terme révolu, (ils le)
changeront en cinq (ans)

VI 3 l.1 nay = né
VI 12 l.1 copies ⟨ Lat. copias, 'armies'
VI 10 l.4 terre = terreur
VI 16 l.1 milve ⟨ Lat. miluus, 'kite'
    l.3   noirs: Nostradamian code
for Benedictines (Cheetham)
    Negrisilve ⟨ Lat. Silva Nigra,
'Black Forest'
VI 20 l.3 vaisseaux, 'naves': thus,
'churches'
    gent ⟨ Lat. gens, gentis,
'people, tribe': often used by
Nostradamus to mean 'army'
VI 21 l.1 du polle artiq: writers of the
time often used the word 'pole' where

we would use 'hemisphere', a word
which they tended to reserve for the
Earth itself (compare Marlowe, for
example)
VI 24 l.1 le sceptre: the celestial ruler:
thus, Jupiter
VI 27 l.2 Selin, 'of Selene the moon-
goddess'
    l.3   laer = l'air
VI 36 l.2 Perousse = Perugia
    l.3   estre = astre
VI 43 l.2 Signe = Seine
    l.3   Tamise, 'Thames': thus,
'England'
    l.4   deceux = déçus
VI 44 l.1 L ris: misprint for L'iris, 'the
rainbow'
    l.3   classe ⟨ Lat. classis, 'fleet'
    l.4   Saxe, 'Saxony' (?)
VI 49 l.1 Tesin = Ticino
    l.4   Pau = Po
    granci = garanti
VI 58 l.2 Syntax unclear. Selin ⟨ Grk.
Selene, goddess of the moon: hence
'crescent, Islam'. Since perdue is
feminine, it would seem to apply to her
rather than to le Sol: hence read Lors
que Selin par le Sol clair perdue (?)
    l.3   simulté ⟨ Lat. simultas,
'rivalry'
VI 62 l.3 gallots = Gaulois,
'Frenchmen'
    l.4   Monech ⟨ Lat. Moneceus,
'Monaco'
VI 64 l.1 pache ⟨ Lat. pax, 'peace-
treaty'
    l.4   classe ⟨ Lat. classis, 'fleet'
VI 66 l.4 enfouetz (⟨ Vulg. Lat.
infodictus ⟨ Lat. infodere) = enfoui
VI 67 l.3 peaultre ⟨ Lat. paluster, -ris,
'foul, dirty, unclean, vicious'
VI 70 l.2 Plus oultre: epithet
historically applied to himself by the
Emperor Charles V
    l.3   loz ⟨ Lat. laus, 'praise'
VI 78 l.1 Selin, 'of Selene' (Greek
moon-goddess): hence, 'lunar, Muslim'
    l.4   Basil ⟨ Grk. basileus, 'king'
VI 80 l.4 croix = croyants, 'believers'
VI 81 l.3 Gennes = Genoa
    l.4   frofaim = faim de froment
(Cheetham)
VI 95 l.1 puis nay = puisné, 'younger
(brother)'
VI 98 l.1 Volsques = Vocae, people of
the Languedoc
VI 100 l.4 Meaning obscure

VII 2 l.4 sonnés, 'found out' (?)
VII 6 l.2 barbare (⟨ Berber) =

(erroneously) 'Arab, Muslim', thus, by Christian extension, 'infidel, heathen'
 l.4 intemptee ⟨ Lat. *intentatus*, 'extended'
VII 8 *l.1 Flora*, 'Florence'
 l.2 fesulan ⟨ Lat. *Faesulae*, 'Fiesole'
 l.3 prins (⟨ Lat. *prehensus*) = pris
 l.4 sexe = secte
VII 10 *l.1 limitrophe du Mans*, 'from near le Mans'
 l.2 exercite ⟨ Lat. *exercitus*, 'army'
 l.3 Gallotz = Gaulois, 'Frenchmen': or possibly = Gallois, 'Welshmen'
  Normans, 'northerners'
 l.4 Caspre (printed *Caſpre*: error for Lat. *Calpe*), 'Gibraltar'
VII 12 *l.2 assemble* = assemblés
VII 15 *l.1 Insubre*, 'Insubria', arca around Milan
VII 19 *l.1 Nicene*, 'of Nice'
 l.3 faict ⟨ Lat. *factum*, 'fact', in absence of French word ⟨ Lat. *fatum*, 'fate'
VII 21 *l.1 Volsicque* ⟨ Lat. *Vocae*, 'people of the Languedoc'
VII 22 *l.2 Yrés*, 'irate', ⟨ Lat. *ira*, 'anger'
 l.4 prins (⟨ Lat. *prehensa*) = prise
VII 23 *l.3 l'aneau*, '(Papal) ring'
VII 25 *l.1 exercite* ⟨ Lat. *exercitus*, 'army'
  expuiser = épuisera
 l.2 pecune ⟨ Lat. *pecunia*, 'money'
 l.3 cuir ⟨ Lat. *corium*, Grk. *chorion*, 'skin, leather'
  cuser ⟨ Lat. *cudere*, 'to mint'
VII 30 *l.4 prinse* ⟨ Lat. *prehensa*, 'taken'
VII 31 *l.3 Allobroges*: ancient tribe from the Savoy region
VII 34 *l.3 venin*, 'poison *or* medicine', by analogy with Grk. *pharmakon*: thus, 'drugs'
VII 37 *l.2 classe* ⟨ Lat. *classis*, 'fleet'
 l.4 stecades ⟨ Lat. *Stoechades* = les Isles d'Hyères
  cap = capitaine
VII 39 *l.3 sus paire* ⟨ Lat. *suspicere*, 'to suspect'

VIII 2 *l.1 le*: misprint for *je*
VIII 4 *l.1 Monech* ⟨ Lat. *Moneceus*, 'Monaco'
 l.3 Logarion: later editions have legation

VIII 6 *l.2 print*: misprint for *prinſe* (= *prinse*) ⟨ Lat. *prehensa*, 'taken'
 l.3 Sardon: possibly Sardinia
  Mauris = mauresques, 'Moors'
VIII 7 *l.1 Verceil* = Vercelli
 l.2 Tycin = Ticino
  paye = paix
 l.4 choir, 'fall'
  faisant maye, 'while May is being celebrated'
VIII 9 *l.4 Barb'* = Barbare, 'Berber': thus (inaccurately) 'Arab, Muslim'
VIII 11 *l.3 Lunage*: anagr. for Lugano
 l.4 par more ⟨ Lat. *per mare*, 'by sea'
VIII 15 *l.1 Aquilon* ⟨ Lat. *aquilo*, 'the north'
 l.3 deux ⟨ Lat. *dux, duces*, 'leader'
  eclypses ⟨ Lat. *eclipsis*, 'failure'
 l.4 Pannons inhabitants of Pannonia, in classical times the region centred on Hungary, which was largely Slav at the time
VIII 16 *l.1 HIERON*; later editions have *Jilson*, 'Jason'
  feit (⟨ Lat. *fecit*) = made
 l.3 s'atacquer = s'attacher
 l.4 Fesulan = fessan, 'broad of bottom', incorporating pseudo-geographical reference to Fiesole, Italy (see VII.8 above)
VIII 19 *l.1 cappe* ⟨ L.Lat. *cappa*, 'cape, priest's cope'
VIII 20 *l.2 urben* ⟨ Lat. *urbem* (acc.), 'town, city'
  pache = pacte
 l.3 pont ⟨ Grk. *pontos*, 'sea'
  pont = tête de pont, 'bridgehead' (deliberate play on words with line 3)
VIII 22 *l.1 Gorsan* = Coursan
 l.2 Tucham: analogical reference to the Revolt of the Tuchins of 1382–4, a peasant rebellion against the Church and aristocracy of Toulouse and elsewhere in south-western France
 l.4 drap = drapeau (?)
VIII 29 *l.1 lon* = dès longtemps
  Saturne = Saint Saturnin (St-Sernin)
 l.4 Capion = Caepio
VIII 30 *l.1 beluezer* = baluchon, 'miner's bucket' (?)
 l.4 locz = lieux
  vasacle = Basacle
VIII 34 *l.2 Secatombe* = hécatombe,

'ritual sacrifice'
    l.3   *delues* ⟨ Lat. *deludere*, 'to play false'
        Brodes = Prov. term for inhabitants of Alpine country around River Isère (⟨ Lat. *Allobroges*); also = O.Fr. *brode*, 'unworthy, dark, swarthy'. See III.92.
    l.4   *Vlme* = mule (anagr.), 'papal slipper'
VIII 38 *l*.2   *emonopolle* = en monopole, 'exclusively'
    l.4   *Nolle*, 'Nola' (near Naples)
VIII 46 *l*.2   *destrois* (⟨ Lat. *districtus*, 'drawn tight') = détroit
    l.3/4   Meaning obscure
VIII 48 *l*.2   *Chaldondon* ⟨ Lat. *Chaldeus*, 'Chaldean, soothsayer, astrologer'
        salvaterre ⟨ Lat. *salvat terram*, 'saves the land'
    l.3   *Saut Castallon* ⟨ Lat. *Saltus Castulonensis*: Sierra Morena (Cheetham)
    l.4   *Verbiesque* ⟨ Med. Fr. *verbier*, 'to chatter' (typically Nostradamian pseudo-geographical play on words)
VIII 49 *l*.1   *Satur.* = Saturne
        ioue, 'Jove, Jupiter'
    l.3   *Tardaigne* = Tardenois, ancient name for Soissons area of France, now in the département of Aisne near the Belgian frontier
    l.4   *Ponteroso*: ⟨ Grk. *pontos*, 'sea' + Lat. *russus*, 'red'
VIII 51 *l*.2   *reprinse* = reprise
    l.3   *pamplation* ⟨ Pampelune, 'Pamplona'
    l.4   *Colongna* = Colonnes d'Hercule, 'Gibraltar' (?)
VIII 54 *l*.2   *selin* ⟨ Grk. *Selene*, goddess of the moon: thus, '(to the) Crescent, (to) Islam'
    l.4   *second banc macelin* (⟨ Lat. *macellum*, 'market'), 'on the back stall of the market'
VIII 60 *l*.3   *mesnie* ⟨ Lat. *mansionem*, 'house(hold)'
    l.4   *terax* ⟨ Grk. *teras*, 'omen, sign, wonder, monster'
        NORLARIS: anagram for Lorraine, signalled by usual capitals
VIII 62 *l*.1   *expiler* ⟨ Lat. *expilare*, 'to plunder'
    l.2   *du rosne* = de Rome (?)
VIII 70 *l*.3   *d'ame* = dame
    l.4   *tertre* ('mound, knoll') = terre, 'land', partly disguised so as to resemble *teſte* (teste), 'head': or

possibly the waking Nostradamus had the typical Babylonian 'tell', or city-mound in mind
VIII 72 *l*.1   *Perusin*, 'of Perugia'
    l.4   *la venne* = *l'aveine* (⟨ Lat. *avena*), former spelling of *l'avoine*, 'oats'
VIII 76 *l*.1   *Macelin* ⟨ O.F. **macelenc* ('maceling' − i.e. mace-man)
VIII 77 *l*.1   *trois* = très, via Lat. *tres* (?)
        annichilez (past participle) ⟨ Lat. *annihilatus*, 'reduced to nothing'
    l.2   *ans sang durera* = (i) ans sans durer a / (ii) ans endurera ⟨ *endurer*, 'to withstand'
VIII 78 *l*.1   *bragamas* ⟨ O.Prov. *briamonso*, 'soldier of fortune' (Cheetham)
VIII 80 *l*.1   *vefue* = veuve
    l.2   *se* (printed *ſe*): misprint for le
    l.4   *boge* = bouge

IX 2   *l*.1   *ouye* = ouïe, 'heard'
    l.3   *assomye*, 'assuaged'
    l.4   *Arimin* = Anagr. for Rimini
        Columna: misprint for Colorno (just north of Parma)
        deboutez = déboutés, 'dismissed'
IX 6   *l*.3   *Ispalme*: anagram of Lat. *mel*, 'honey' + *apis*, 'bee'
    l.4   *Barboxitaine*: compression of Lat. *(Aheno)barbus occitan(us)*
IX 9   *l*.3   *trible*: misprint for *crible*
IX 10 *l*.2   *verrier* ⟨ Lat. *verres*, 'boar'
    l.4   *forrier* ⟨ Lat. *foranus*, 'foreign', *foris*, 'outside'
IX 12 *l*.3   *figulier* ⟨ Lat. *figulus*, 'potter'
IX 15 *l*.1   *Parpan* = Perpignan
IX 16 *l*.1   *castel* (S. Fr. 'castle') = Castile (?)
    l.3   *Ribiere* = Rivière, 'Riviera'
    l.4   *desnier ont* = dénieront
IX 20 *l*.1   *Reines* = Rheims: see IV.46 for a similar transposition
    l.2   *Deux pars vaultorte*, 'two parts deviously'
        Herne = Ierne = Reine
        pierre = piéride, 'Muse, butterfly' (esp. cabbage white)
    l.4   *cap.* ⟨ Lat. *caput*, 'head'
IX 28 *l*.1   *voille* ('sail') = 'ship, fleet'
        symacle ⟨ Grk. *symmachis*, 'allied'
        Massiliolique ⟨ Lat. *massilioticus*, 'of Marseille'
    l.2   *Pannons* ⟨ Lat. *Pannonia*, area centred on Hungary

l.3 *sinus* ⟨ Lat., 'bay'
Illirique, 'Illyrian,
Dalmatian'
l.4 *vast* ⟨ Lat. *vastum*,
'devastation'
Socile = Sicile, 'Sicily'
Ligurs = Ligurians, former
tribe of northern Italy
IX 30 *l.2* *Phanaticque* ⟨ Lat. *Sinus
Flanaticus*: Gulf of Kvarner
l.3 *Cap.* = capitaine
raves = ravages
l.4 *Gaddes* ⟨ Lat. *Gades*: Cadiz
(Cheetham)
IX 31 *l.2* *Cassich* ⟨ Grk. *Cassiterides*,
'tin islands' (Cornwall and the Scillies)
IX 32 *l.2* *laze* ⟨ Grk. *laas*, 'stone'
capitolin, 'of the Roman
Capitol, or government'
l.4 *classe* ⟨ Lat. *classis*, 'fleet'
Methelin, 'Mitilini' (Lesbos)
IX 33 *l.1* *d'Annemarc* = de Danemark
l.2 *Guion* (O.Fr.), 'guide,
leader'
l.3 *l'unde de sainct Marc*, 'the
waters of Venice'
IX 37 *l.3* *Tholose* = Toulouse
IX 38 *l.2* *Aemathien* ⟨ Lat. *Emathia*,
'Macedonia and Thessaly'
IX 41 *l.1* *Chyren*: anagram for
'Henryc(us)'
soy = se
l.3 *Chanignon* = Canino (Italy)
l.4 *duc* ⟨ Lat. *dux*, 'general,
leader'
IX 42 *l.1* *Gennes* = 'Genoa'
l.2 *Monet* = *Monech* ⟨ Lat.
Moneceus, 'Monaco'
l.3 *Barbare*, 'Berber', thus
(erroneously) 'Arab, Muslim, infidel,
heathen'
classe ⟨ Lat. *classis*, 'fleet'
l.4 *poulse* (⟨ Lat. *pulsus*) =
poussé
IX 43 *l.1* *crucigere*: 'cross-bearing'
l.2 *Ismaëlites*, 'sons of Ishmael':
thus, 'Arabs'
l.3 *raviere* ⟨ ravir, 'to ravish,
snatch'
l.4 *eslites* = élues, 'chosen'
IX 44 *l.1* *Migres, migre* ⟨ Lat. *migrare*,
'to go'
l.2 *RAYPOZ*: anagr. of PAY.
ROZ = pays rose
l'a ruent = la ruée
IX 46 *l.3* *dessouz l'umbre des courges*
= sous ombre de (Prov.) coucoureou,
'under the pretext of imbecility' (?)
l.4 *carne omination* ⟨ Lat. *carne
ominatum*, 'entrail-reading'

IX 51 *l.1* *se banderont*, 'they shall
resist'
l.2 *par paix se minera* = par le
pays se (dissé)minera
l.4 *monde*, 'people, everybody'
IX 55 *l.4* *sang, feu* = s'enfuit
IX 56 *l.1* *camp* ⟨ Lat. *campus*,
'(battle)field': thus, 'army'
Noudan = Houdan
Goussan ville =
Goussonville (rather than
Goussainville in north-east Paris)
l.2 *Maiotes* ⟨ Grk. *Maiotai*,
'Scythians'
l.4 *deux* = ducs ⟨ Lat. *dux*,
'leader, general'
legne ⟨ O.Prov. *legna* ⟨ Lat.
lignum, 'wood'
IX 60 *l.1* *Cornere*: misprint for
coronete, 'ornamental headdress',
dim. of O.Fr. *corone* ⟨ Lat. *corona*,
'crown'
l.2 *d'Almatie*, 'Dalmatia'
l.3 *Ismaël*, 'Ishmael': thus,
'Arab'
l.4 *ranes* = 'ranulas' (cysts
under tongue) ⟨ Lat. *rana*, 'frog':
hence, 'strange tongues'
IX 61 *l.2* *cita nova* (O. Prov.) = cité
nouvelle: thus, 'Villeneuve'
IX 64 *l.4* *Cap.* (⟨ Lat. *caput*, 'head'),
'captain'
IX 67 *l.1* *Lizer* = l'Isère
l.2 *Valen. cent* = Valence sont
l.4 *crest* = créscent
foy = fidèles
IX 68 *l.1* *mont Aymar* = Montélimar
IX 69 *l.4* *Langoult*: misprint for
Langouſt (Langoust) ⟨ O.Prov.
langosta ⟨ Lat. *locusta*, 'grasshopper'
IX 71 *l.1* *trixe* ⟨ Grk. *thrix*, 'hair,
wool, fleece'
IX 72 *l.2* *Tholossain*, 'of Toulouse'
IX 73 *l.1* *ceiulee* = cérulé, 'azure,
blue'
l.3 *ban* = bannira (?)
l.4 *la hurne*, 'the water-pot'
(Babylonian Aquarius)
IX 75 *l.1* *Ambraxie* = Ambracia (now
Arta, western Greece)
IX 83 *l.4* *infidelle* = infidèles
voguera ⟨ Lat. *vocare*, 'to
call'
IX 84 *l.1* *hecatombe*, 'ritual slaughter'
IX 85 *l.3* *par foy pay roy* = parfois
parroi
Phocé ⟨ Lat. *Phocaea*,
'Marseilles'
IX 92 *l.2* *expugner* ⟨ Lat. *expugnare*,
'to storm'

IX 93 *l.4 Haemathion* ⟨ Lat.
Emathius, 'Macedonian' (possible
reference to Alexander the Great)
IX 95 *l.1 exercite* ⟨ Lat. *exercitus*,
'army'
    l.2 apamé ⟨ Grk. *apamao*, 'to
cut off'
    l.3 Milannoile (misprint for
Milannoiſe), 'Milanese' (?)
IX 99 *l.1 Vent Aquilon*, 'the north
wind'
    l.2 chauls (⟨ Lat. *calidus*) =
chauds
    l.3 piege ⟨ O.Prov. *piegi*,
'harmful' (Cheetham)
IX 100 *l.1 pugne* ⟨ Lat. *pugna*, 'battle'
          superè ⟨ Lat. *superatus*,
'overcome'
    l.2 naves = Lat. *naves*, 'ships'

X 3 *l.1 en* = ans
    l.2 l'aschera = lâchera
X 5 *l.2 neuf Arriens*, 'a new Arrian
(Greek soldier, statesman and
historian)'
    l.3 Carcas = Carcassonne
          Tholosse = Toulouse
    l.4 Lauragues: region of south-
western France extending into the
Pyrenean foothills around the upper
Garonne and Aude
X 6 *l.1 Sardon*: misprint for Gardon
          Nemans = Nîmes
X 7 *l.2 aemethien* (⟨ Lat. *Emathius*),
'from Macedonia and Thessaly'
    l.3 vin, sel, 'wine and/or wit'
    l.4 Hem. mi deux Phi = en
mi-défi, 'in mid-defiance'
X 10 *l.1 adulteres* ⟨ Lat. *adulterium*,
'corruption, crime'
X 11 *l.2 posthume*, 'posthumous',
thus 'last-born'
    l.4 Duc ⟨ Lat. *dux*, 'general,
leader'
          à Tende = attendre
X 23 *l.3 arc* ⟨ Lat. *arca*, 'ark': thus,
'ship'
    l.4 ribe ⟨ Lat. *ripa*, 'shore' (*cf*
'Riviera')
X 27 *l.4 Lespe* = l'épée
X 58 *l.1 felin*: misprint for ſelin
(*selin*), 'of Selene the moon-goddess':
hence, 'lunar, of the Muslim crescent'
    l.2 Aemathien (⟨ Lat. *Emathius*),
'Macedonian'
    l.3 perecliter, 'to imperil'
    l.4 Phossens ⟨ Lat. *Phocaea*,
Marseilles
          ponant, 'occident': thus,
'west'

X 60 *l.4 nolte* ⟨ Lat. *nolitus*,
'unwanted'
X 65 *l.3 aspre* ⟨ Lat. *asper*, 'harsh'
          coche, 'notch, score-mark'
X 66 *l.2 tempiera* = (t')empierrera,
'will pave (you)'
    l.3 Reb ⟨ Lat. *ruber*, 'red'
X 69 *l.3 alles* ⟨ O.Fr. 'crowd'
    l.4 Ambellon = Ambès (?)
X 72 *l.2 deffraieur*: misprint for
deſfraieur (*desfraieur*) ⟨ O.Fr.
desfrayer, 'to defray, settle, pay up'
    l.3 Angolmois: pun on
Angoulême/Angoumois, used as
anagram for *Mongolois*
X 73 *l.2 Iovaliste*, 'man of Jupiter':
hence, 'man of God'
X 74 *l.3 eage* = age
    l.4 entres = enterrés, 'buried'
X 79 *l.2 somentrée* = psaume entrée
    l.3 fleur de lys, 'French'
    l.4 contree ⟨ O.Prov. *contrada*,
'country'
X 87 *l.1 Nisse* = Nice
    l.3 Antipolles ⟨ Lat. *Antipolis*,
'Antibes'
          genisse (here m., therefore
not 'heifer'!) = genêt ('broom'), ⟨
masculinised form of Lat. *genistal*
genesta (the more normal modern
word *balai* comes originally from the
Breton word for the same plant)
X 95 *l.2 or*: misprint for *au*
X 100 *l.2 pempotam* ⟨ Grk. *pan*, 'all'
+ Lat. *potens*, 'powerful'
    l.3 copies ⟨ Lat. *copia*, 'troops'

Additional Centuries

XII 36 *l.3 classe* ⟨ Lat. *classis*, 'fleet'
    l.4 vast ⟨ Lat. *vastare*, 'to lay
waste'
          la roche, Gibraltar
XII 59 *l.1 pache* = pacte
XII 65 *l.2 avent* ⟨ Lat. *adventus*,
'advent, arrival'

Présages

31 *l.1 classe* ⟨ Lat. *classis*, 'fleet'
          Ister, classical name for Danube
    l.2 holcades ⟨ Grk. *holkas, -ados*,
'transport vessel, barge' (*cf* Eng. 'hulk')
          Ceres = Persephone, goddess of
the isle of Sicily
    l.3 Flor, 'Florence'
40 *l.1 De maison sept*, 'seven of the
(ruling) house'
41 *l.1 predons* ⟨ Lat. *praeda*, 'booty'

BIBLIOGRAPHY

1 Brennan, J.H., *Nostradamus; Visions of the Future* (Aquarian, 1992)
2 Cannon, D., *Conversations with Nostradamus: His Prophecies Explained*, Vol. 2 (America West, 1990)
3 Cheetham, E., *The Final Prophecies of Nostradamus* (Futura, 1989)
4 Cheetham, E., *The Prophecies of Nostradamus* (Corgi, 1973)
5 Clarke, A.C., *Profiles of the Future* (Pan, 1973): quotations by kind permission of David Higham Associates
6 Dixon, J., *My Life and Prophecies* (Muller, 1971)
7 Fontbrune, J.-C. de, *Nostradamus 1: Countdown to Apocalypse* (Pan, 1983)
8 Glass, J., *The Story of Fulfilled Prophecy* (Cassell, 1969)
9 Hewitt, V.J. and Lorie, P., *Nostradamus: the End of the Millennium* (Bloomsbury, 1991)
10 Hogue, J., *Nostradamus and the Millennium* (Bloomsbury, 1987)
11 Laver, J., *Nostradamus or the Future Foretold* (Mann, 1973)
12 Lemesurier, P., *The Armageddon Script: Prophecy in Action* (Element, 1981): quotation by kind permission of Element Books Ltd
13 Lemesurier, P., *Gospel of the Stars: The Mystery of the Cycle of the Ages* (Element, 1990)
14 Lemesurier, P., *The Great Pyramid Decoded* (Element, 1977)
15 Lindsey, H., *The Late Great Planet Earth* (Lakeland, 1970)
16 Loog, C., *Die Weissagungen des Nostradamus* (Berlin, 1921)
17 Pitt Francis, D., *Nostradamus: Prophecies of Present Times?* (Aquarian, 1984)
18 *Prophesies of Nostradamus, The* (Avenel, N.Y., 1975)
19 Roberts, H.C., *The Complete Prophecies of Nostradamus* (Grafton, 1985)
20 Sabato, M. de, *Confidences d'un voyant* (Hachette, 1971)
21 Sabato, M. de, *25 ans à vivre?* (Pensée Moderne, 1976)
22 Tomas, A., *Beyond the Time Barrier* (Sphere, 1974)
23 Woldben, A., *After Nostradamus* (Spearman, 1973)

INDEX OF PREDICTIONS QUOTED

GENERAL INDEX

If you have enjoyed this book, you may be interested in other titles published by Piatkus. All are by authorities in their field and are written in a clear and easy-to-follow format. Titles include: